English Legal System
Student text

Hutchinson Professional Studies Series (LLB)

Student texts
Constitutional Law
Contract Law
Criminal Law
English Legal System

Cases & Materials
Constitutional Law
Contract Law
Criminal Law
English Legal System

In Preparation
Administrative Law
Commercial Law
Company Law
Evidence
Family Law
Jurisprudence & Legal Theory
Land Law
Succession
Law of Tort
Public International Law
Revenue Law
Law of Trusts

HUTCHINSON PROFESSIONAL STUDIES SERIES

LLB
English Legal System
Student Text

By Tacey Aquino, LL.B, Barrister
Jane Blessey, M.A.(Oxon), Solicitor
Leslie Blake, LL.B, LL.M., A.K.C., Barrister

Editorial Advisory Panel
Chart University Tutors

Hutchinson

London Melbourne Sydney Auckland Johannesburg

Hutchinson Education

An imprint of Century Hutchinson Ltd
62-65 Chandos Place, London WC2N 4NW

Century Hutchinson Australia Pty Ltd
PO Box 496, 16-22 Church Street, Hawthorn,
Victoria 3122, Australia

Century Hutchinson New Zealand Ltd
191 Archers Road, Glenfield, Auckland, New Zealand

Century Hutchinson South Africa (Pty) Ltd
PO Box 337, Bergvlei, 2012 South Africa

First Published 1988 by Hutchinson Education
© Chart University Tutors Ltd 1988

Printed and bound in Great Britain by
Scotprint Ltd., Musselburgh

ISBN 0 09 1824 21 4

HELP US TO HELP YOU

The Hutchinson – Chart LL.B series is prepared to the highest possible standards. We have in preparing the student text borne in mind the needs of law students.

In our efforts constantly to improve the standards. We invite comments from you. If you feel there are ways in which the student text can be improved, please tell us. We will do our best to improve our next edition and will incorporate any helpful suggestions in our longer-term planning.

Thank you for your help. The comments form is set out below.

EDITORIAL PANEL
Jane Blessley
Leslie Blake
Nicholas Bourne
Tracey Aquino
Sept '88

To: The Editorial Advisory Panel
    Chart University Tutors
    200 Greyhound Road,
    London W14 9RY,
    England.

Name_____

Address_____

_____

_____Tel_____

Student Text title_____

_____

_____

_____

_____

_____

_____

CHART UNIVERSITY TUTORS

200 Greyhound Road, London W14 9RY, Telephone: 01-385 3377
Telex: 266386 · Fax: 01-381 3377

FAR EAST SUBSIDIARY

Chart Tutors Sdn Bhd 58 Jalan Tuanku Abdul Rahman 50100 Kuala Lumpur, Malaysia. Telephone: 03-293 5337

Chart University Tutors has a long and distinguished record of training students in the legal profession and prides itself on the pursuit of academic excellence and this is reflected by our results and by the number of our students who gain places to research into Law and subsequently enter practice as first class advocates.

We are proud of our past students who have graduated with us and who are flying our flag in their professions.

Commitment and conviction in seeing to the progress of all our students rank top in our priorities and we invite students who are not yet part of Chart University Tutors to act today and become part of the growing tradition.

NICHOLAS BOURNE
PRINCIPAL

TRACEY AQUINO
DIRECTOR OF STUDIES

SONNY LEONG
REGISTRAR

Please send me further details (please tick)

London LL.B (External)   Full Time ☐   Part Time ☐   Home Degree ☐
'A' Levels   Full Time ☐   Part Time ☐   Home Study ☐
Bar Finals   Full Time ☐

Name ....
Address ....
Telephone (Home) ....
(Office) ....

LLB

ENGLISH LEGAL SYSTEM

TABLE OF CONTENTS

Page

LLB

ENGLISH LEGAL SYSTEM

LESSON 1 (STUDY)

11. MAJOR DIVISIONS OF ENGLISH LAW

11.1 *Introduction*

The entire corpus of English law can be divided up in a number of different ways using different sets of criteria. As we are here studying the English legal system – i. e. its machinery, institutions and procedures (adjective or procedural law) rather than the specific ingredients of particular actions (substantive law) – we shall draw our first distinction according to the courts in which proceedings would begin.

The most obvious division in the English courts' system is between the criminal and the civil structures. The term 'civil law' is being used to describe disputes between individual legal personalities e.g. in the areas of contract, tort and property, and not to mean the Roman law based legal systems found on the Continent.)

11.2 *Civil and criminal law – history*

The English legal system in its infancy did not distinguish between a crime and a civil wrong. The wrongdoer who killed, stole, or deliberately damaged property was treated in the same way as the careless man who accidently killed or injured another person, or who inadvertently removed or damaged another person's property. The remedy in all such cases was restitution of the property taken or the payment of compensation to the party who had suffered loss (or to his family). Thus Sir Henry Maine (1822-1888) was able to write as follows in his famous book, *Ancient Law* (1861):

> Now the penal law of ancient communities is not the law of Crimes; it is the law of Wrongs, or, to use the English technical word, of Torts. The person injured proceeds against the wrong-doer by an ordinary civil action, and recovers compensation in the shape of money-damages if he succeeds.

> (Maine, *Ancient Law*, Chapter X, 'The Early History of Delict and Crime')

According to Sir Henry Maine, 'the greatest gap in ancient civil law will always be caused by the absence of Contract'. In early English law, the only causes of action were those derived from the concept of 'trespass', trespass to the person, trespass to goods (including livestock), and trespass to land. We may date this period as 1189 to 1285. The first date is known as 'the date of legal memory'. It represents the year in which King Henry II died, and King Richard I ascended to the throne. Prior to the work of Henry II there was no 'common law of England', only local customs. The date 1285 represents the year in which King Edward I signed the *Statute of Westminster II*. This statute gave approval to the creation of new writs, and therefore to new causes of action, if those writs were *in consimili casu*, i.e. similar to pre-existing writs. In practice, this permitted the common law to adapt to new situations, and to the requirements of an increasingly commercial society. It reversed an earlier attempt by the feudal lords to restrict the powers of the Royal Courts by prohibiting the creation of new writs. (During a brief period of ascendancy, the feudal lords had compelled King Henry III to sign the *Provisions of Oxford 1258* which prohibited the creation of new writs by the clerks of the Royal Courts.)

After 1285 trespass was supplemented by new and more sophisticated causes of action (known as 'actions on the case' or as 'trespass on the case'). Nuisance, slander, negligence and contract all developed, sooner or later, from this innovative procedural change in the common law writ system.

Criminal law is different from all these changes because it gradually became a legal system in its own right. It separated itself from the ordinary courts of law and from the ordinary rules of procedure. However different negligence may be nowadays from trespass to the person, or contract from slander, all civil actions are tried in the same courts, and are amenable to the same, or to very similar, rules of procedure (including the use of written pleadings). Criminal law, however, possesses its own courts, its own rules of evidence, its own procedures, and (of course) its own particular methods of dealing with those defendants against whom it gives a judgment.

11.3 *Civil and criminal law – the reasons for the split*

The reason why criminal law breaks away from civil law in all sophisticated legal systems is a matter for historians and for anthropologists to explain. It is not, of course, a problem that need worry lawyers, otherwise than as a matter of academic interest. Sir Henry Maine (who was, undoubtedly, the greatest authority on this aspect of jurisprudence) observed that 'all civilised systems agree in drawing a distinction between of fences against the State or Community and offences against the Individual' *(Ancient Law*, Chapter X). We may, however, attempt to list some probable reasons why English law is divided into civil and criminal law:

(a) *The desire of the Plantagenet Kings of England* (especially Henry II (1154-1189) and Edward I (1272-1307) *to centralise government*, to diminish the power of the local courts and the feudal lords, to prevent disorder, to discourage private vendetta and to protect the coinage. The Kings of England, therefore, identified certain wrongs as being directed against 'the King's peace', and insisted on removing such cases to the Royal Courts. This is an example, in England, of a more general reason, namely:

(b) *The decline of tribalism, the break-up of feudalism, and the growth of the state.* The deliberate use of force becomes the monopoly of the state, and any person committing a crime of violence is seen as usurping the power of the state and, thus, constituting a threat to the state itself.

(c) *The inefficiency of civil justice* against persons of a criminal disposition. Criminals often have no money to pay compensation since, almost by definition, they destroy and damage more than they create. They are often able to evade the service of proceedings, and/or the enforcement of civil judgments made against them. In short, they do not cooperate with the process of the civil courts.

(d) *The influence of religion.* The actual state of mind of the perpetrator of a wrongful act is seen as a decisive factor: murder is seen as a more serious crime than manslaughter, and accidental killings are seen as civil matters only.

(e) *The rise of individualism.* Once a man is entitled to own his own property, separate from his tribe, or his family, or other social group, it is no longer possible to exact compensation from that social group for any wrongdoing which he commits. Each man is then to be held accountable for his own transgressions and (for the reasons given above) he may be subject to criminal sanctions applied to him personally.

(f) *The efficiency of the criminal law* to achieve certain social objectives. In modern times, Parliament has created 'crimes of a regulatory nature' not for the purpose of imposing great punishments, but because the criminal law is an efficient method of imposing standards, e.g. in the field of road traffic, public health, health and safety at work, town and country planning and so on. In such cases the enforcement of the law does not wait for a victim to suffer injury or loss, but the state takes action to punish (usually with a fine) any person who creates a dangerous or undesirable state of affairs. In practice, the existence of the criminal offence usually achieves its purpose because of the desire of almost all persons to obey sensible laws.

The origins of the English criminal law can be traced to legislation promulated in 1166 *(Assize of Clarendon)* and 1176 *(Assize of Northampton)*, legislation which extended Royal jurisdiction to cases of theft, murder, robbery, counterfeiting and arson. (It should be noted, in passing, that statutes were often named, during this period, after the town or city where the King signed them.)

12.   CRIME AND TORT

12.1   *Introduction*

In dealing with the characteristics of, and differences between, crime and tort it is necessary to answer the following questions in relation to each branch:

(a)   What is the essential nature of crime and of tort?

(b)   Who begins proceedings?

(c)   Is there a time limit within which an action must be brought?

(d)   Who can be prosecuted/sued?

(e)   What are the differences in the conduct of the proceedings?

(f)   What is the ultimate aim of criminal proceedings/actions in tort?

12.2   *The essential nature of crime and of tort*

Both are 'wrongs' in the sense that someone or something that belongs to some person will have suffered or have been threatened with harm.

Crimes are wrongs which are considered to be detrimental to the well-being of society as a whole as well as to the particular individual against whom they are perpetrated. For example, if A stabs B, this not only causes harm to B but threatens the order which must prevail in a civilised society. Because of this, it is the Crown (usually) which instigates proceedings and the individual wronged has no power to stop these. The offence that is being prosecuted is only incidentally the offence that was committed against himself – what is being prosecuted is, in effect, the affront to the order of society as a whole. Of course, what is considered disruptive to society in this sense at one point in time can cease to engender concern at another and, conversely, something which initially is thought not to affect society at large later becomes a matter of widespread concern, thereby attracting the penalties of the criminal law.

Two examples falling into the first category stem from the less paternalistic attitudes to morality by the Church and state which have come about in the latter half of the twentieth century: by the *Sexual Offences Act 1967* it is no longer a criminal offence simply to be a homosexual; under the *Abortion Act 1967* there is provision for an abortion to be carried out without breaking the law.

An example of the second category is the motor car. Traffic offences in the twentieth century fall within the ambit of the criminal law, whereas in the nineteenth and early part of the twentieth century, damage caused by the careless driving of a possibly defective vehicle was thought to be a matter purely between the driver of the vehicle and the person who suffered the damage. With the rise of the production motor car, this state of affairs could not be allowed to continue – it was a matter which affected an increasingly large number of members of society.

The criminal law is not static. Note that it is not a question of something suddenly ceasing to be actionable or becoming actionable. There are still circumstances under which homosexuals and persons performing abortions can be prosecuted, and there is certainly nothing to prevent a person injured by a careless motorist from bringing his own action in tort. When considering the substance of the criminal law, the thing to be considered is whether it is an act which affects the public at large or simply the individuals involved. Another way of distinguishing criminal law from contract, tort and property, therefore, is to describe them as public law on the one hand and private law on the other.

Torts are wrongs which are redressable in the courts at the suit of the individual who has suffered damage as a result of the defendant's act. They are not seen as being as widespread in their effect as crimes, which is why it is entirely up to the individual concerned whether or not he brings his case. By the same token, he can also waive his right to bring proceedings. Tort thus falls within the sphere of private law, as the matter is perceived as affecting only the two parties directly involved.

Note: It is not the case that any wrong that is not a crime must be a tort. If an action is to be brought in tort, it must concern a right which the courts are prepared to recognise. Lord Macmillan in *Donoghue v Stevenson (1932) AC 619* said: 'The categories of negligence are never closed', but it is perhaps more realistic to say that the categories of negligence (or of anything else) are never *finally* closed. Although the law of tort, as part of the common law, will develop and expand to meet changing needs, this is not to imply that it exists to allow people to take every instance of injured feelings into the courts.

This is perhaps best illustrated by example. Suppose Mr Perfect, of regular habits, takes the 8.10 train every day from the suburbs to Central London. He likes to have the corner seat on the left in the front carriage. Usually he manages to get it. His fellow commuters know about this, and they will say to each other: 'Better not sit there, old boy: that's Perfect's seat. He'll go mad if you're sitting there'. Although they may seem to be recognising some right of Mr Perfect, it is not a right that would be enforced in a court of law – even though not being able to have that seat could upset Mr Perfect's entire day. Suppose, though, that Mr Perfect is happily esconced in the seat when, at the next station, another commuter, also a hot contender for that particular position, boards the train. He is so incensed by Mr Perfect's presence in the seat he regards as 'his' that he hits him. Mr Perfect would then have a good cause of action: not because of the threat to his train seat, but because the law recognises a person's right to be free from physical attack.

You may at this point ask: when the commuter hit Mr Perfect, did this give rise to criminal proceedings or to an action in tort? The answer is: both. Just as it is possible for an insulting act to be neither criminal nor tortious, so it is possible for another act to be both criminal and tortious.

12.3 *Parties to the proceedings*

Criminal proceedings are usually brought in the name of the Crown (Regina or Rex, abbreviated to 'R'). Sometimes the name of the prosecutor will be that of a police official. Before bringing the case, the police will have made enquiries to ensure that they have sufficient evidence to charge the suspect with the crime. It is possible for an individual to bring a private prosecution, but in practice it is very rare since the Prosecution of Offences Act 1985, once a decision to prosecute has been made, the conduct of the prosecution is n the hands of the Crown Prosecution Service.

An action in tort is a civil action. Proceedings are started by one of the parties directly involved in the dispute that the court is being asked to settle. That person is called the 'plaintiff'. In both civil and criminal cases the other party is the 'defendant'.

12.4 *Time limits within which an action must be brought*

In criminal offences, the saying is that 'time never runs against the Crown', and so the answer is that there is no time limit.

In tort actions, the plaintiff must bring his action within a certain period of time. In purely private actions, it would be grossly unfair if, 10 or 20 years after the event, the defendant found himself served with a writ in respect of something he had long since forgotten about and for which his evidence had been destroyed. The periods of limitation which are applicable to any given case are contained in the *Limitation Act 1980*. This subject can be a complex one and properly belongs to the study of the law of tort. It will be sufficient if you are aware that:

(a) *s.2* sets the normal limitation period as being six years from the time when the cause of action arose;

(b) *s.11* reduces this to three years in cases of personal injury where the cause of action is based on negligence, nuisance or breach of duty. The limitation preiod in defamation cases is also 3 years.

12.5 *Who can be prosecuted/sued*

Children (known to the law as minors since the *Family Law Reform Act 1969 (s.12)*) are protected from the rigours of the criminal law by a number of statutory provisions and presumptions of law as to their capacity.

S.50 Children and Young Persons Act 1933 states that it shall be conclusively presumed that no child under the age of 10 years can be guilty of any criminal offence. This is not really a presumption but is essentially a rule of law.

There is a rebuttable presumption of law that a person aged 10-14 is *doli incapax*. This means that he is incapable of forming the intent *(mens rea)* necessary to commit a criminal offence. Thus, someone of this age may be prosecuted, but the prosecution will have to prove that there is capability to form the intent necessary to commit the crime. This is referred to as proof of 'mischievous discretion'.

There are no such restrictions on capacity in relation to liability in tort.

12.6 *Differences in the conduct of the proceedings*

Criminal cases are dealt with in the criminal courts – Magistrates' Courts, the Crown Court, the Divisional Court of Queen's Bench Division, the Court of Appeal (Criminal Division) and the House of Lords.

Those instigating the action are the Prosecution and the person alleged to have committed the offence is referred to as the 'accused' or the 'defendant'. For the accused to be found guilty, the prosecution must prove the case against him 'beyond reasonable doubt': *Woolmington v D.P.P. (1935) AC 123*. There have been a number of attempts by the judiciary to explain the meaning of that phrase to juries in such a way that they will be aware of the very high standard of certainty required before they can convict the accused. Consider the following cases:

R v Summers (1952) 1 All ER 1059 per Goddard CJ:

> ... juries should simply be told that they must see that the evidence satisfies them so that they can feel sure when they return the verdict of guilty.

Miller v Minister of Pensions (1947) 2 All ER 372 per Denning J:

> ... the evidence must reach the same degree of cogency that is required in a criminal case before an accused person is found guilty. That degree is well settled. It need not reach

certainty, but it must carry a high degree of probability. Proof beyond reasonable doubt does not mean proof beyond the shadow of a doubt. The law would fail to protect the community if it admitted fanciful possibilities to deflect the course of justice. If the evidence is so strong against a man as to leave only a remote possibility in his favour which can be dismissed with the sentence 'of course it is possible, but it is not in the least probable', the case is proved beyond reasonable doubt, but nothing short of that will suffice.

Ferguson v The Queen (1979) 1 All ER 877:

... You must be satisfied beyond reasonable doubt so that you feel sure of the defendant's guilt.

Consider the following remarks of Lawton LJ in *R v Yap Chuan Ching (1976) 63 Cr App Rep 7:*

Perhaps it is not irrelevant in the year 1976 for the court to take judicial notice of the fact that one of the popular forms of entertainment nowadays on television is a series of reconstructed trials which have a striking degree of realism. Most jurors nowadays know something about the burden and standard of proof before they ever get into the jury box ...

... in most cases ... judges would be well advised not to attempt any gloss upon what is meant by 'sure' or what is meant by 'reasonable doubt'. In the last two decades there have been numerous cases before this court, some of which have been successful, some of which have not, which have come here because judges have thought it helpful to a jury to comment on what the standard of proof is. Experience in this court has shown that such comments usually create difficulties. They are more likely to confuse than help.

Civil cases are dealt with in the civil courts' structure – County Court, High Court (in the case of tort in the Queen's Bench Division of the High Court), Court of Appeal (Civil Division), House of Lords.

The person instigating the action is described as the 'plaintiff', and the person against whom the action is brought is referred to as the 'defendant'.

For the defendant to be held liable, the plaintiff must prove his case 'on a balance of probabilities'. This means that, at the conclusion of the evidence, the judge (or jury if there is one) must consider that it is likely that the plaintiff's account of events is more correct than the defendant's account.

Denning J stated in *Miller v Minister of Pensions (1947) 2 All ER 372:*

... the case must be decided according to the preponderance of probability. If at the end of the case the evidence turns the scale definitely one way or the other, the tribunal must decide accordingly, but if the evidence is so evenly balanced that the tribunal is unable to come to a determinate conclusion one way or the other, then the man must be given the benefit of the doubt. This means that the case must be decided in favour of the man unless the evidence against him reaches the same degree of cogency as is required to discharge a burden in a civil case. That degree is well settled. It must carry a reasonable degree of probability, but not so high as is required in a criminal case. If the evidence is such that the tribunal can say: 'we think it more probable than not', the burden is discharged, but, if the probabilities are equal, it is not.

Therefore the prosecution in a criminal case must prove to a higher standard than the plaintiff in a civil case.

12.7 The ultimate aim of proceedings

The distinction is often sharply drawn in the form: the aim of criminal proceedings is to punish the offender; in tort it is to compensate the victim. This 'never the twain shall meet' view is a gross over-simplification.

Consider the following points:

(a) The object of criminal proceedings has been variously described:

(i) to punish the offender and thus exact retribution on behalf of society;

(ii) to prevent the offender from repeating the conduct;

(iii) to deter others from similar conduct;

(iv) to reform the offender;

(v) to protect society from the dangers posed by having the offender in its midst, i.e. by imprisoning him. A person's liberty cannot be taken away from him by a civil court, only by a criminal court with its higher standard of proof.

At various stages in the development of the criminal law different objectives have been given priority. Ultimately a balance must be struck between the rights of the offender and the needs of society.

(b) The same action is capable of being both a crime and a tort. The fact that criminal proceedings are instituted is no bar to the victim pursuing his remedy in tort. In addition, in the course of the criminal proceedings themselves:

(i) *s.35(1) Powers of Criminal Courts Act 1973* allows a criminal court to make an order for compensation to the victim of the offence for which the accused has been convicted in respect of 'any personal injury, loss or damage' *whether or not the victim has a right of action in tort.*

Note that the aim is compensation: any order made under the Act is not to be regarded as a fine payable to the victim rather than to the state.

The court must take into account the means of the defendant, and there is an upper limit of £2,000 per offence in magistrates' courts, although in the Crown Court there is no such limitation;

(ii) *s. 28 Theft Act 1968* provides that a person convicted of an offence under the Act may be ordered by the criminal court to make restitution to the victim.

(c) The alleged aim of the law of tort is compensation to the plaintiff rather than punishment of the defendant.

However, damages may be exemplary (or punitive) where the defendant's conduct towards the plaintiff is, in the court's opinion, deserving of punishment. The circumstances in which exemplary damages can be (not must be, may be) awarded were laid down by Lord Devlin in *Rookes v Barnard (1964) AC 1129* and discussed at length by the House of Lords in *Cassell & Co Ltd v Broome and Another (1972) 1 All ER 801.*

12.8 *Burden and standard of proof*

The burden of proof (sometimes known as the 'onus of proof') is the duty of proving all (or any) of the facts-in-issue in civil or criminal proceedings. The location of this duty with one party or the other can be decisive to the outcome of a case.

The general rule is that the burden of proof 'rests upon he who alleges, not on he who denies'. However, in civil cases it is common for the defendant to raise new issues in his defence (or in his counterclaim). If he does this, he will bear the burden of proving these facts. Thus (for example) if a plaintiff alleges breach of contract in his statement of claim and the defendant denies the existence of the contract, or denies the alleged breach, the plaintiff will have the burden of proof and will have to call evidence to show the existence of the contract (and its relevant terms) and to show that the defendant failed to comply with his obligations under that contract. If, however, the defendant admits the existence of the contract in his defence, and admits that he has conducted himself in the manner alleged by the plaintiffs but alleges that the plaintiff has made him the victim of a misrepresentation, he (the defendant) will have the burden of proof on this issue. He will have to show that the representation was made by the plaintiff (or one of his agents); that he (the defendant) relied upon that representation when entering into the contract; and that this representation was false. The case of *Joseph Constantine v Imperial Smelting Corporation (1942) AC 154* is an important example of how this principle works.

P entered into a contract (known as a 'charterparty') to charter a ship from D. The ship failed to arrive at the time and place agreed, and P suffered financial loss. P sued D for breach of contract. D admitted the existence of the contract and also admitted that the ship had failed to arrive at the time and place agreed. D went on to allege that the ship had suffered an explosion in one of its boilers and further alleged that this amounted to the defence known as 'frustration of contract'. P did not dispute that the boiler had exploded, but denied that the defence of frustration of contract applied. P averred that the explosion had been caused by D's negligence, not by some circumstance beyond his control. In fact, there was no evidence to show why the boiler had exploded. (There were three equally possible explanations, only one of which was tantamount to negligence on the part of D.)

It was held by the House of Lords that it was for P to prove that the explosion had been caused by the negligence of D. It was not for D to prove that the explosion had arisen from some non-negligent cause. Accordingly (in the absence of any evidence one way or the other), D was entitled to rely on the defence of frustration of contract.

However, the accused bears the burden of overcoming the evidential burden which is not really a burden of proof at all. This requires the accused to adduce some evidence to raise the issue of the defence. What this 'some evidence' amounts to is a matter of law for the trial judge: *R. V. Jeyasena (1970) AC 618.*

Note: If P had denied that the boiler had exploded, or had averred that the explosion was irrelevant to the non-arrival of the ship, he would not have had to prove this denial. The burden of proof would have remained on D to prove his defence, namely the existence of an event which had effectively prevented the ship from arriving as and when agreed. (In the *Joseph Constantine case*, D was clearly capable of proving this, and it would only have added to the costs of the case for P to have denied such an obvious fact.)

In criminal law, the burden of proof operates in a much more favourable way to the defendant. If the defendant puts forward a defence (e.g. self-defence or provocation as a defence to a charge of murder) he does not have to prove that defence. The burden of proof remains on the prosecution to *disprove* this defence. *Woolmington v DPP (1935) AC 462* is an example of this principle at work.

D was charged with murdering his wife with a gun. He admitted killing his wife, but alleged that this had been an accident. The judge directed the jury that once the prosecution had proved that D had killed his wife, the burden of proof shifted to D to show that the killing had been accidental.

It was held by the House of Lords that it was the duty of the prosecution to prove every element in the offence charged, including the mental element. Thus the prosecution had to prove that D had killed his wife with malice aforethought, not accidentally.

In certain exceptional circumstances (which are likely to arise more frequently since the decision of the Court of Appeal (Criminal Division) in *R v Hunt (1986) Crim LR 172)*, the burden of proof rests upon the defendant to prove some part of his defence to a criminal charge.

The *standard of proof* is the *extent* to which a fact (or a series of facts) must be proved. In civil proceedings the standard of proof is 'the balance of probabilities' (sometimes described as 'the preponderance of probabilities'). This indicates that the successful party to a civil case will be the one whose evidence (including the evidence of his witnesses) succeeds in being (to any extent at all) more probable as an explanation of the disputed facts than the evidence of the other party. If the judge is unable to detect any such preponderance, e.g. because there is no evidence at all on the matter in question, or because all explanations are equally likely, then the party who had the burden of proof will fail. (The judge is duty-bound to give judgment for one party or the other.)

In criminal law, the standard of proof is higher than in civil law. In *Miller v Minister of Pensions (1947) 2 All ER 372* Denning J (as he then was) contrasted the civil standard of proof with the criminal standard of proof, and described the latter as follows:

> That degree [of proof] is well settled. It need not reach certainty, but it must carry a high degree of probability. Proof beyond reasonable doubt does not mean proof beyond a shadow of a doubt. The law would fail to protect the community if it admitted fanciful possibilities to deflect the course of justice. If the evidence is so strong against a man as to leave only a remote possibility in his favour which can be dismissed with the sentence, 'of course it is possible, but not in the least probable', the case is proved beyond reasonable doubt, but nothing short of that will suffice.

If for any reason the defendant bears the burden of proving any fact in a criminal trial, the standard of proof required of him is *not* 'proof beyond reasonable doubt', but merely the civil standard of proof ('balance of probabilities'): *R v Carr-Briant (1943) 1 KB 607.*

If, in a civil case, the plaintiff alleges that the defendant has committed a criminal offence (or *vice versa*), e.g. driving without due care and attention, or some offence of fraud, the standard of proof does not change. The standard remains the civil standard ('balance of probabilities'): *Hornal v Neuberger Products (1957) 1 QB 247; Post Office v Estuary Radio (1968) 2 QB 740.*

However, the accused must attain a higher degree of proof within the civil standard, i.e. a higher degree of probability or cogency. This higher degree of probability increases with the seriousness of the crime alleged

12.9 *The effect of a criminal conviction on civil proceedings*

It is axiomatic that many criminal offences also amount to civil wrongs (although the terminology may be different in the two systems of law). The following is a list of the more obvious examples:

Crime	Civil wrong
Murder	Trespass to the person (tort)
Manslaughter	Trespass to the person, or negligence (tort)
Assault	Trespass to the person (tort)
Battery	Trespass to the person (tort)
Criminal damage	Trespass to land, or trespass to goods (tort)
Theft	Trespass to goods (tort) or breach of trust
Reckless driving	Negligence (tort)
Driving without due care	Negligence (tort)
Conspiracy	Conspiracy (tort)
Offences involving deception	Deceit (i.e. fraud) (tort) or misrepresentation or breach of contract or breach of trust

Of course, the ingredients of a civil wrong are often different from the ingredients of a criminal offence. It is not always necessary to prove a mental element in a civil wrong (e.g. trespass to land) and (unlike civil law) it is not always necessary to show that there has been a victim in the case of a criminal offence (e.g. reckless driving). However, it is obvious that a conviction for (for example) reckless driving, or driving without due care, will be highly relevant to a civil claim for negligence brought by a pedestrian (or another motorist) against the same defendant in respect of the same incident. There is also a further difference in terminology:

Criminal law	Civil law
Prosecutor (usually 'the Crown')	Plaintiff
The accused (more usually 'the defendant')	Defendant
Prosecution/prosecute	Civil action/sue
Illegality/illegal	Unlawfulness/unlawful
Verdict	Judgment
Guilty/Not guilty	Liable/Not liable (usually expressed as 'Judgment for the plaintiff/defendant')
Sentence	Order
Fine	Damages

Because of the high degree of relevance of some criminal convictions to some civil claims, *s.11 Civil Evidence Act 1968* provides as follows:

> In any civil proceedings the fact that a person has been convicted of an offence by or before any court in the United Kingdom or by a court-martial there or elsewhere shall ... be admissible in evidence for the purpose of proving, where to do so is relevant to any issue in those proceedings, that he committed that offence, whether he was convicted upon a plea of guilty or otherwise and whether or not he is a party to the civil proceedings; but no conviction other than a subsisting one shall be admissible by virtue of this section.

(The reference to 'subsisting convictions' is a reference to the fact that a conviction ceases to 'subsist' if it is quashed by a higher court.)

13. TORT AND CONTRACT

13.1 Introduction

Having considered the differences between criminal law and (through the medium of the law of tort) civil It is necessary to turn to the distinctions which exist among the branches of the civil law itself.

Why these distinctions should exist within the civil law is largely a matter of history. Briefly, the early common law courts would not hear just any case in which a person felt he had a grievance. (That this remains true today has been demonstrated in the discussion of tort above.) The main difference between, say, the eighteenth century and the present day is that procedure (or form) played a far more dominant role than it does now. Proceedings were started by the issue of a writ in which the cause of action was stated. If a plaintiff's cause of action did not fit into one of these recognised forms, then the courts would not hear his case. 'No writ, no remedy', was how the saying went. The development of these forms of action is beyond the scope of this text. Even today, however, the courts find that problems can arise as a result of categorisation of rights at law imposed by the rigidity of the old forms of action. As Maitland put it in a much-quoted phrase, 'The forms of action we have buried but still they rule us from their graves', and it would be hard to understand the problems faced by the House of Lords in *Donoghue v Stevenson (1932) AC 562*, for example, without some appreciation of the latter-day importance and present-day pervasiveness of these old forms.

The jurisdictional institutions themselves are so important in the English legal system. The strength of the common law has lain, and still does lie, in its ability to adapt to changed circumstances, without any break in its own continuity. It is thus inevitable that vestiges of practices and procedures will continue to linger after their true function has disappeared.

The law exists not only to sort out disputes between individual legal personalities, but also to preserve order within the society in which we all live and go about our business. So it is in everybody's interests to submit their disputes to some kind of recognised arbitration procedure, of which the courts of law form the most widely known, but by no means the only, one.

Contract, tort and property are all divisions of civil – as opposed to criminal – law. They deal with disputes between individual legal personalities. The term 'legal personalities' is used because the law does not equate human personality with legal personality. For example, a company has legal personality independent of the human individuals who make up its membership, and so the parties to a dispute over the terms of a contract may be a company on the one hand, and a private person on the other. Similarly, a disagreement may arise between a government department and an individual member of the public. In both cases, the dispute is nonetheless between two legal personalities.

In examining the differences between tort and contract. It is necessary to ask the following questions:

(a) What is the essential nature of tort and of contract?

(b) Who can bring proceedings?

(c) Is there a time limit within which an action must be brought?

(d) Who can be sued?

(e)   Damages are a remedy in contract and in tort. Is there any difference in the basis on which they are awarded?

13.2   *The essential nature of tort and of contract*

Rights in tort exist independently of any express agreement. For example, if A places his rubbish in my garden, I have a right of action against A in trespass. It is not necessary to show the existence of an agreement whereby A agreed not to dump rubbish in my garden. It would clearly be impractical if the law were to require this, since I would then have to establish an agreement with everybody (including people I did not know!) if I wanted to guarantee that my garden would be rubbish-free. A legal system which required action of this type would quickly fall into disrespect.

Thus duties in tort are duties which are owed to everyone, and no express agreement is necessary to establish the right of one party and the corresponding duty on the other not to infringe that right. It is the law which establishes what these rights and duties are.

Duties owed under a contract, on the other hand, do arise by express agreement. Further, English law recognises the freedom of parties to agree to more or less whatever terms they choose, the main proviso being that the courts will not enforce an agreement which is for the performance of some act which itself is *illegal.*

Note that within the terms of a contract between two parties, it is possible for them to come to an agreement about the extent to which one party will be liable in tort to the other for the purposes of the contract. If the parties do agree to restrict their rights in tort, then they cannot subsequently frame actions in tort, rather than in contract, to recover the wider liability they had expressly agreed to curtail.

The principle that people are free to agree to restrictions on their rights in tort for the purposes of contractual dealings is subject to the *Unfair Contract Terms Act 1977.*

Therefore, the principle that parties are free to agree to whatever terms they may settle on between themselves is subject to statutory intervention. In particular, Parliament has given considerable protection, in the latter half of this century, to the consumer in such Acts as the *Unfair Contract Terms Act 1977* (above), the *Consumer Credit Act 1974*, the *Sale of Goods Act 1979*, the *Trade Descriptions Act 1968*, the *Supply of Goods and Services (Implied Terms) Act 1981* and so on.

Finally, on this topic of the essential nature of contract and of tort, note that the same act or omission can sometimes be grounds for an action in contract and an action in tort. Medical negligence cases are a good illustration: the surgeon was in breach of contract with the patient (see also *s.2(1) Unfair Contract Terms Act 1977* (above)) *AND* he carried out his work in a *negligent* manner *which caused injury.*

13.3   *Parties to the proceedings*

Anyone who suffers damage as a result of an infringement of their rights in tort can bring an action against the person who owed them a duty and breached that duty. This includes a minor, who sues through his 'next friend'.

In contract, however, only the parties to a contract may sue upon it. This is known as the doctrine of privity of contract. For example, if my elderly neighbour agrees with a builder that she will pay him £500 to extend her house, but he fails to carry out the work, despite the fact that she paid him a deposit, I may feel very sorry for her. But the law will not allow me, in my capacity as a private individual, to sue the builder for breach of the contract. That contract was not made between the builder and myself. I am not a party to it. In everyday language 'what business is it of mine?' Or, as the court would have it, the doctrine of privity of contract would defeat my attempt to enforce the contract on her behalf.

Difficulties have arisen, however, when a third party suffers damage as a result of a breach of contract. Not being a party to the agreement, he cannot sue on the basis of it. Any remedy he might have, therefore, will lie in tort. This was the situation in *Donoghue v Stevenson (1932) AC 562*. The facts of the case are as follows.

The plaintiff had been out one evening for a walk with a friend. They stopped at a cafeteria, where the friend purchased a bottle of ginger-beer for the plaintiff. The ginger-beer bottle was opaque, and the top fastened on with a metal fastening. On the side of the bottle was a label with the name and address of the manufacturer. The owner of the cafe poured some of the ginger-beer over some ice-cream in a glass (an ice-cream soda) and the plaintiff drank some. When he 'topped up' the glass with the rest of the ginger-beer, the decomposed remains of a snail floated out. The plaintiff was horrified, and she suffered gastroenteritis from the contaminated ginger-beer that she had already drunk. She sued the manufacturer in the tort of negligence.

The court had to decide whether the manufacturer owed a duty of care to the plaintiff. She had no contractual relationship with him. Any contract that existed was between the manufacturer and the owner of the cafe to whom he supplied the ginger-beer, or between the friend who had purchased the ginger-beer (i. e. actually paid for it) and the owner of the cafe who had sold it to her. The plaintiff herself was a party to neither contract which, of course, meant that if she had tried to bring an action in contract, the doctrine of privity would have defeated her claim. Any chance of success thus lay in tort. The questions with which the court had to deal were:

(1)   Did the manufacturers (respondents in the House of Lords) owe a duty of care to the plaintiff?

(2)   Was the relationship between the manufacturer and the plaintiff sufficiently proximate for such a duty (if established) to be owed by the manufacturer to her or were they too remote from each other?

The judges who were in favour of allowing the appeal were aware that they were setting new and wider liability in the tort of negligence. Those who dissented (i.e. who would have said that she did not have any rights against the manufacturer of the contaminated ginger-beer) contended that to allow the action would 'open the floodgates for litigation', in other words, that the courts would be swamped with cases of this type. The plaintiff succeeded.

13.4   *Time limits within which an action must be brought*

In contract, the *Limitation Act 1980* provides that actions based on breach of a simple contract must be commenced within six years. If the contract was made by deed, or if it relates to an action for the recovery of land, the period is twelve years.

Time begins to run from the moment at which breach of the contract actually occurred. If the defendant deliberately concealed the true state of affairs from the plaintiff, however, time will begin to run from the moment that the breach was discovered or should reasonably have been discovered.

13.5   *Who can be sued*

This question involves the issue of capacity. Minors, subject to a few exceptions (most notably contracts for 'necessaries'), cannot be sued on their contracts, even if they misrepresent themselves as being of the age of majority, and despite the fact that the other party acted in good faith.

They can, however, be sued in tort. So, what of those acts that are both torts and breaches of contract? In general, the courts have strongly resisted attempts to enforce contracts entered into by minors by the device of framing the action in tort. Where the tortious act can be cleanly separated from the contract, however, the action will be allowed. (Compare *Jennings v Rundall (1799) 8 Term Rep 335 at p.336* and *Burnard v Haggis (1863) 14 CBNS 45.*)

Only the parties to a contract may sue upon it. Who the legal personalities are will be ascertained by referring to the contract itself.

In tort, the position is somewhat more complicated. If a servant commits a tort while acting in the course of his employment, then his employer may be vicariously liable for his tort. This subject is complex, e.g. who is a servant? When can he be said to be acting in the course of his employment? etc. and properly belongs to the study of the law of tort itself.

The phenomenon of insurance is another factor which should not be over looked when discussing the parties in tort actions, particularly in the cases arising out of road traffic accidents and injuries received at work. It is common practice for the motorist's or employer's insurance company to meet the plaintiff's claim and then to take over the plaintiff's cause of action against the defendant.

13.6 *Damages as a remedy both in contract and in tort*

The aim of an award of damages in contract is to place the parties relatively in the positions that they would have been had the contract been performed, i.e. to make the final standing of the two parties the same as it would have been had the contract not been breached.

Sometimes the contract itself will contain a clause as to the measure of damages payable in the event of breach, in which case the dispute will be as to whether the conduct of the defendant amounts to such as to bring the clause into operation. Damages in contract are said to be 'liquidated'.

When damages are awarded in tort, they are said to be 'unliquidated', or 'at large'. The aim is to compensate the plaintiff for the harm he suffered, and to restore him to the position that he would have been in had the tort not been committed. As the consequences of tortious acts are often in the nature of personal injury or disability, or damage to reputation, the courts find considerable difficulty in assessing an appropriate sum.

14. *PROPERTY*

14.1 *Introduction*

Property law is a division of law in its own right, but not in the same way as the other three branches of law previously examined.

Property has always occupied a special place in English law, mainly because of the importance of land as a source not only of wealth, but of political power, in early times. In fact, it could be said that it was largely as a result of the need for the early kings to maintain a firm grip on what was happening on their land that central courts were instituted at all. Until that time law had been administered on a purely local basis.

Property today, and dealings with it, are governed largely by statute, most notably the property legislation of 1925, which was virtually a codification of the law of property.

Property is not, of course, confined to land and goods. In addition to realty and personalty, recent years have seen the growth of intellectual property. This can be summarised as property in ideas. The notion is not new: the first *Copyright Act* was passed in 1709 and in this century we have the *Patents Act 1949*, the *Trade Marks Act 1938* and the *Copyright Act 1956*. It is only in recent years, however, that the term 'intellectual property' has come into everyday use, mainly as a result of advances in technology which make it necessary to give legal protection to architectural designs and computer programs, to give but two instances.

The law of property, therefore, is almost entirely to be found in statutory provisions. If, however, these provisions do not provide the answer to the particular question before the courts, it will be necessary for the judges to look at the relevant branch of the common law.

LLB

ENGLISH LEGAL SYSTEM

LESSON 2 (STUDY)

21. *SOURCES OF ENGLISH LAW*

    21.1   INTRODUCTION

22. *FORMAL SOURCE*

23. *HISTORICAL SOURCE*

    23.1   INTRODUCTION
    23.2   THE COMMON LAW
    23.3   EQUITY
    23.4   STATUTE LAW
    23.5   CUSTOM
    23.6   THE LAW MERCHANT
    23.7   CANON LAW

24. *LEGAL SOURCE*

    24.1   LEGISLATION
    24.2   EEC LEGISLATION
    24.3   CASE LAW
    24.4   CUSTOM
    24.5   FOREIGN LAW

25. *LITERARY SOURCES*

    25.1   LAW REPORTS
    25.2   BOOKS OF AUTHORITY
    25.3   TEXTBOOKS
    25.4   STATUTES
    25.5   TRAVAUX PRÉPARATOIRES

21. SOURCES OF ENGLISH LAW

21.1 Introduction

The phrase 'source of law' has a number of different meanings, and it is important for the student to determine in what context the phrase is being used.

22. *FORMAL SOURCE*

A formal source of law is the 'power' that gives law its validity, i.e. the reason why law is recognised and obeyed. This is a question of jurisprudence and many conflicting theories exist. Custom, tradition, fear of punishment, the need to conform are all formal sources.

23. HISTORICAL SOURCE

23.1 Introduction

A historical source is something from which our present law has derived. Therefore, one needs to look to the past in order to explain how the law was produced and developed.

23.2 The Common Law

(a) *Introduction*

Before the Norman Conquest there was no unified system of law for the whole country. Local areas were largely autonomous and had their own systems of courts and local law. William the Conqueror introduced a strong central government and from this emerged a system of justice which was common to the whole country, i.e. *the Common Law*. The King appointed commissioners to travel around the country dealing with the King's affairs and some of these commissioners had judicial powers-they were the first royal judges, usually known as itinerant justices. Their jurisdiction included both civil matters (i.e. disputes between subjects) and criminal matters. The courts were known as assizes.

(b) *The courts of Common Law*

In addition to the Courts of Assize, various courts were later created which sat in London and dealt with specific matters:

(i) *Court of the King's Bench* – originally dealt with criminal and some civil matters;

(ii) *Court of Common Pleas* – dealt with civil actions, especially land disputes;

(iii) *Court of Exchequer* – dealt with tax cases and some civil actions.

The law administered by the royal courts depended on a system of *writs*, i.e. written commands issued by the Lord Chancellor ordering the defendant to attend court and show why the plaintiff should not be given judgment. Originally, there was no limit to the different types of writ but statutes in the thirteenth century forbade the creation of new writs unless they were analogous to the old. This step severely restricted the development of the Common Law because a plaintiff would have no remedy if he could not fit his case into one of the existing categories of writ.

These categories of writs were known as the *forms of action*.

(c) *The defects of the Common Law*

Although the Common Law provided a uniform system of law for the first time, it suffered from four major defects:

(i) after the *Provisions of Oxford 1258* no new writs could be issued without the consent of the Curia Regis. This severely impeded the further development of the law;

(ii) the system of pleadings was very formal. Pleadings had to be very specific, and any error made by the litigant or his adviser would result in the case being thrown out of court;

(iii) the Common Law suffered from a lack of appropriate remedies. The only remedy available was damages which, though available as of right, was only given after the event. The law had no means of preventing a legal wrong being committed or continued;

(iv)   there was virtually no right of appeal available from decisions of the Common Law courts. Although an appeal was found upon an error on the face of the record, this gave very little scope upon which litigants could appeal.

23.3 *Equity*

(a) *Introduction*

Equity developed primarily as a response to the defects of the Common Law. It provided a system by which litigants could appeal from the decisions of the Common Law courts, without having to draft complex and formal pleadings to a court which developed both new rights and a new set of remedies which gave effect to those rights.

(b) *The Court of Chancery*

When litigants failed to obtain satisfaction from the royal judges, they often appealed directly to the King. Later it became common for these appeals to be dealt with by the King's principal officer, the Lord Chancellor. Because the Lord Chancellor was usually a churchman, he tended to settle these appeals on the basis of morality and fairness, i.e. in accordance with equitable principles.

The system became so popular that a permanent court was set up – the *Court of Chancery*, presided over by the Lord Chancellor. This court dealt with cases:

(i)   where the application of the rigid Common Law rules applied by the royal judges produced an unjust result, e.g. where land had been transferred without the formality of a deed and the Common Law refused to recognise the transaction;

(ii)   where the Common Law refused to recognise the plaintiff's rights, e.g. the royal judges would not enforce trusts which, therefore, had to be dealt with by the Court of Chancery;

(iii)   where the Common Law recognised the plaintiff's rights but failed to provide an adequate remedy, e.g. the only Common Law remedy for breach of contract was damages, whereas the Court of Chancery could order the defendant to carry out the contract (*specific performance*).

In time, the Chancellors built up their own series of rules and precedents which became known as *Equity*.

These include:

(i)   the *doctrine of laches* which states that an equitable right will not be enforceable if the plaintiff delays unreasonably. At Common Law an action must generally be commenced within six years of an event (*Limitation Act 1980*) unless it is in respect of personal injury when it is three years;

(ii)   an *injunction* which is an order of the court instructing someone to do something (*mandatory injunction*) or restraining him from doing something (*prohibitory injunction*). Sometimes, where the matter is urgent, a plaintiff will ask for an *ex parte injunction*. This is a temporary injunction granted by a judge (normally in chambers) on the evidence of one party only pending a full hearing of the case in court when both parties will present their views.

Because Equity acted *in personam* (i.e. against the person, rather than, as at Common Law, against his property) it was able to ensure the attendance of the defendant before the court (by means of the subpoena) and to ensure that its judgments were enforced (by means of specific performance and injunction) as in each case a failure to comply with the order would result in imprisonment for contempt of court.

(c) *The relationship between the Common Law and Equity*

(i)   Whereas the Common Law was a complete body of law, Equity only developed in order to remedy the defects of the Common Law. As Maitland said Equity assumes the existence of the Common Law; it did not attempt to rival the Common Law system, but simply became a gloss or appendix upon it.

(ii) Although to begin with the Court of Chancery was willing to recognise new rights (e.g. the trust and mortgages), abandoning the rigidity of the Common Law (so much so that at one stage Equity was said to vary with the length of the Chancellor's foot!) it eventually began, like the Common Law, to adhere to a system of precedent and became almost as rigid.

(iii) While legal remedies are granted as of right, equitable remedies are purely discretionary. They will be granted only where it will be just and equitable to do so – applying the equitable maxims: he who comes to Equity must do Equity; he who comes to Equity must come with clean hands.

(iv) Until the *Judicature Acts 1873-75* Common Law and Equity were applied in different courts. If litigants were dissatisfied with the judgment of the Common Law courts, they had to commence entirely different proceedings in the Court of Chancery to obtain equitable relief, and an injunction to prevent enforcement of the Common Law rights.

(v)   The *Judicature Acts 1873-75* totally reorganised the system of courts. The High Court of Justice and Court of Appeal were set up, with all courts being empowered to apply the rules of Common Law and Equity. Although the legislation did not fuse the substantive rules of law, any division of the High Court may apply either rules of law, and award any remedy, and they are specifically directed by the legislature (*s.25*) that whenever there is any conflict between Common Law and Equity, the rules of Equity are to prevail.

23.4 *Statute law*

Early legislation was rare. It was made by the King in Council, which had both Parliamentary and judicial functions, and was therefore difficult to distinguish from Common Law. By the seventeenth century, however, Parliament, comprising of the Monarch, Lords and Commons, had become established as the main legislative body and its legislation was accepted as supreme law.

In the last century legislation has become the most important legal source of law, transcending Common Law and Equity. It has codified and altered the Common Law and Equity and defined the jurisdiction of the courts. It differs from Common Law and Equity in that they have developed new principles slowly and piecemeal by applying existing principles to new circumstances. Legislation can alter the law dramatically and coherently by Act of Parliament to repeal existing laws, or create entirely new laws, e.g. the laws relating to sex and race discrimination.

23.5 *Custom*

(a) *Introduction*

Law has its origin in custom. Early codes such as the Twelve Tables of Rome and the Laws of the Anglo-Saxons are not true exceptions to this as they constituted collections of updated customs.

Usage is a generally observed course of conduct which arises spontaneously out of habit or imitation. If certain conditions are fulfilled the law recognises and enforces usage as custom when it has come to be regarded as obligatory by the persons to whom it applies.

(b) *General customs*

The foundation of English law is the unwritten Common Law. There are no statutory definitions of murder, assault, libel, false imprisonment, negligence, or the consideration required for contracts not under seal. The traditional doctrine is that the Common Law of England consists of general customs of the realm.

To a great extent it is true of earlier times that the Common Law consisted of general immemorial customs, but not entirely. Some part of the law applied by the royal courts, which in the Middle Ages was attributed to general customs of the realm, included legislative provisions whose statutory origin has been forgotten; and it was also supplemented by principles which early judges had derived from Roman civil and canon law, feudal notices and ideas of natural reason. But custom was extremely important and it was a task of the King's judges to weld the variety of local customs into a consistent whole.

It is the case now that general customs are no longer a creative source of English law, as they have all become embodied in the system of case law or been replaced by legislation.

(c) *Local custom*

Local customs are not nearly so important at the present day owing to the effects of legislation. They are largely to be found in rights of way and common.

A local custom is always an exception to the general law, but it must not be contrary to a statute or to a fundamental principle of the Common Law. This is not a question of proving the existence of a custom, but of whether the custom if proved will be allowed by the courts. Thus in *Noble Durell (1789)* a local custom that every pound of butter sold in a certain market should weigh 18 ozs was held bad for a statute of Charles II had enacted that a pound avoirdupois should be 16 ozs everywhere. It automatically ceased to be custom on the passing of the statute.

Local custom is a variation of the Common Law applying either to persons generally within a locality, or to a specific class of persons within a locality, e.g. Borough English, Gavelkind, right to play sport on common land, rights of fishermen to dry nets on land, etc.

Several matters have to be proved by one party in a dispute where a custom is alleged. These are shown in the following paragraphs.

(d) *The existence of the custom must be proved*

This involves showing that it has the necessary antiquity. Ideally this should be since *time immemorial* which is arbitrarily set at 1189 (first year of Richard I's reign).

In practice it is enough to show that the custom has existed for a long period (and that no one can remember a time at which it did not exist) and that there is no proof that it did not or could not have existed in 1189.

In *Simpson v Wells (1872) LR 7 QB 214* Simpson was charged with obstructing a public footpath by setting up a refreshment stall. Simpson relied on the local *statute sessions fair* custom – and it was proved that the *custom* of setting up stalls had existed for years. His defence failed because the prosecution proved that statute sessions were set up after 1189 by a statute of Edward III in the fourteenth century.

Nevertheless, once the general custom is proved, post-1189 variations of details are allowed: So a customary right to play all kinds of lawful games on certain land did extend to cricket in the eighteenth century, even though cricket was unknown in 1189. Also in *Mercer v Denne (1904) (1905) 2 Ch 538* the custom of fishermen in a certain area to dry their nets on private land was considered valid, even though they dried their nets in a modern manner.

Vaughan Williams LJ said:

> The fact is that reason recoils from the proposition that legal memory goes back to an arbitrary date at the beginning of the reign of Richard I AD 1189, and, if one finds proof of uninterrupted modern usage, there is a natural inclination to presume the previous existence of the custom right back to 1189, even though the facts may be such as to force upon reason the conclusion that the modern usage could not in fact have been adopted for more than a few generations. Judges, therefore, presume everything possible which would give a custom origin, and find in favour of a manifestly modern custom as being an extension which falls within the reason of so much of the modern usage as may well have existed throughout legal memory.

(e)   *Continued enjoyment must be proved*

This enjoyment is not necessarily of the exercise of the custom, but enjoyment of the right to do so. (e.g. a right of way which is sometimes exercised on only one day a year to indicate that that right is still being claimed).

(f)   *Peaceable, open enjoyment, not by reason of consent or licence must be proved*

(i)   Cannot be a custom if only enjoyed by show of force;

(ii)   cannot be a custom if exercised secretly (no case: but see acquisition of easements by prescription);

(iii) cannot be a custom if only exercised because of consent. *Mills v Colchester Corporation (1867) LR 2 CP 476:* there is no general custom for local fishermen to use an oyster fishery because the right to fish has always depended on the grant of a licence (i.e. permission).

(g)   *The requirement of certainty*

How can one prove that the custom has existed from 1189 if one does not know what it is? Therefore, the limits of the right must be fairly closely defined.

In 1339 a usage of Hereford was pleaded that a man might sell his land when he could measure an ell (45 inches) and count up to 12 pence, but Sharedelowe J said:

> The usage is contrary to law, for one person is twenty years old before he knows how to measure an ell, and another person knows how when he is seven years old.

(h)   *The custom must have been regarded as obligatory*

Custom is regarded as a variety of law – a deviation from the general law. Therefore it must be regarded as legally obligatory just as the law is generally regarded, e.g. one can have a custom that the local landowners should contribute towards the upkeep of a bridge, the amount varying depending on the value of the landholdings. But you cannot have a custom whereby the landowner may contribute what he pleases towards the upkeep – for there is no obligation to contribute at all.

(i) *The custom must not be unreasonable*

It is for the party disputing the custom to prove that it is invalid because it is unreasonable, either in 1189 or today or (of course) both. For example, in *Bryant v Foot (1868) LR 3 QB 497* a fee of 13 shillings could not be a custom because 13 shillings in 1189 would have been unreasonable. (Note that the whole of the Manor of Birmingham was worth only £1 in 1087!)

There is also the possibility of legal unreasonableness, e.g. because one of the basic principles of the law is ignored. For instance, there is a basic principle that property should not be confiscated: if it is taken away, there should be compensation. Therefore, it cannot be a custom to take minerals from land without compensating the landowner. See *Wolstanton Ltd v Newcastle-under-Lyme Corporation (1940) AC 860:* the basic principle was that the judgment of disputes should be impartial: no man can be a judge in his own cause.

23.6 *The law merchant*

This had its origins in the customs of medieval merchants and was later developed by a body of courts administering their own rules. Like ecclesiastical law, it differs from the 'Englishness' of Common Law and Equity as it has a 'European flavour' based on much of Roman Law.

Since the courts of the merchants were not Common Law courts, they were uninhibited by the rules of those courts and it is to this fact that the concept of negotiability owes its existence.

Partnership, agency, insurance and negotiable instruments are four areas of law which have law merchant as their main source, but during a period of codification much of the law merchant was put into statutory form. The *Bills of Exchange Act 1882*, the *Partnership Act 1890* and the *Sale of Goods Act 1893* are all examples of merchant law-based codifications.

23.7 *Canon law*

This is the law of the Western or Catholic church and it influenced the development of English law in two ways:

(a) it formed the basis of many of the concepts developed by the lay courts (Common Law courts and Court of Chancery), e.g. the element of moral fault in crime, and the moral content of equity resulting from the influence of the early Chancellors who were churchmen;

(b) it was an area of law independent of the Common Law and administered by separate ecclesiastical courts. In Anglo-Saxon times there were no separate church courts. These were established after the Norman Conquest and initially had wide jurisdiction over clergy and lay people. Although this was reduced in the seventeenth century, the ecclesiastical courts continued to have jurisdiction over lay people in matrimonial and probate matters until 1857. Since that date these courts only have jurisdiction over matters affecting members of the church which are not within the jurisdiction of the ordinary courts, e.g. church doctrine or ceremony.

24. LEGAL SOURCE

A legal source is the law that the courts apply and to which notice is taken when coming to a decision. It is the authority for a proposition of law.

24.1 *Legislation*

This is the most important legal source. Since Parliament is sovereign, legislation takes priority over all other sources of law.

(a) *United Kingdom statut*

The main considerations are:

(i) what is a statute, and how does it come into being?

(ii) reasons for statutes;

(iii) the types of law that statutes create;

(iv) various categories of statutes;

(v) operation of statutes;

(vi) how do the courts, to whom it falls to say what the exact words of the statute mean, go about interpreting statutes?

(b) *What is a statute?*

A *statute* is the basic unit of that source of law referred to collectively as *legislation*. In England, another word for 'statute' is *Act of Parliament*. Legislation is the formulation of law by the appropriate organ of state (the *legislature*), in such a manner that the actual words used are themselves an integral part of the law – the exact shades of meaning which can be read into the words used are of vital importance when the time comes for the practical application of the law.

Although it is probably not true to say that judges do not make law themselves today (because they manifestly do make law by the way they manipulate the doctrine of precedent, distinguishing unpopular decisions and extending desirable decisions by analogy), legislation is certainly the quickest, easiest and most common way of developing law (by extending, changing and repealing) in modern systems.

In England, Parliament has unlimited legal power to create, alter and repeal English law. Even the Act of Accession to the EEC is technically repealable. An Act of Parliament is *passed* (made law) by being *read* and debated upon in both Houses of Parliament (Commons and Lords) and, if not defeated by majority vote at any stage, being signed by the Queen (i.e. receiving the Royal Assent).

Not all legislation is directly enacted by Parliament: a mass of detail (e.g. the fuel regulations) is usually completed by what is called *subordinate* or *delegated legislation*.

Since most of the problems concerning Acts of Parliament arise from quibbles as to meaning, it is therefore important that they should be as accurately and concisely drafted as possible.

(c) *Reasons for statutes*

    (i)   Case law may need revision by an Act of Parliament, e.g. the decision in *Rookes v Barnard (1964) 1 All ER 467* altered by the *Trade Disputes Act 1965.*

    (ii)   Creation of a completely new law which has never existed even in case law, e.g. the *Trade Descriptions Act 1968.*

    (iii)   Replacement of an old Act by a new one, e.g. the *Theft Act 1968* replaced the *Larceny Act 1916.*

    (iv)   Consolidation laws – in order to piece together in one statute all previous statutes concerned with a particular branch of the law, e.g. the *Companies Act 1948* consolidated the *Companies Acts 1929 & 1947.* The *Employment Protection Consolidation Act 1978* consolidated various labour law provisions.

    (v)   Codification – this is greater in scope than consolidation for, as well as piecing together various statutes, it also accumulates relevant case law into one or a few volumes of written law. The other emphasis of codification is that it tends to simplify and clarify existing law rather than to effect substantial alterations to it, e.g. the *Offences Against the Person Act 1861*, the *Sale of Goods Act 1979.*

(d) *Types of laws created by statutes*

    (i)   The *Finance Act* – a collection of taxes – passed each year.

    (ii)   Social legislation – laws concerned with the location of industry, immigration, local government laws, town and country planning, safety regulations, public utility matters, e.g. rules regarding laying of pipe-lines and telegraph wires, etc.

    (iii)   Criminal law – e.g. the *Theft Act 1968*, the *Criminal Damage Act 1971*, the *Offences Against the Person Act 1861*, etc.

    (iv)   Civil law – e.g. the *Law Reform (Frustrated Contracts) Act 1943*, the *Animals Act 1971*, the *Occupiers' Liability Act 1957*, the *Wills Act 1837*, the *Law Reform (Contributory Negligence) Act 1945*, the *Unfair Contract Terms Act 1977.*

(e) *Categories of legislation*

    (i)   *Acts of Parliament* – the contents of the Act are set out in various publications, though reference to the present day Act is through the *Queen's Printer's Copy* published by Her Majesty's Stationery Office and on sale to the public. This office publishes these copies in annual volumes and also publishes annually an *Index to Statutes in Force* for reference purposes. In addition, the Incorporated Council of Law Reporting publishes annually texts of Acts taken from the Queen's Printer's copies.

        Method of citation – short title, calendar year and chapter number, e.g. *Torts (Interference with Goods) Act 1977*, Chapter 32.

    (ii)   *Delegated legislation* – this is the vast body of rules, orders, regulations and bye-laws created by subordinate bodies under specific powers delegated to these bodies by Parliament.

        One of the advantages of delegated legislation is that it enables regulations to be made and altered quickly without need (usually) for placing them before Parliament. The vital feature which distinguishes Parliament from any other person or body having legislative power is that the latter are not sovereign.

Delegated legislation is valid only if it lies within the legislative powers conferred by Parliament, i.e. is *intra vires*.

The highest form of delegated legislation is an *Order in Council* which is nominally an order of the Privy Council consisting of the Sovereign and her Privy Councillors. Many Acts are brought into operation by Order in Council, the power to make an order being contained in the Act itself. In fact, though not in theory, an Order in Council is generally made by the Government and merely sanctioned by the Privy Council. The effect is to confer wide legislative power upon government departments: *s. 2 (2) European Communities Act 1972.*

An Order in Council and certain other regulations are published in the *Statutory Instruments* by the Queen's Printer and are available at Her Majesty's Stationery Office.

Citation is by calendar year and a number, often followed by the short title, e.g. *1971 No. 1292 (L 33) Supreme Court of Judicature – The Crown Court Rules 1971.*

(iii) *Autonomic legislation* – this differs from delegated legislation in that private bodies and organisations are given power by Parliament to legislate for their members, e.g. the Church of England, General Medical Council and Law Society. It does not affect the public, but it does in a negative sense in that any individual who causes a breach of regulations created by an autonomous body may commit a civil wrong.

(iv) *Administrative quasi-legislation* – this phrase (invented by Sir Carleton Kemp Allen) refers to Codes of Practice, Non-Statutory Rules, Guidance Notes and other publications (by whatever name known) which are admissible evidence in a court of law, and can be interpreted in much the say way as (but less strictly than) an Act of Parliament or Statutory Instrument – but which are not, in themselves, a form of legislation. Examples are the Immigration Rules, the Codes of Practice issued under the *Health and Safety at Work Act 1974*, the *Employment Act 1980* and the *Police and Criminal Evidence Act 1984*. These publications are made by a Secretary of State (or by some other named public body) under a statutory duty to make and publish appropriate provisions by way of guidance or advice. A common form of words giving effect to such publications is to be found in *s.66(10) & (11) Criminal Evidence Act 1984. Sub-s. (10)* provides that breach of a Code of Practice shall not 'of itself' render a police officer liable to any criminal or civil proceedings. *Sub-s. (11)* provides that the Code shall be admissible evidence in civil and criminal proceedings 'and if any provision of such a code appears to the court or tribunal conducting the proceedings to be relevant to any question arising in the proceedings it shall be taken into account in determining that question'. One of the oldest and best known pieces of quasi-legislation is, of course, the *Highway Code* which, in addition to referring to particular legal obligations, also gives guidance and advice on road safety. This is made admissible evidence in civil and criminal proceedings by *s.37(5) Road Traffic Act 1972*. The Immigration Rules (made under *s. 3 (2) Immigration Act 1971*) are more 'legislative' in appearance than most forms of quasilegislation. These 'rules' must be approved by both Houses of Parliament, and so they mimic the procedure used in making certain statutory instruments. However, they are *not* statutory instruments, and they are not interpreted by the courts in the same way as a statutory provision: *R v Immigration Appeal Tribunal, ex parte Alexander (1982) 1 All ER 763.*

(f) *Operation of statutes*

(i) *Geographical operation* – there is a presumption that an Act of Parliament is operative throughout the whole of the United Kingdom unless a contrary intention appears in the Act itself.

A statute is in fact often expressly limited to England and Wales, owing to the special character of Scots law.

Some statutes are expressed to extend to crimes committed abroad (although UK legislation has no force in foreign countries), but anyone committing such crimes can be called to account if charged in England. See the *Treason Act 1352* and the case of *Joyce v DPP (1946) 1 All ER 186* and *s. 3 Marine Broadcasting Offences Act 1967* on pirate radios.

(ii) *Temporal operation* – the presumption is that an Act of Parliament is operative on the day it receives the Royal Assent. A later date may sometimes be mentioned in order to give to whom the Act concerns a chance to abide by the new rules, e.g. the *Highways (Miscellaneous Provisions) Act 1961* did not come into force until 1964. This delay was for the purpose of enabling highway authorities, upon whom a new duty to maintain highways was imposed, to effect such repairs as were necessary to comply with the stringent provisions of the Act.

There is not always a time stated in the Act, e.g. the *Civil Evidence Act 1968*, of which certain sections shall come into force on such day as the Lord Chancellor may, by order made by Statutory Instrument, so appoint, e.g. the *Fair Trading Act 1973* was to come into operation on such day as the Secretary of State by order made by Statutory Instrument should appoint. It in fact came into operation on 14 September 1973.

Note: Delegated legislation generally comes into force when it is passed, but *s.3(2) Statutory Instruments Act 1946* provides that, where a person is charged with contravening the provisions of a Statutory Instrument, it shall be a defence to prove that the Statutory Instrument had not been issued by Her Majesty's Stationery Office at the date of the alleged contravention, unless it is proved that at that date all reasonable steps had been taken for the purpose of bringing the purpose of the Instrument to the notice of the public, or of persons likely to be affected by it.

(iii) *Retrospective operation* – the presumption against a statute being retrospective in its effect. This presumption is particularly strong where the statute in question creates criminal penalties or tax obligations as would operate to deprive a person of a vested right in property.

However, statutes, e.g. the *Finance Act 1936*, aimed at preventing tax avoidance, are sometimes expressed to be retroactive and therefore there seems to be no irrebuttable presumption against retroactivity in the case of statutes of this type. Also *s. 1(2) War Damage Act 1965* operated to remove vested rights to compensation from the Crown; it was exceptional in that it was also expressed to apply to proceedings commenced before the Act came into force: *Burmah Oil Co v Lord Advocate (1964) 2 All ER 348*.

(iv) *Ending of a statute* – no statute becomes obsolete by the passing of time.

A statute may come to an end by *express* or *implied repeal*. A statute is *expressly* repealed either when repealed by another Act devoted only to repeal, e.g. the *Statute Law (Repeals) Act 1971* (which repealed more than 170 separate statutes in whole or in part) or, when repealed by another Act which creates new law and repeals previous enactments in whole or in part. Repeals are set out in a Schedule to the new Act. An example is the *Theft Act 1968* which repealed the *Larceny Act 1916*, and many other previous enactments.

Implied repeal occurs where two statutory provisions are inconsistent with one another. In this situation the later provision impliedly repeals the earlier to the extent of inconsistency.

Note: It must be an Act of the same type, e.g. a Public Act cannot repeal a Private Act of Parliament.

24.2 *EEC legislation*

(a) *Introduction*

EEC law, which applies to the 12 Member States, is essentially concerned with customs duties, agriculture, free movement of labour, services and capital, transport, and restrictive trade practices. Regulation of the coal, steel and nuclear energy industries is provided for under the treaties and law relating to the other two communities, viz. the *European Coal and Steel Community* (ECSC) and the *European Atomic Energy Community* (EURATOM).

Most English domestic law, such as criminal law, contract, tort, land and family law remains unaffected.

(b) *Applicability*

Where EEC law has direct internal effect, it can affect citizens in their private capacity, and can impose monetary penalties under civil proceedings relating to industrial and commercial activities. The effect of the *European Communities Act 1972* (passed by the Westminster Parliament) is to override existing English law so far as it is inconsistent, and Parliament is expected to refrain from passing legislation inconsistent with EEC law for the time being in force.

By the *European Communities Act 1972* effect was given to the treaties by which the UK agreed to join the EEC, ECSC and EURATOM.

Accession to the EEC was effective for the UK as from 1 January 1973.

s.2(1) European Communities Act 1972 provides for the application in this country of laws made by the treaties and by existing or future self-executing Community Regulations, questions of interpretation and, in the case of Regulations, validity being decided by, or in accordance with principles laid down by, the European Court.

There is also a limited power under *s.2(2)* to issue Statutory Instruments giving effect to Community Directives and either to be laid in draft for approval by resolutions of each House (of the Westminster Parliament) or to be subject to annulment by resolution of each House.

(c) *Forms of EEC legislation*

(i) *Regulations* – these are made by the Council of Ministers and the *European Commission* (which is situated in Brussels) under *Article 189 Treaty of Rome*.

Regulations are of general application in the 12 Member States and become part of the domestic law of each member state without, for example, the Westminster

Parliament needing to take cognisance of them. Some may give rise to consequent subordinate legislation, or may require repeal or amendment of existing Acts.

(ii) *Directives* – these are the equivalent of British delegated legislation and are binding in principle. It is left to the member countries to decide up on the means of giving them legal and administrative effect, e.g. in the UK by an Act of Parliament. This is dealt with under *s. 2 European Communities Act 1972.*

(iii) *Decisions*

These are also made by the Council of Ministers and the European Commission under *Article 189 Treaty of Rome.*

Decisions are of more particular application and are also immediately operative, but may require administrative or legislative action to make them effective.

(d) *Law-making in the EEC*

A substantial number of types of EEC law come from the Council of

Ministers acting in most cases on proposals put forward by the Commission and published in draft, and it may be months (and sometimes years) before a final decision is taken. Such legislative proposalsmust be referred to the European Parliament at Strasbourg before the Council of Ministers take the final decision, though the Council is in no way bound by opinions of the European Parliament.

Thus all important legislative proposals of the EEC are published in draft at an early stage and this gives the legislatures of member countries a chance to exert influence on the formative stages of law-making.

(e) *Interpretation*

The European Court has jurisdiction to give preliminary rulings on the interpretation of the treaties of the Community and of acts of the various Community institutions under the *Treaty of Rome* and the treaties setting up the ECSC and EURATOM.

Lord Denning adopted a restrictive approach to when matters should be referred to the European Court in *Bulmer v Bollinger (1974) Ch 401* but there has been an increasing tendency to refer doubtful matters. However, he used the opportunity to make a statement on how European legislation should be interpreted. He urged English judges to avoid examining words in meticulous detail, and to look instead at the purpose or intent of the legislation. The *Treaty of Rome* should serve as an inspiration, and if there is a gap in the legislation, the judges should fill it by trying to ascertain what the drafters of the legislation would have done.

24.3 *Case law*

(a) *Meaning and importance*

Case law is the body of law which is contained in judicial decisions, as distinct from the law contained in legislation.

In many countries legislation is regarded as the normal type of law, supplemented by decisions of the judges on the interpretation of the statutes. This is so of most continental countries where these *codes* are regarded as the only source of law. In England, in the absence of such codes, it was for many centuries left to the judges to formulate legal principles based on their experience and common sense. Law evolved in this way is technically known as judge-made or case law and is so termed because it is based on decisions made in actual cases which come before the courts. As stated earlier, such law is sometimes referred to as Common Law as opposed to statute law, i.e. that which emanates from Parliament.

The Common Law is constantly changing, adapting to new conditions and circumstances. One of the problems in the legal systems of those countries using a codified law is that unless the code is constantly updated and reformed, it may stagnate and present the judges who must interpret it with extremely complicated problems. In France, the prevailing codes are still the Napoleonic codes; the judges have needed considerable ingenuity to adapt these to cover problems associated with the industrial and technological revolutions.

The Common Law system of judge-made law is said to be *declaratory*, i.e. a decision of a court operates retrospectively, declaring what the law is (and has been) rather than what it shall be. It is because of this that judges can claim that they are not making new law, but merely deciding a novel case in accordance with existing legal principles. This is the so-called 'declaratory theory', but it will be seen below that the judges *do in reality make law* when dealing with unprecedented situations, 'distinguishing' earlier cases and interpreting statutes.

(b) *Case law as a source of law*

Case law may be a source of law in two ways:

(i) where no statute covers the point at issue the judge declares the existing Common Law principle which applies. Historically, case law is extremely important and Common Law and Equity were created by case law. As legislation became a more important source of law the areas of law which were and are now developed solely by case law have been reduced. However, it is still important in areas not covered by statute and large parts of the law of contract and tort are still based to a large extent on case law;

(ii) where judges interpret a statute, their decision may become a secondary source of law, the statute itself being the primary source.

(c) *Meaning of judicial precedent*

When a judge decides a case before him his judgment will have been based on some legal principle or process of legal reasoning – logically and practically it is desirable that in all future cases of a similar kind where the material facts do not substantially differ, that the same process of legal reasoning should apply.

The desirability of his *following* the earlier decision can be seen in several ways, and one advantage is that it leads to certainty and fairness. People who have based their conduct on the decision in the earlier case do so in the belief that they are doing what is correct and lawful. It would be unfair and would bring the law into disrepute as being uncertain if, the next time a similar problem came before a court, a different process of legal reasoning was used.

In England, if the necessary conditions are satisfied – i.e. if the court which decided the first case is suitably related to the court which is in the process of trying the second similar case – the decision of the first court would be not merely persuasive but actually binding.

Example

If Court 2 considers that the legal reasoning and facts in Case 1 are applicable to Case 2, they must apply that legal reasoning (even if privately the judges do not agree with it).

(d) *What is meant by a decision?*

Every case which reaches a conclusive result in a court of law has a specific *decision* in one sense of the word – this type of decision is the order which the judge issues, e.g. 'I find that X owes Y £800'. This decision is called *res judicata* and is binding on X and Y only. The decision in this sense is not the decision which constitutes the precedent for future cases.

The binding decision referred to in the previous paragraph is the legal reasoning upon which the judge came to his decision. This forms the binding decision or *precedent. It is the rule of law contained in the decision, i. e. the ratio decidendi.*

(e) *Ratio decidendi*

This process of legal reasoning produces the *ratio decidendi* (the reasoning behind the decision). The court deciding a case does not state what is its *ratio decidendi* that is for later courts to discover.

(f) *The difference between res judicata and ratio decidendi*

The cases of *Re Waring (1942) Ch 309* and *Re Waring (1948) Ch 221* illustrate the difference.

By his will, Waring left legacies to H and L *free of income tax.* A dispute arose between the legatees and the executors of Waring's estate as to what amount should be paid to the legatees. H contested this in the Court of Appeal in *Re Waring (1942).* The Court of Appeal decided that the amount to be paid to H was the legacy *minus* the income tax. H did not appeal to the House of Lords.

In 1946 the House of Lords decided a similar case (between entirely different people) differently from *Re Waring (1942).* In fact, the House of Lords said that the Court of Appeal was wrong in that case-or, in technical terms, the House of Lords overruled the Court of Appeal. It said the Court of Appeal had used the wrong *ratio decidendi.* After H and L heard of the 1946 House of Lords decision they both applied to the court to have their legacies sorted out.

In *Re Waring (1948)* the court held:

(i) that H, who had been a party to *Re Waring (1942)*, was bound by the actual decision in that case and had to take his legacy minus income tax. This was because the matter *vis-à-vis* H was *res judicata;*

(ii) that L, who had not been a party to *Re Waring (1942)*, could take advantage of the 1946 House of Lords case overruling the legal reasoning or *ratio decidendi* in *Re Waring (1942)* and could claim his legacy before income tax was deducted.

In *Re Waring (1942)* the two decisions were:

(i) the *res judicata* (actual decision) – H can only receive his legacy minus income tax;

(ii) the *ratio decidendi* the legal reasoning upon which (i) was reached.

It was the *ratio decidendi* that was overruled in the 1946 House of Lords case. H remained personally bound by it but L was not a party and therefore could take advantage of the 1946 case.

(g) *How to find the ratio decidendi of a case*

A judgment in a case usually contains:

(i)   a statement of facts, with emphasis laid on the cases considered by the judge to be material to his decision;

(ii) an account of the process of reasoning used by the judge in deciding what the legal consequences of the material facts should be. Here the judge will look at earlier cases to find if there is one on a par with the one he is deciding. If there is not, he looks for analogous cases;

(iii) the actual decision.

The *ratio decidendi* is discovered from all three parts of the court's judgment, e.g. *Donoghue v Stevenson (1932) AC 562* as applied in *Grant v Australian Knitting Mills (1936) AC 85*.

The decision in *Donoghue v Stevenson* was that if a snail was in a bottle, the manufacturer owed a duty of care to Mrs D and had to pay money compensation in the form of damages.

In *Grant v Australian Knitting Mills* it was decided that the *ratio decidendi* in *Donoghue v Stevenson* was based on the neighbour principle. The decision was that the manufacturer owed a duty of care to Grant and had to pay money compensation in the form of damages.

How did the court in *Grant v Australian Knitting Mills* discover what the *ratio* of *Donoghue v Stevenson* was, in order to decide whether or not the principle in *Donoghue v Stevenson* applied to the *Grant v Australian Knitting Mills* facts?

Judges deciding *Grant's case* would look at the actual decision in *Donoghue* together with the judgments delivered by the judges in *Donoghue v Stevenson*, and would try to discover what facts and principles of law were used in order to produce the actual decision.

(h) *What were the facts essential to the decision?*

To some extent it was fairly easy to determine which facts the court in *Donoghue v Stevenson* regarded as material because by this time the facts in the case would have been twice filtered to exclude obviously irrelevant matters:

(i)   in the pleadings;

(ii) by judges in *Donoghue v Stevenson* themselves.

Therefore, the judges in *Grant's case* could take it as read that the most obviously irrelevant facts had been omitted from the judgments in *Donoghue v Stevenson* (hence no references to the colour of Mrs D's hair, or to the reason why her friend bought her the ginger-beer, or to whether it was a rainy day, etc.). However, the judges in *Grant* would be aware that even in the House of Lords' judgments in *Donoghue v Stevenson*, some facts would be mentioned that were not regarded by the court in *Donoghue v Stevenson* as material. This is inevitable because the court likes to give a brief resumé of the factual situation in question, and this cannot generally be done without mentioning some irrelevant facts, e.g. the fact that the café was an ice-cream parlour, the date of the incident, etc.

However, from the judgments in *Donoghue v Stevenson*, the court in *Grant* would discover that the material facts were:

(i)   S manufactured ginger-beer intended to be consumed;

(ii)   at some time during the bottling process, a snail entered the bottle, which would not have occurred if S had taken reasonable steps to protect the ginger-beer;

(iii) Mrs D became ill as a result of consuming the ginger-beer.

(i)   *What general principles of law were cited?*

    (i)   Nineteenth century cases had established a tort of negligence comprising four main elements:

        (1)   the defendant must owe a duty of care to take reasonable steps not to injure the plaintiff;

        (2)   the defendant must have broken his duty;

        (3)   it must have been reasonably foreseeable that someone would suffer from the breach;

        (4)   the plaintiff did in fact suffer from the breach of duty.

    (ii)   To whom is a duty of care owed? Lord Atkin stated in *Donoghue v Stevenson:*

        ... Who then is my neighbour? The answer seems to be persons who are so closely and directly affected by my act that it ought reasonably to have them in contemplation as being affected when I am directing my mind to the acts or omissions which are called in question.

(j)   *What was the decision in Donoghue v Stevenson?*

S, the manufacturer of the ginger-beer, owed a duty of care to Mrs D which he broke (by not preventing the snail from getting in the bottle). Mrs D had been injured. S owed her a duty of care and paid damages since he had breached that duty.

Therefore, the court in *Grant v Australian Knitting Mills* would come to the conclusion that, where a manufacturer provides consumer goods, he owes a duty to the ultimate consumer to ensure that no harm occurs to the consumer by reason of defects in the goods, caused by the manufacturer failing to take reasonable steps to ensure that the goods are of good quality.

Then, applying the above reasoning to the facts in *Grant's case:*

(i)   the Australian Knitting Mills manufactured consumer goods (woollen underpants). Therefore, the defendants owed a duty of care to the ultimate wearer of these goods;

(ii)   at some time a defect occurred (a foreign body causing dermatitis) which was not reasonably prevented by the Australian Knitting Mills;

(iii) Grant was injured.

Accordingly, Grant was entitled to damages.

These two cases are closely allied but the doctrine of precedent allows a case being applied by analogy to wider issues, e.g. in *Hedley Byrne v Heller (1964) AC 465* where the *Donoghue v Stevenson* principle was held to apply to negligent statements. A duty of care is owed to persons whom one knows will rely on one's advice, i. e. one's neighbour under the *Donoghue* test.

(k)   A formula for finding the ratio decidendi of a case

Basically it is: *Material facts + Principles + eq Decision.*

> *Case 1*:   Facts + Principle = X, Y, Z
>
> Court says Y and Z are material to decision
>
> Decision re Y and Z = A

> *Case 2*:   Facts + Principle = W, X, Y, Z
>
> Court says Y and Z are material, W and X are not
>
> Therefore, follow Case 1.

> *Case 3*:   Facts = V, Y, Z
>
> Court says all are material
>
> Therefore, do not necessarily follow Case 1 (because one extra material fact, namely V, may alter the decision) but use Case 1 as analogy

(l)   *Obiter dicta*

Not every statement of law in a judgment is binding. Only statements based on facts found in that particular case and on which the decision is based form the *ratio* of the case. All other statements are merely comments of the judge, which are called *obiter dicta.*

These observations of the judge are not strictly relevant to the facts in issue and they are not binding. However, they may help other judges in the future in that they will illustrate a line of reasoning and as such are persuasive authority.

If you remember, part of a judge's judgment is usually taken up with discussions of general legal principles which might be applicable to the case in hand. Not all those principles will be embodied in the *ratio decidendi* but, if the judge made a serious statement of principle, it will be regarded as persuasive in a later case, even if it was only used as a means of explanation, an illustration or an analogy in the earlier decision. Thus, if in a particular case a judge finds for the defendant on facts A, B and C, but says in his judgment that had the facts been A, B and E he would have given judgment for the plaintiff, that latter statement is obviously not part of the *ratio decidendi* because the judge was not deciding facts A, B and E. However, if in a later case, facts A, B and E crop up, another court would regard the judge's statement concerning his probable reaction to facts A, B and E (an *obiter dictum*) as being persuasive: the latter court is not bound because the statement was not a *ratio decidendi*, but it would only depart from the *obiter dictum* if it clearly thought it was wrong.

The extent to which the *dictum* is persuasive depends on the degree and lucidity of the reasoning given, the court and the judge, whether other judges have found it persuasive and the age of the case.

(m)   *Other persuasive authorities*

As well as *obiter dicta* there are other persuasive precedents:

(i)

> *Decisions of inferior courts*

(i) *Decisions of inferior courts*

Some precedents are binding if there is a special relationship between the present court and the court that decided the earlier case. This special relationship will be explained in more detail later but basically a court is bound by the decision of a court higher than it in the hierarchy, and sometimes by its own earlier decisions.

However, if that special relationship is absent, the earlier decision will not be binding but it will be persuasive. For example:

(1) In 1974 a High Court judge decided that the outcome of a particular case should be X. In 1984 another High Court judge is faced with the same kind of case and, although he is not bound by the 1974 decision, it is nevertheless persuasive, and he will only depart from it if there is a compelling reason.

(2) In 1974 the Court of Appeal decided that the outcome of a particular case should be X. In 1984 the House of Lords is faced with a similar case. The 1974 decision is not binding since the Court of Appeal is inferior to the House of Lords in the hierarchy, but the decision is persuasive, and the House of Lords will only reach a different decision if the Court of Appeal was obviously wrong.

(ii) *Decisions of foreign courts*

There is a tendency for English judges to draw analogies with cases decided by foreign courts, and to regard such decisions as persuasive.

Scotland and Eire have separate legal systems but the decisions of their courts may be regarded as persuasive. Similarly, decisions of Commonwealth countries and the USA are persuasive since their legal systems are based on the Common Law.

(iii) *Decisions of the Judicial Committee of the Privy Council*

These decisions are not strictly binding and even a first instance judge is free to ignore them. This court is a special court outside the normal hierarchy and deals with appeals from overseas courts. In practice most of the Privy Council judges are also judges in the House of Lords.

In 1961 the Privy Council decided an appeal from Australia in a case called *The Wagon Mound (1961) 1 All Er 404*. This case concerned the recovery of damages for negligence and conflicted with a decision of the Court of Appeal in *Re Polemis (1921) 3 KB 560*. In 1964, in *Doughty v Turner Metals (1964) 1 QB 518*, the Court of Appeal followed the Privy Council decision in preference to the earlier Court of Appeal decision.

24.4 *Custom*

In a limited sense the courts will also recognise and give effect to a valid custom. For the circumstances of when this applies, see paragraph 23.5.

24.5 *Foreign law*

On occasion, especially in cases on wills and family matters, the English courts are required to take account of rules of foreign law. Such rules are proved in evidence by calling an expert to appear as a witness and to say what the foreign law is.

As a member of the community of nations and of international organisations such as the United Nations, the United Kingdom is often a party to international agreements.

These international agreements, or treaties, govern relationships between states and their obligations. This international law is not automatically recognised and enforced by the English courts.

The status of these treaties as far as the English courts are concerned can best be understood by considering the *Treaty of Rome 1957*. This was the Treaty to which Britain had to become a signatory in order to enter the Common Market. The Treaty provisions are not part of English law in their own right: Parliament had expressly to implement them as such by passing the *European Communities Act 1972*. It was as a result of action by the UK Parliament that they became a source of law as defined above. Thus, international law is not a source of law unless and until the UK Parliament expressly enacts that it should be so. (It should be noted that secondary legislation of the EEC, as contained in Regulations and Directives, for example, is not international law but law of the EEC which is an autonomous entity having legal personality in its own right.)

So what of the treaties to which the UK is a signatory?

Relationships between sovereign states – the purview of international law – are generally the province of the executive rather than the judiciary. Their nature is political rather than legal: if a dispute arises between the UK government and that of another state, the matter could not be resolved either by the English courts or by the national courts of the other country, for neither would have the power to make decisions which could be enforced in the other jurisdiction. Negotiations would be handled by government ministers. It is true that the United Nations exists to assist in disagreements between states, but its resolutions lack coercive force in the sense in which we use that term when talking about domestic law. UN resolutions have their strength in a political context since the two countries become aware of likely world reaction to their intended actions; fear of economic and political consequences may achieve the desired result.

In practice, despite the lack of sanctions in the legal sense, international law, as contained in the *Charter of the United Nations* as in other treaty obligations, is generally perceived as binding and are widely obeyed. Thus, while international law cannot be regarded as a source of law under the definition adopted here, it is nonetheless a point of reference in foreign affairs for much the same reasons as the conventional sources of law are a point of reference for the individual citizen.

25. *LITERARY SOURCES*

A literary source is the document in which a legal source is recorded.

25.1 *Law Reports*

The basic rule is that a judge may only rely on precedents which are vouched for by a member of the Bar present when judgment was given; or which the judge is aware of personally. Although a barrister may cite a case in which he appeared, or a judge rely on a case in which he sat in judgment, this is relatively rare and precedents cited or relied on are almost always those contained in Law Reports.

Thus, the doctrine of judicial precedent depends on law reporting. Indeed, the current doctrine really commenced with the beginning of a reliable system of law reporting.

The history of law reporting falls into three main periods:.

(a)   *The Middle Ages* – the *Year Books;* rather inaccurate notes of cases, prepared by counsel.

(b)   *1500 to 1865* – commercial law reporting by a large number of publishers, often restricted to certain branches of the law.

(c)   *1865 to date* – a system of law reporting which is partly private and partly official. In 1865 the Incorporated Council of Law Reporting for England and Wales was established to publish reports of decisions in important cases quickly and cheaply. Representatives of both the barristers' and solicitors' professional bodies are members of the Council. It publishes two semi-official series of reports known as the *Law Reports* and the *Weekly Law Reports.* There are also several series of reports which are published by private publishers, e.g. the *All England Law Reports. The Times* and the *Independent* newspapers also publish cases of interest either the day after or within a few days of judgment being given. In addition, there are specialised series of reports, e.g. *Simon's Tax Cases* which report only tax cases.

Cases are cited by reference to the relevant series of reports, the year of the decision and the page in the report, e.g. *Hedley Byrne & Co v Heller & Partners (1963) 2 All ER 575* shows that this case is reported in the *All England Law Reports* of 1963, Volume 2, at p.575.

It must be realised that only a small proportion of cases are reported. Many cases – particularly criminal cases – are solely concerned with establishing facts. It is only when the law to be applied to the facts is in dispute that the decision is of importance as a precedent, and is, therefore, recorded in the Law Reports.

25.2 *Books of authority*

This is a convenient place to introduce another, albeit minor, source of law-*books of authority*, which are old textbooks.

The general rule is that, as textbooks only describe the law in that they set out the author's opinion of what the law is, they are not a source of law and cannot be regarded as authority. However, certain very old textbooks have become generally accepted as *books of authority.* These books are those which were written during a period of inadequate law reporting and were the main source of law at that time. Not all ancient books of English law have become authorities; only those of certain authors – not surprisingly almost all of these were judges. The last generally accepted book of authority was published in 1765.

25.3 *Textbooks*

Modern textbooks are of ten consulted for guidance but are not regarded as books of authority. The court may accept and approve the opinion of the author and to this extent they are persuasive authority. There used to be a rule that a textbook could only be cited in court if the author was dead. However, this rule no longer exists and several writers have had the pleasure of persuading the judges through their own work during their lifetime.

25.4 *Statutes*

The Queen's Printer's copy of a statute is the literary source where legislation may be found.

25.5 *Travaux préparatoires*

Where a UK court needs to interpret provisions made in response to international agreements or treaties, the court may refer to the preparatory working papers that led to the signing of the treaty.

LLB

ENGLISH LEGAL SYSTEM

LESSON 3 (STUDY)

31. *HISTORICAL DEVELOPMENT OF THE COURT STRUCTURE*

31.1 *Introduction*

As a result of a number of factors, two of which were the number of courts which had developed and the conflict between some of the courts, extensive reforms were carried out in the nineteenth century. This produced a court structure which is, to a large extent, much the same today. For an appreciation of the current law and the court structure it is necessary to know in outline the reforms that were made, and these are discussed below.

31.2 *Common Law*

In Anglo-Saxon times there was no unified system of law for the whole country. The law varied from area to area and depended on whom had invaded and settled in the area and what local customs, often based on oral traditions, had grown up. There was no coherent general theory of law and there was little distinction between civil and criminal wrongs. There were courts but they enforced the local laws and the procedure was primitive, e.g. trial by ordeal.

English law is regarded as stemming from one of the most decisive events in English history, the Norman Conquest, whereby William of Normandy became King of England in 1066. As the conqueror William did not impose Norman law on the English nor abolish the jurisdiction of the existing courts nor change existing customary laws. Indeed, he stated that the laws dispensed should be the existing laws.

However, the jurisdiction of the existing local courts gradually declined and the law was gradually unified as a result of a number of factors:

(a) The King's Council *(Curia Regis)*, an assembly of the King and the more important nobles, lords, bishops, etc., and the predecessor of Parliament and the courts, introduced strong central government and developed national unity.

(b) A feudal system was established throughout the country whereby the King owned all the land. Feudalism had existed before 1066, in that the owner of land would grant part of his estate to tenants in exchange for loyalty and services (e.g. military services). William centralised and extended this by appropriating all the land to himself and granting holdings to his followers. They in turn make grants of the land granted to them. The King, however, ultimately *owned* all the land (as the Queen still does in theory today).

(c) Representatives of the King appointed by the King's Council were sent from Westminster to check the local administration in all parts of the country. Initially, these representatives had administrative functions, e.g. recording land, wealth, collecting taxes, etc., but gradually they developed a judicial capacity and became the original royal judges.

As their judicial function increased they became known as *itinerant justices*. The country was divided into circuits which they toured regularly, returning to Westminster between circuits where they compared the customs of the different areas. By selecting the best customs and applying them outside that local area these itinerant justices gradually unified the local customary laws.

(d) The principle of *stare decisis* (let the decision stand) developed, whereby decisions made would be followed by other judges in subsequent cases. This helped to unify the law and made it more certain. This principle is the foundation of the current doctrine of judicial precedent, which is based on the concept that judges do not make the law but merely declare what the existing law is.

(e)   The functions of the King's Council became more distinct and split off to form separate departments or courts. This happened in the following order:

   (i)   *The Court of Exchequer* – initially formed as a department dealing with revenue, which split into an administrative department and the Court of Exchequer which dealt with tax cases and some civil actions.

   (ii)   *The Court of Common Pleas* – set up to deal with disputes between persons (civil actions) and called 'common pleas' because it dealt with the pleas of commoners as opposed to pleas of the Crown (criminal cases).

   (iii)   *The Court of King's Bench* – the last to separate and as a result more closely associated with the King. It dealt with criminal and some civil matters and had a supervisory role over inferior courts.

(f)   The development of the *writ system*, whereby the King, as the fount of justice, would grant a writ to enable a person to seek justice from the King (in the King's courts) when he could not obtain it in the local courts. As the use of these writs increased the civil jurisdiction of the local courts declined.

31.3 *Defects in the Common Law*

The procedure in the Common Law courts was very technical. To start civil proceedings the person taking the action (the plaintiff) purchased a writ from the Chancery, the office of the Chancellor, who was the King's principal minister. A writ was a formal document issued in the name of the King by the clerks in the Chancellor's office. It set out the plaintiff's claim or 'cause of action' against the other person (the defendant) and required the defendant to show why the plaintiff's claim should not be granted.

The statement of the plaintiff's claim was prepared by the Chancery and was in a standard form. A register of writs was kept. The plaintiff would select the writ with the statement which was most suitable to his claim. If there was no suitable writ the clerks in the Chancery might draft a new writ.

However, over time the judges refused to accept new writs on the basis that they effectively created new law and in 1258 the *Provisions of Oxford* forbad the issue of new writs. This draconian measure was alleviated to a degree by the *Statute of Westminster II 1285* which allowed the courts to issue writs which were similar to existing writs. However, despite this, the Common Law remained extremely rigid and dominated by the writ system.

The phrase used to describe the Common Law – *ubi remedium ibi ius* where there is a remedy there is a right – effectively sums up the position.

31.4 *Common Law – What it means*

The term 'Common Law' is used in several ways:

(a)   the law common to all the country – as opposed to local law;

(b)   the law which developed under the Norman kings, administered by the Common Law courts – as opposed to Equity;

(c)   the law which developed through judges' decisions, beginning with the principle of *stare decisis* (above) and now of judicial precedent as opposed to statute law; and

(d)   the English law as opposed to a foreign system of law such as Roman law.

31.5 *Equity*

As a result of the rigidity of the Common Law injustices occurred. When people were unable to obtain justice in the Common Law courts, they sometimes petitioned the King, complaining of the injustice and requesting him to intervene and provide relief, which he had the power to do. Originally the King in Council decided what relief would be granted on these petitions. As the petitions grew in number the King delegated the determination of relief to the Chancellor, who controlled the issue of writs by the Chancery and who, as a churchman, was also known as 'the Keeper of the King's Conscience'.

The petitions usually complained of injustices:

(a)   where the application of the rigid Common Law rules applied by the royal judges produced an unjust result, e.g. where land had been transferred without the formality of a deed and the Common Law refused to recognise the transaction;

(b)   where the Common Law refused to recognise the plaintiff's rights, e.g. the royal judges would not enforce trusts (see below) which, therefore, had to be dealt with by the Chancery Court;

(c)   where the Common Law recognised the plaintiff's rights but failed to provide an adequate remedy, e.g. the only Common Law remedy for breach of contract was damages, whereas the Court of Chancery would order the defendant to perform the contract *(specific performance)* (see below).

The Chancellor was not bound by the formal rules of the Common Law courts when he determined these petitions and he granted relief (still in the name of the King) on the grounds of morality, fairness and conscience which formed the basis of the equitable principles which developed.

The number of petitions increased and by the end of the fifteenth century the Chancellor began to issue decrees in his own name and the Court of Chancery was established. This was a permanent court, independent of the King and the Common Law courts, presided over by the Chancellor.

As cases were decided on the basis of conscience, the early Chancellors used their own discretion in their judgments. Although this did result in flexibility it also gave rise to uncertainty, and it was said that 'equity varies with the length of the Chancellor's foot'. However, over time a body of rules and procedures was developed which became known as 'Equity' and can be summarised as follows:

(a)   *New rights were recognised*

The most important rights recognised solely by Equity were those created under a *trust*. A trust is established when one person, the *settlor*, settles property on another, the *trustee*, ordering him to look after it for the benefit of a third, the *beneficiary:*

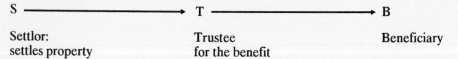

S ⟶ T ⟶ B

Settlor: Trustee   Beneficiary
settles property   for the benefit

The beneficiary need not be and usually is not a party to the arrangement by which the trust property is transferred to the legal ownership of the trustee by the settlor. Under the law of contract, the beneficiary could not enforce the arrangement: no consideration has been provided and B is not privy to the arrangement, but Equity will enforce the trust against the trustee on the basis of justice and fairness.

(b) *New remedies were created*

(i) *Injunctions* – which are orders of the court instructing someone to do something *(mandatory injunction)* or restraining him from doing something *(prohibitory injunction)*. Sometimes, when the matter is urgent, a plaintiff will ask for an *ex parte injunction*. This is a temporary injunction granted by a judge (normally in chambers) on the evidence of one party only, pending a full hearing of the case in court when both parties will present their views.

(ii) *Specific performance* – ordering performance of an obligation under a contract or trust. Common Law merely gave damages f or non-performance of a contract.

(iii) *Rectification* – an order correcting a written document so that it reflects the true intentions of the parties.

(iv) *Rescission* – an order rescinding a contract, to restore the parties to the contract to their pre-contractual positions.

(c) *New procedures were created* – as the Court of Chancery was not bound by the procedures of the Common Law courts, it developed its own: Including subpeona, evidence on oath, information on interrogatories and the process of discovery.

31.6 *The need for reform*

The Court of Chancery (Equity) became very popular and friction developed between it and the Common Law courts. The courts could (and did) issue contradictory orders, e.g. the Common Law courts might enforce a contract which the Court of Chancery rescinded. The Court of Chancery began the practice of issuing *common injunctions* to prevent the institution or continuance of proceedings at Common Law which were inequitable. Although the injunction was addressed to the parties it effectively limited the jurisdiction of the Common Law courts. However, the conflict continued and was brought to a head in the *Earl of Oxford's case* in 1615. Magdalen College owed money to a merchant. The college wanted to discharge this debt by granting the merchant a piece of land it owned in Aldgate. However, it was forbidden by statute to grant leases of this land for more than 21 years. In an attempt to circumvent the provisions of the statute the college granted the land to the Crown who in turn agreed to grant it to the merchant. The merchant then sold the land to the Earl of Oxford who spent more than £10,000 erecting buildings on it. The college then claimed the land back on the ground that the original grant was void because it was prohibited by statute. The Common Law courts held that it was void. The Earl of Oxford therefore applied to the Court of Chancery for relief.

The Chancellor issued an injunction preventing the parties from enforcing the Common Law judgment. The matter was referred to the King who upheld the validity of the common injunction. Although the Chancellor's power to issue a common injunction was not seriously challenged after the *Earl of Oxford's case*, there were still difficulties.

By the nineteenth century the rules of Equity had become almost as rigid as those of the Common Law. Reform was clearly needed for a number of reasons:

(a) the two separate court systems whereby a person might have to take two actions, one in the Common Law courts for damages and one in the Court of Chancery for an injunction;

(b)   the common injunction which could prevent a person who had been successful in the Common Law court from obtaining his remedy;

(c)   the continuing rigidity of the Common Law procedure;

(d)   the organisation of the Court of Chancery where there were too few judges, too many officials, and instances of bribery and corruption which resulted in court actions being slow and expensive;

(e)   the separate ecclesiastical court which had jurisdiction over lay people;

(f)   the local courts which had dispensed the law reasonably, quickly and cheaply had been absorbed to a large extent into the Common Law courts which were expensive and slow, and there was no system of courts to deal with small civil claims;

(g)   the inadequate and complex system of appeals.

31.7   *The reforms carried out*

Although there were some reforms in the middle of the nineteenth century (e.g. the removal of matrimonial and probate matters from the ecclesiastical courts in 1857 and the creation of a system of county courts in 1846) the principal reforms were undertaken by the *Judicature Acts 1873 & 1875* which effected reforms in two areas:

(a)   *The Supreme Court of Judicature*

The jurisdiction of all the superior courts of Law and Equity (except certain Chancery Courts which have now been abolished) was transferred to one court, the *Supreme Court of Judicature*. This court is divided into two parts, the High Court and the Court of Appeal.

The High Court took over jurisdiction formerly exercised by the three Common Law courts, the Courts of Chancery, the Ecclesiastical Courts and the Court of Admiralty. Originally, there were five divisions of the High Court:

(i)   Chancery Division;

(ii)   Probate, Divorce and Admiralty Division (wills, wives and wrecks!);

(iii) Queen's Bench Division;

(iv)   Common Pleas Division;

(v)   Exchequer Division.

In 1880 the Common Pleas Division and Exchequer Division were merged into the Queen's Bench Division.

The Court of Appeal was established by the *Judicature Acts* with permanent judges to hear appeals from courts of first instance. The Court of Appeal took over jurisdiction formerly exercised by the Court of Exchequer, the Court of Appeal in Chancery and other appellate bodies.

(b)   *Fusion of Common Law and Equity*

It is clear from the earlier discussion of Law and Equity that these two branches of law developed separate substantive rules and separate rules of procedure. The main effect of the *Judicature Acts 1873 & 1875* on the relationship between Law and Equity was to fuse the administration of these separate systems, so that it became possible to bring an action and seek remedies at Common Law and Equity at the same time and in the same court. This brought an end to the wasteful duplication of judicial work, which was caused by some cases having to be pursued first at Common Law and then in Equity, and it also avoided the inconvenience to the parties in having to find the appropriate court for their particular complaint, and for the particular remedy which was sought.

It must be emphasised, however, that this did not also mean the fusion of the rules of Common Law and Equity. The distinction between the two remains as will become apparent later.

However, the *Judicature Acts* did deal with certain substantive matters and declared that 'if there was any *conflict* between rules of Law and Equity, those of Equity should prevail'.

In addition, until the *Judicature Acts*, appeal to the House of Lords was an appeal to all the lay peers entitled to sit in the House; obviously many were not qualified in law and had no legal experience. The *Appellate Jurisdiction Act 1876* provided for the creation of law lords – salaried life peers who were legally qualified – to exercise the House's judicial function.

It is only convention that keeps the non-law lords from taking part in judicial sessions.

The House of Lords is not part of the Supreme Court of Judicature.

32.   *THE ADMINISTRATION OF THE LAW*

32.1   *The courts*

Although the *Judicature Acts 1873 & 1875* reformed the court structure and other reforms have been made since then, the structure of the English courts remains complicated. A diagram of the structure is set out below:

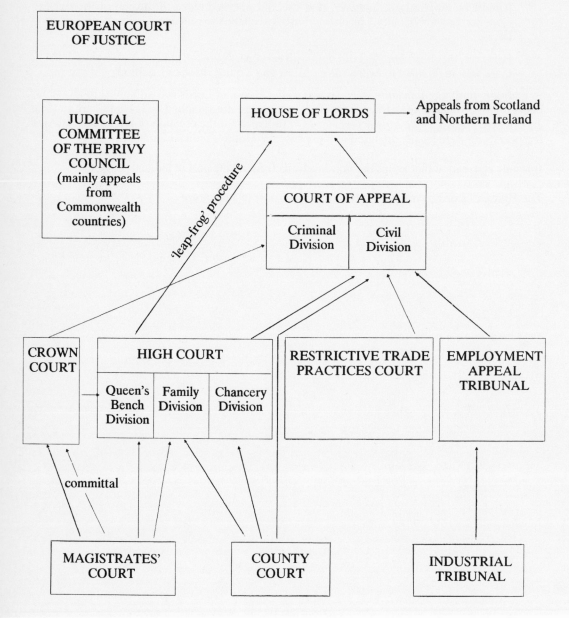

(a)   The main courts are the House of Lords, Court of Appeal, High Court, Crown Court, Magistrates' Court and County Court. The European Court of Justice is important in respect of matters of European law. The jurisdiction and composition of each of these courts is discussed in the remainder of this section.

(b)   The other courts, the Judicial Committee of the Privy Council, the Restrictive Trade Practices Court and the Employment Appeal Tribunal (which is a *court* despite its name) have more specialised functions and are discussed in the next section.

(c)   In addition, there are tribunals, i.e. bodies set up by Parliament for particular purposes, such as the Industrial Tribunals which deal with employment disputes. An outline of the types and functions of tribunals is set out in Lesson 12 (civil procedure).

32.2   *The European Court of Justice*

The supra-national element in the European Community needs to be cemented by an effective court. The most important functions of the Court are to ensure that the law is enforced, irrespective of political considerations; to act as a referee between the Member States and the Community as well as between the Community institutions inter se; and to protect the rights of the individual from infringement by the Community bureaucracies. These functions are especially important in view of the fact that the democratic element is still weak in the community.

Therefore, this court has two main functions:

(a)   to hear complaints from member states of the Commission that a member state is in breach of its obligations under the Treaties and to review the legality of the acts of the Council and the Commission; and

(b)   to decide points of Community law which come up in the course of litigation in the national courts (*Article 177* references).

Article 177 of the EEC Treaty

The first reference from the UK to the European Court was *Van Duyn v Home Office (1974) 3 All ER 178.* A Dutch national was refused entry into the UK on the grounds of her association with the Church of Scientology. The UK government had declared the practice of scientology socially harmful. Miss Van Duyn had arrived in England to take up a position at a college set up by the Church of

Scientology. She claimed that the refusal to allow her to take up employment was contrary to *Article 48* of the Treaty – freedom of movement between member states for the purpose of employment. The Home Office denied that *Article 48* conferred any individual right on the person concerned. This case raised sufficient questions of the proper interpretation of EEC law for a reference to the European Court within *Article 177* to be necessary.

The European Court decided that a member state might prohibit, on grounds of public policy, an individual from entering its territory where the individual is associated with an organisation which the member state considers to be socially harmful *(Van Duyn v Home Office (No. 2) (1975) Ch 358).*

The European Court is made up of one judge from each of the member states (currently 12) who are assisted by four Advocates General. They are obliged publicly to present reasoned conclusions on cases submitted to them.

The court has its own rules of procedure, but these must be unanimously approved by the Council.

The Court has no machinery to enforce judgments against individuals or companies. It is left to each state to provide enforcement machinery. There is no machinery for enforcing judgments against states except pressure from the other members of the Community. In the tachograph case ('the spy in the cab'), EEC law required compliance by 1 January 1978. The British government failed to comply with the deadline and the Commission brought the UK before the Court which ruled that there had been a breach of Community law. Within one month of the order to the UK to comply, the government announced that it would comply.

An individual has no direct access to the court and in most cases the ultimate court of appeal is the House of Lords, but if he takes action in the national courts the courts must follow the European Court on issues of Community law. If the court is in doubt over the question it has a discretion to refer to the European Court, but if it is a hearing of the final court of appeal it must refer the issue under *Article 177.*

32.3 *The House of Lords*

Originally the Curia Regis (King's Court), which existed before Parliament, exercised all the powers of government including judicial functions. When Parliament became established, the Upper House retained the judicial powers, which were exercised by the full House, every member of which could take part in the proceedings. This was considered unsatisfactory so in 1876 the *Appellate Jurisdiction Act* for the first time provided for the appointment of salaried life peers to exercise the House of Lords' judicial function.

On appeal to the House at least three judges must sit (usually five); these can be the Lord Chancellor, Lords of Appeal in Ordinary (the law lords) and peers who are generally appointed from the ranks of the Court of Appeal. Just as the non-law lords have a right to sit on judicial sessions, but rarely exercise this right, the law lords have a right to take part in political debates but rarely do so.

There must be at least seven law lords but not more than 11; this number can be increased by Order in Council.

If on appeal the House is equally divided, then the appeal must be dismissed. This rarely happens in practice as it is usual to appoint an odd number of judges to sit. Its jurisdiction is mainly appellate and is part civil and part criminal.

(a) *Civil* – cases from the Court of Appeal or from the High Court, using the leap-frog procedure introduced in 1969. Leave to appeal required from Court of Appeal/High Court *or* the House of Lords itself.

(b) *Criminal* – cases from the Divisional Court of the Queen's Bench Division and from the Court of Appeal (Criminal Division). An appeal will only lie with the leave of the Appeals Committee of the House itself, and only after the lower court has certified that a point of law of general public importance is involved.

32.4 *The Court of Appeal*

This is the appeal court of the Supreme Court established by the *Judicature Acts 1873 & 1875.* The members of the court can be divided into two categories:

(a) *Ex officio members* – Lord Chancellor, Lord Chief Justice, Master of the Rolls, President of the Family Division, former Lord Chancellors, Lords of Appeal in Ordinary. Of these generally the Master of the Rolls (civil cases) and the Lord Chief Justice (criminal cases) sit in the court.

(b) *Appointed judges* – Lord Justices of Appeal who are the regular judges of the court. There must be not less than eight or more than 28 Lord Justices.

Any number of appeal courts may sit at the same time but appeals must be heard by at least three judges, though in certain situations, e.g. applications for leave to appeal in criminal cases, the case can be heard by one judge. Occasionally, five or more judges sit but such a court has no additional authority.

(a) *Civil Division* – it hears appeals from the High Court, County Courts, Restrictive Trade Practices Court, Employment Appeal Tribunal and various other tribunals.

(b) *Criminal Division* – appeals by convicted persons, and appeals against sentence, from Crown Courts. There is no right of the prosecutor to appeal against an acquittal in the Crown Court but the court may consider points of law referred to the court by the Attorney-General.

32.5 *The High Court of Justice*

Brought into being by the *Judicature Acts 1873 & 1875*. Until the *Administration of Justice Act 1970* the Divisions of the High Court were:

(a) Queen's Bench;

(b) Chancery;

(c) Probate, Divorce and Admiralty.

The 1970 Act redistributed the probate and admiralty work and gave the title of *Family Division* to the new third Division.

32.6 *The Queen's Bench Division*

The head is the Lord Chief Justice supported by over 40 *puisne* (High Court) judges.

(a) *Civil*

(i) Original Court – most major civil actions in contract and tort.

(ii) Appeal Court from:

(1) an *interlocutory order* (an order made while proceedings are in progress) of a Queen's Bench Master;

(2) certain tribunals;

(3) civil proceedings in magistrates' courts.

The Division contains two specialist courts:

(i) an Admiralty Court;

(ii) a Commercial Court.

(b)   *Criminal (Divisional Court)*

    (i)   Original Court – very rarely an offence on indictment can be transferred to the Queen's Bench Division either because it is complicated or because a trial in the local Crown Court is unlikely to be given a fair hearing.

    (ii)   Appeal Court from magistrates' courts on a case stated.

(c)   *Supervisory (Divisional Court)*

The court:

    (i)   may issue a writ of *habeas corpus* when a person is unlawfully detained. This writ instructs the jailor to bring the person to the court and justify the detention or release him;

    (ii)   makes *prerogative orders*

        (1)   *mandamus* (commanding the performance of a publicly owed duty, e.g. for a magistrates' court to *state a case* for appellate consideration);

        (2)   *prohibition* (commanding an inferior court or tribunal not to conduct an improper trial);

        (3)   *certiorari* (e.g. to quash a decision of an inferior court or tribunal).

32.7   *The Chancery Division*

Presided over by the Vice-Chancellor who is supported by 11 *puisne* judges.

The Division deals with cases involving:

(a)   *Original Court*

    (i)   Matters previously the province of the Court of Chancery-(Equity) – trusts, rectification of contract documents, specific performance, most aspects of land law;

    (ii)   partnerships;

    (iii) bankruptcy;

    (iv) contentious probate (disputed wills and intestacies);

    (v)   company matters (Company Court);

    (vi) revenue cases.

The Chancery Division contains the specialist Patents Court.

(b)   *Court of Appeal*

    (i)   Revenue cases from General or Special Commissioners (a single judge may hear such appeals);

    (ii)   bankruptcy cases from county courts (Divisional Court, at least two judges) except appeals from county courts in London which are dealt with by the Bankruptcy Court of the Chancery Division.

32.8 *The Family Division*

The head is the President supported by 17 *puisne* judges.

The Division deals with cases involving:

(a) *Original Court*

    (i)   Divorce and maintenance;

    (ii)   property disputes between spouses;

    (iii) wardships of infants *(wards of court)*, formerly a Chancery Division matter;

    (iv)   adoption;

    (v)   guardianship;

    (vi)   legitimacy.

(b) *Appellate (Divisional Court)*

    (i)   Appeals from magistrates' courts in connection with adoption orders, etc;

    (ii)   appeals from county courts in connection with guardianship of infants.

32.9 *The Crown Court*

(a) *Introduction*

The Crown Court is administratively under the direct control of the Lord Chancellor, and so are the other types of courts both civil and criminal above the level of magistrates' court.

(b) *Jurisdiction*

This court has exclusive jurisdiction:

    (i)   over offences tried on indictment by a jury;

    (ii)   hearing appeals from a summary trial from the magistrates' court;

    (iii) sentencing persons committed to it for sentence by the magistrates' court;

    (iv)   to hear original pleadings in a few civil matters, e.g. applications for removal of prohibition from possessing a firearm, licensing, and also in some civil appeals, e.g. rating, betting and gaming licences – not very common.

(c) *Administration*

For the purpose of administration, England and Wales are divided into six Circuits:

    (i)   Midland and Oxford;

(ii)   North-Eastern;

(iii) Northern;

(iv)   South-Eastern;

(v)   Wales and Chester;

(vi)   Western.

In each Circuit the court service is headed by a *Circuit Administrator*. Below the Circuit Administrator, who has a relatively small staff at the circuit headquarters itself, there are in each Circuit a number of *Courts Administrators* who have overall responsibility for the running of all locations of the High Court, Crown Court and County Courts in their respective areas. The day-to-day organisation of the courts themselves is in the hands of *chief clerks* at the various court centres. As signed to each Circuit are two *Presiding Judges* who would have a general responsibility for the Circuit and a particular responsibility for matters affecting the judiciary.

(d)   *Crown Court centres*

The Crown Court, as well as the High Court and County Courts, has the power to sit anywhere on any day and at any time in England and Wales according to directions given by or on behalf of the Lord Chancellor, although there are regular places where the Courts sit, known as Crown Court Centres; they are divided into first tier, second tier and third tier.

Outside London there are 23 first tier centres where sittings of the High Court are also held, and where both High Court and Circuit judges sit in the Crown Court.

There are 19 second tier centres which differ from the first only in that no High Court work is taken.

There are 46 third tier centres, where the Crown Court is visited by Circuit judges only, to deal with the less important criminal work.

To summarise:

(i)   *First tier* – are served by High Court and Circuit judges, and they deal with both civil and criminal cases, hearing all classes of criminal offences.

(ii)   *Second tier* – are also served by High Court and Circuit judges hearing all classes of criminal offences *but they do not deal with civil cases* so that, from the point of view of the administration of the criminal law, there is no difference between first and second tier centres.

(iii) *Third tier* – are limited to criminal cases and are served by Circuit judges and Recorders so that their jurisdiction is limited. They hear Class 3 and Class 4 offences, i.e. less serious offences.

32.10 *The County Court*

The County Courts are the local courts dealing exclusively with civil cases. These are grouped into Circuits and at least one Circuit judge is as signed to each group.

The County Court's main areas of jurisdiction are:

(a)   actions founded on contract or tort where the claim does not exceed £5,000;

(b)   actions for the recovery of land where the net annual value for rating does not exceed £1,000;

(c)   certain Equity proceedings where the sum involved does not exceed £30,000, e.g. administration of estates of deceased persons, declaration and execution of trusts:

(d)   the jurisdiction conferred by the *Matrimonial Causes Act 1967* that certain County Courts be divorce courts to hear undefended matrimonial cases.

The *Administration of Justice Act 1972* introduced a power to refer proceedings to arbitration where the claim does not exceed £500 (or more where the parties consent to arbitration). The advantage of arbitration is that it provides a procedure for 'small claims' which is not only expeditious but inexpensive and informal.

32.11 *The Magistrates' Court*

The Magistrates' Courts are often considered analogous to the County Courts but dealing with criminal as opposed to civil issues. Despite this, the Magistrates' Courts do have some civil jurisdiction.

The civil jurisdiction of the Magistrates' Court is varied; it concerns itself with the recovery of certain civil debts (e.g. rates), renewal and revocation of licences and domestic proceedings.

The criminal jurisdiction of the Magistrates' Court is extensive, covering summary offences, i.e. offences of a minor character carrying a maximum penalty of six months' imprisonment or a fine of £2,000, or both. They also try triable either way offences if the accused consents.

The magistrates have extensive jurisdiction over offences committed by, and other matters concerning, children and young persons. The court sits as a juvenile court with as little formality and publicity as possible.

The Magistrates' Court also holds committal proceedings for indictable offences.

It is a measure of the volume of the work done by the Magistrates' Court that it deals with 98% of all criminal cases.

The magistrates can try any summary offence committed within their county, but they cannot usually try an offence committed outside the county: *s.2(1) Magistrates' Courts Act 1980*.

If the offence is one that is triable either way (see later for explanation) and the magistrates try the case summarily, they are not limited to offences committed within the county.

No child under the age of ten can be guilty of a criminal offence but otherwise courts have jurisdiction over every accused except for those who can claim sovereign, diplomatic or other immunity. A person who commits a summary or indictable offence usually appears in the Magistrates' Court of the district in which he committed the offence.

The basic rule is that English courts exercise jurisdiction only over offences committed in England and Wales.

33. SPECIALIST JUDICIAL BODIES

33.1 Introduction

There are courts with special jurisdiction which are not included in the basic court structure. There are also tribunals, which are not courts but which are recognised as having the power to settle disputes.

33.2 Specialist courts

(a) *Judicial Committee of the Privy Council*

The Committee, which advises the Crown, is drawn from members of the Judicial Committee of the House of Lords and sometimes includes Commonwealth judges.

It hears appeals from courts outside the UK. The Privy Council has jurisdiction to hear appeals from the Isle of Man, the Channel Islands, British Colonies and Proectorates (e.g. Gibraltar, Hong Kong) and also from the highest court of independent Commonwealth countries (e.g. New Zealand). However, certain Commonwealth countries have their own equivalent courts and do not use the Privy Council (e.g. Canada).

Decisions of the Privy Council in Commonwealth cases are merely of persuasive authority, and English courts are not therefore bound by its decisions.

It also hears appeals from ecclesiastical courts and the General Medical Council, relating to Church affairs and disciplinary matters of the General Medical Council.

(b) *Restrictive Practices Court*

This Court considers agreements which restrict prices or the conditions of supply of goods. Under the *Fair Trading Act 1973* it has jurisdiction to hear proceedings brought by the Director of Fair Trading against a trader who trades unfairly, e.g. one who is consistently in breach of contract.

It does not actually form part of the High Court, although it is of the same standing. An unusual feature of the court is that it includes laymen among its members – it consists of a High Court judge sitting with two laymen. An appeal lies to the Court of Appeal (Civil Division).

(c) *Coroners' Courts*

These are courts of ancient jurisdiction (the word 'coroner' is derived from the word 'crowner' or 'king's man'). The duty of a coroner is to hold an 'inquest' (i. e. an inquiry) into any unexplained or suspicious deaths in his area. (He also has jurisdiction in the case of bodies brought back to England from abroad.) The proceedings are inquisitorial in nature (not adversarial) and lawyers representing parties are only allowed to question witnesses with the permission of the coroner, after he has asked his own questions. In some cases, he sits with a coroner's jury (e.g. deaths in police custody). The purpose of the inquest is to return a verdict showing the cause of and reason for the death, e.g. 'accidental death', 'suicide', or 'unlawful killing'. An inquest can, however, return an 'open verdict' if there is not sufficient evidence to explain the reason for the death.

A coroner also has jurisdiction in cases of alleged 'treasure trove' – gold and silver found buried in the ground. This belongs to the Crown if the coroner comes to the view that these items were deliberately buried by some unknown person for safe-keeping.

(d) *Courts-Martial*

These exercise jurisdiction over members of the armed forces. Their jurisdiction is concurrent with civilian courts, except that murder, manslaughter, treason and rape committed within the UK cannot be tried at a court-martial.

Procedure is essentially similar to a trial in the ordinary criminal courts. The trial will be before at least three officers who are assisted by a judge-advocate from the Judge-Advocate-General's Department. Acquittal is final, whereas a finding of guilt is subject to confirmation by a superior officer.

Appeal is to the Courts-Martial Appeal Court which consists of members of the Court of Appeal, judges of the Queen's Bench Division nominated by the Lord Chief Justice and various other persons of legal experience appointed by the Lord Chancellor. Further appeal lies to the House of Lords.

(e) *Ecclesiastical Courts*

In each diocese there is a *Consistory Court* presided over by a *chancellor*, who must be at least 30 years of age, and be either a barrister of at least seven years' standing or have held high judicial office.

The jurisdiction of these courts is mainly concerned with investigating allegations of misconduct or neglect of duty by the clergy.

Appeal lies to the *Court of Arches* at Canterbury, presided over by the *Dean of the Arches*, or to the *Chancery Court* of York, presided over by the *Auditor*. Appeal from these two courts lies to the Privy Council.

Jurisdiction equivalent to that of the Consistory Courts is exercised over bishops and archbishops by *Commissions of Convocation*.

(f) *Naval Courts*

A Naval Court may be summoned by an officer in command of one of HM ships on any foreign station, on a complaint to him that requires immediate investigation, or where any British ship is wrecked, abandoned or lost. The court consists of naval officers, and it must investigate the matter judicially.

Appeal lies to the Divisional Court of the Queen's Bench Division, and thence to the Court of Appeal.

(g) *Prize Courts*

Prize Courts are established in time of war to decide whether or not a ship and/or its cargo can be seized by the Crown as 'prize'. Certain facts relevant to this jurisdiction can be established by Prerogative Order in Council, e.g. whether or not a particular nation is an ally, enemy or a neutral state, and whether or not certain ports are to be blockaded or to be denied to the ships of certain nations. But the law itself which is administered by a Prize Court is international law and this cannot be changed by the Royal Prerogative: see *The Zamora (1916) 2 AC 77*.

(h) *The Employment Appeal Tribunal*

This Tribunal sits at St James's Square in London (and also in Edinburgh) to hear appeals from industrial tribunals. Although it is called a 'tribunal', it is in fact presided over by a High Court judge (assisted by a trade unionist and a representative of an employers' organisation). Appeals lie from the Employment Appeal Tribunal direct to the Court of

Appeal (Civil Division) and so it has the same status as the High Court itself. It only hears appeals on points of law and (for this reason) Legal Aid is available to individuals who cannot afford legal representation in the Employment Appeal Tribunal. However, strict rules of appearance do not apply, so that (for example, trade union representatives are entitled to appear on behalf of their members. The majority of appeals to the Employment Appeal Tribunal are concerned with complex points of law relating to unfair dismissal, redundancy payments, and sex (or race) discrimination in employment.

'Unfair dismissal' is a statutory concept. It was first introduced into English law by the *Industrial Relations Act 1971*. It is now embodied in the *Employment Protection (Consolidation) Act 1978* and in a body of 'case law' reported in specialist law reports (e.g. *Industrial Relations Law Reports* and the *Industrial Cases Reports*). 'Unfair dismissal' does *not* necessarily depend upon the employer having committed a breach of contract towards the employee. Most cases arise after the employer has given proper notice of dismissal to his employee, or has paid him 'salary *in lieu* of notice'. This means that the employee does not usually have any Common Law right to sue in the High Court or County Court for breach of his employment contract (known as an action for 'wrongful dismissal'). However, the modern policy of Parliament is to recognise that even a lawful dismissal can be 'unfair' – and so the law of 'unfair dismissal, allows certain dismissed employees (with two years' service or more) to challenge their dismissal in an industrial tribunal. The burden of proof then shifts to the employer to show that he acted reasonably in deciding to dismiss the employee, and adopted fair procedures in implementing this dismissal. The law of unfair dismissal has been one of the largest 'growth areas' in English law in the last 15 years. The Employment Appeal Tribunal has recently attempted to decrease the financial burden on employers of such disputes by discouraging appeals from industrial tribunals unless a clear error of law can be discerned.

In most cases, the approach of the Employment Appeal Tribunal has been to treat the industrial tribunal as an 'industrial jury' whose decisions should be accepted without appeal.

(i)   *The Lands Tribunal*

This (like the Employment Appeal Tribunal) is a tribunal enjoying equal status with the High Court. Appeals lie from the Lands Tribunal direct to the Court of Appeal. The Lands Tribunal is essentially an expert valuation tribunal concerned with disputes about the value of land, and legal interests in land. It primarily deals with the following matters:

(i)   compulsory purchase valuations;

(ii)   appeals from local valuation courts about the rateable value of land;

(iii)   compensation claims in certain town and country planning disputes; and

(iv)   disputes about restrictive covenants on land.

Such cases are heard by a 'member' of the Lands Tribunal who may be legally qualified, but who is always an expert in valuation methods. These disputes are of ten highly technical, and expert witnesses are usually called by both parties to the case. Legal Aid is available to litigants who cannot afford the legal costs and the costs of expert witnesses.

(j)   *Court of Chivalry*

This is one of the ancient feudal courts and it is presided over by the Earl Marshal. It determines disputes over the right to use armorial bearings.

(k) *Tribunals and inquiries*

(i) *Tribunals*

Various tribunals have been established by statute with differing functions which may be administrative or judicial. Some of these are subject to the supervision of the Council on Tribunals. A few examples are given here.

(ii) *Domestic tribunals*

Private and professional as sociations have established *domestic tribunals* to determine disputes or exercise disciplinary functions within the profession, e.g. the Disciplinary Committee of the General Medical Council, the Solicitors' Disciplinary Tribunal. Some of these tribunals are set up by statute, in which case there may be a statutory right of appeal.

(iii) *Industrial tribunals*

These perform various judicial functions, e.g. hearing complaints concerning redundancy payments and unfair dismissal. Appeal on a point of law lies to a Divisional Court of the Queen's Bench Division. However, now that the provisions of the *Employment Protection Act 1975*, which brought the Employment Appeal Tribunal into existence, are operative, appeal lies to that Tribunal in most cases.

(iv) *Criminal Injuries Compensation Board*

This was established under the prerogative powers of the Crown to provide *ex gratia* payments to victims of crimes of violence.

LLB

ENGLISH LEGAL SYSTEM

LESSON 4 (STUDY)

41.   *JUDICIAL REASONING*

41.1 *Introduction*

Judges have always been reluctant to admit that they make law. Traditionally they have said that they 'declare' law, not make it. In order to fully discuss the question, three main areas should be considered:

(a)   statutory interpretation;

(b)   judicial precedent;

(c)   judicial inventiveness.

42. STATUTORY INTERPRETATION AND CONSTRUCTION

42.1 Introduction

Although it is Parliament which produces an Act of Parliament, the real enforcement and application of the individual statute is a matter for the courts. For whenever there is a dispute as to what a particular section of an Act means, it is the judges in the courts who will decide what the law should be regarded as being.

Interpretation is the process whereby the meaning of words used in a statute is ascertained.

Construction is the process whereby uncertainties or ambiguities in a statute are resolved.

Thus all statutory provisions require interpretation whereas only uncertain or ambiguous provisions require construction.

42.2 Interpretation and construction

All matters which come before a court must be to some degree interpreted so that their legal significance may be assessed. It is generally said that there are three fundamental principles to be applied to interpreting and construing statutes:

(a)   the *Literal Rule;*

(b)   the *Golden Rule;* and

(c)   the *Mischief Rule.*

42.3 The Literal Rule

It is the task of the judge to ascertain the intention of Parliament when interpreting legislation. In order to do this, words in the statute must be given their ordinary and natural meaning and, if they have only one meaning, that is deemed to be the intention of Parliament, even if the result is considered ludicrous or unlikely. No reference may be made to extrinsic evidence or other parts of the Act, such as the long or short title, and this literal rule can only be used if the words are unambiguous. If the words are capable of more than one meaning, then the Literal Rule cannot be applied, and problems arise where the statute has been carelessly drafted.

In *Prince of Hanover v Attorney-General (1956) Ch 188* the court had to interpret the meaning of a statute in which one section applied to 'all lineal descendants of the Electress Sophia'. The *Preamble*, which is an introductory paragraph at the beginning of the Act, stated 'during your Majesty's lifetime'. The court held that it was not possible to refer to the *Preamble*, since the words in the section had only one meaning, and that must be the meaning that Parliament intended.

In *IRC v Hinchy (1960) 1 All ER 505* the court had to interpret a section of the *Income Tax Act 1952* which dealt with fines imposed for tax avoidance when someone sent in an incorrect tax return. The section provided for the forfeiture of 'a sum of £20 plus treble the tax which he ought to be charged under this Act'. The court held that this meant that the unfortunate taxpayer should forfeit treble the tax payable, not just treble the tax he had not paid because of the inaccurate tax return.

In *Fisher v Bell (1961) 1 QB 394* a shopkeeper was displaying a flick-knife in his shop window and he was charged with an offence of offering an offensive weapon for sale. The court held that he was not guilty since the display of goods in a shop window is not an offer, but an invitation to treat.

Thus the words were given their ordinary meaning, even though Parliament surely must have intended this type of situation to be governed by the Act.

The application of the Literal Rule can lead to absurd results and the courts have sometimes tried to adopt a more flexible approach.

42.4 *The Golden Rule*

This is sometimes called the purposive approach, and words are to be given their ordinary and natural meaning in so far as is possible, but only in so far as that meaning does not produce absurdity. If there is absurdity, then the court will try to modify the strict grammatical meaning so as to give the provision a rational meaning.

In *R v Allen (1872) LR 1 CRR 367* the defendant was charged with bigamy under *s. 57 Offences Against the Person Act 1861*. The section provided that 'whosoever, being married, shall marry any other person during the lifetime of the former husband or wife ... shall be guilty of bigamy'. If the words 'shall marry' are given their strict literal meaning, then no one could commit the offence since it is impossible to marry if you are already legally married. Therefore, the court gave the words a more suitable, wider meaning in that it interpreted 'shall marry' as meaning 'goes through a ceremony of marriage'.

In *Alder v George (1964) 1 All ER 628* members of a peace organisation which was in favour of unilateral disarmament were charged with 'obstruction in the vicinity of a prohibited place' contrary to the *Official Secrets Act 1920*. They had been demonstrating in an airfield which was a prohibited place. The court interpreted 'in the vicinity' as meaning 'in or in the vicinity of'.

One of the judges who most favoured the Golden Rule was Lord Denning who said:

> the literal meaning of the words is never allowed to prevail where it would produce manifest absurdity or consequences which can never have been intended by the legislature.

The rule is not a new development; it was first formulated in *Becke v Smith (1836) 2 MXW 195*:

> It is a very useful rule in the construction of a statute to adhere to the ordinary meaning of the words used, and to the grammatical construction, unless that is at variance with the intention of the legislature to be collected from the statute itself, or leads to any manifest absurdity or repugnance, in which case the language may be varied or modified to avoid such inconvenience, but no further.

However, the application of the Golden Rule is open to criticism in that it depends entirely on the wishes of the individual judge. He is, by using this rule, stating what the intentions of Parliament are without reference to the strict meaning of the statute. In doing this, it may be argued that he is substituting his own view of what the law should be for what Parliament has expressed in the legislation. As such the judge is usurping the function of Parliament and, even if the result of the Literal Rule is absurd or undesirable, it is for Parliament and not the judiciary to change the law.

42.5 *The Mischief Rule*

If the words of a statute are ambiguous or incomplete and therefore not saved by either the Literal or Golden Rules, then the court will look at the Act to see what was its purpose and what mischief in the Common Law it was designed to prevent.

The rule was first enunciated in *Heydon's Case (1584) 3 Co Rep 7a.* It states that if the above situation applies, then the court may:

(a)   consider the law as it stood before the Act;

(b)   consider the mischief intended to be remedied by the Act;

(c)   consider the remedy actually provided;

(d)   consider why that remedy was given.

Examples of the application of this rule:

Gorris v Scott (1874) LR 9 Ex 125. By an Order in Council made under the authority of *s. 75 Contagious Diseases (Animals) Act 1869*, it was provided, with the object of preventing the spread of contagious disease, that any ship bringing sheep or cattle from abroad should have the space provided for such animals divided into pens containing secure footholds.

The defendant neglected his duty, and in consequence some of the plaintiff's sheep, which the defendant was in the course of transporting from Hamburg to Newcastle, were washed overboard and lost. The plaintiff founded his action upon the defendant's breach of the Order. It was held that, since the purpose of the Order was to prevent the spread of contagious disease and not to guard against the danger of the property being washed overboard, the claim failed.

In *Smith v Hughes (1960) 2 All ER 859* under the *Street Offences Act 1959* prostitutes who tapped on windows from the inside of houses in order to a attract the attention of passers-by were held guilty of soliciting 'in the street' in order to meet the objects of the statute.

In theory, the Mischief Rule should only be applied if literal interpretation does not produce a result.

Here the court can look at titles and Schedules of Acts as well as previous laws but not at non-legal matters such as *Hansard.* For example, does injury as the result of a breach of statutory duty give rise to an action for damages? The court would look to see what purpose lay behind the imposition of statutory duty: was the duty imposed for the protection of all people or for a special class in limited circumstances?

Before 1882 if one wished to sue a married woman one had to join the husband in the writ. The *Married Women's Property Act 1882* stated that the husband need not be joined. Did this mean that in future writs would be invalid if he were joined? See *Edwards v Porter (1925) AC 1* where it was held: No; the mischief was the invalidity arising from the failure to join; it was not intended to make the joinder invalid.

In *Wycombe Marsh Garages v Fowler (1972) 1 WLR 1156* a man took his car to the garage for testing so that he could get a MOT test certificate. The garage failed the car. The garage said that two car wheels had tread-lift. In fact the wheels were later subjected to extensive testing and were found to have mould-drip. Existence of mould-drip instead of tread-lift should have meant that the certificate should have been given. The garage was prosecuted under *s.1 Trade Descriptions Act 1968* for applying a false trade description to the wheels. Conviction by the magistrates was quashed. It was held that the mischief to be prevented was that goods might be sold or provided with false descriptions. This Act was not concerned to prevent people from giving honest advice and to punish them criminally if they got the answer wrong. Parliament did not intend that this

Act should apply to such a situation. Therefore words even though literally seeming to apply do not in fact do so.

42.6 *The purposive approach*

A more modern approach to statutory interpretation is to recognise that Parliament does not (nowadays) only intend to suppress 'mischief' when it passes a statute. Modern legislation (reflecting the role of a modern state) often desires to bring about social benefits, or to comply with international obligations. In recognition of this fact, some judges (particularly Lord Scarman) have propounded the 'purposive approach' to statutory interpretation. This approach asks what the true *purpose* of Parliament was in passing the legislation (whether it was to suppress a mischief or to promote a benefit or to secure conformity with an international obligation, or to achieve any other purpose at all). This is often called finding 'the presumed legislative intent'. It is, of course, the antipathy of the literal approach. Thus, in *Fothergill v Monarch Airlines (1980)* the House of Lords refused to give the word 'damage' (in the *Carriage by Air Act 1961*) its literal, dictionary, meaning, and held that (for the purposes of airline travel) it included 'loss' of property, as well as damage to property. Thus the plaintiff was prevented from claiming compensation for certain items stolen from his suitcase because he had failed to report the loss to the airline within the seven-day time limit for reporting 'damage to baggage'. As the time limit was laid down in an international treaty (the 'Warsaw Convention') and this treaty formed part of the *Carriage by Air Act 1961*, it was not appropriate to apply a strict constructionalist approach. Lord Scarman said:

> The trial judge's error was, I think, to construe the provision as though it were merely a term of a ticket contract. It is much more than that. It is part of a convention intended to unify the rules relating to the carriage of persons and goods by air ... I consider it our duty to interpret, if it be possible, Article 26(2) in a way which is consistent with the purpose of the convention ...

Lord Scarman also took the view that it was permissible, in such a case, to look to the legislative history *(les travaux préparatoires)*, the international case law *(la jurisprudence)* and the writings of jurists *(la doctrine)* as aids to interpreting the international obligations adopted by the British Parliament.

Another example of the 'purposive approach' is the decision of the House of Lords in *Mandla v Lee (1983)*. In this case the House of Lords interpreted the phrase 'ethnic group' (in *s.3 Race Relations Act 1976)* to include members of the Sikh religion, even though the literal meaning of 'ethnic' connotes a racial group. (The defendant had argued that Sikhs were not racially different from Punjabis who were not Sikhs.) The House of Lords interpreted the word 'ethnic' so that it covered distinct communities who shared a long history and cultural tradition, as did the Sikhs. (The defendant was therefore held to have unlawfully discriminated against a Sikh schoolboy by refusing to admit him to his school because of his turban.)

However, the 'purposive' approach does not work satisfactorily in criminal law since (in the case of statutes creating a criminal offence) the paramount rule is that any ambiguity must be interpreted in favour of the defendant: *R v Bloxham (1982) 1 All ER 582;* but see *R v Shivpuri (1986) 2 WLR 988.*

42.7 *Conclusion*

In interpreting a statute the court will decide whether or not a particular wording is ambiguous.

The Preamble or Long Title of a statute may be looked at if there is any ambiguity in the statute, but not otherwise.

Ambiguity arises through an error in drafting, whereby the words used in a statute are found to be capable of bearing two or more literal meanings, e.g. the *Restriction of Offensive Weapons Act 1959* made it an offence 'to offer for sale' certain offensive weapons including flick-knives.

In *Fisher v Bell (1961) 1 QB 394* a shopkeeper who displayed weapons of this type in his window was held to be not guilty of an offence under the Act, because in contract law the display of goods in a shop window does not constitute an offer.

Where the subject-matter of a statute is a branch of the law which is intrinsically complex, such as landlord and tenant or income tax, it seems to be virtually impossible to choose language which is entirely free from ambiguity and uncertainty.

Uncertainty is far more common. It occurs where the words of a statute are intended to apply to various factual situations, and the courts are called upon to decide whether or not the set of facts before them amounts to a factual situation envisaged by the Act, e.g. the use of the words 'road', 'house', 'ship', 'premises', 'vehicle', etc. For example, the *Telegraphs Act 1* as passed before the invention of the telephone – does it extend to telephones? Yes: the courts presume that Parliament foresaw the invention: *Taylor v Goodwin (1879) 4 QBD 228* and *Maxwell on Interpretation of Statutes*.

Also does a particular commodity fall into a particular category for the purposes of a particular Act? For example, are frozen yogurts dairy produce or ice cream confectionery? Is an orange squeezed by hand a 'manufactured drink' for the purposes of taxing of bottled orange juice? See *Customs & Excise Commissioners v Savoy Hotel Ltd (1966) 2 All ER 299*. This matter is sometimes simplified a little by the modern practice of containing in the particular Act a definition section for the purposes of that Act.

Whichever of the three approaches (Literal, Golden, Mischief) to interpretation is adopted, the court is still bound to interpret the words of the Act before it. If interpretation disclosed an uncertainty or ambiguity the court will then be bound to construe the statute. Judges themselves have formulated a large body of rules for the interpretation and construction of statutes.

42.8 *Criticisms and ideas for reform*

Although skilled draftsmen try and provide for every contigency and the courts have a number of aids and devices they can employ, problems continuously arise over the interpretation of Acts of Parliament. Sometimes a situation arises known as a casus omissus «» an omitted case. That is something which should have been provided for but has been omitted. In *Seaford Court Estatess v Asher (1949)* Denning L.J. (as he then was) advocated that in such cases the court in finding out the intention of Parliament and implementing it should fill in the gaps they had left. However, this approach was roundly criticised by Lord Simonds in the House of Lords in *Magor & St Mellons R.D.C. v Newport Corporation (1952) AC 189*. He said that a judge should give effect to 'the meaning of what Parliament has said and not what Parliament omitted to say'. He described the Denning approach as 'a naked usurpation of the legislative role.' In effect Parliament should change any absurdities not the courts.

These cases highlight a conflict which existed and to a certain degree still does between those who look to what the Act intended and that school which in effect adopts as pure literal approach.

The Denning approach has been called the 'Social Policy Approach'. i.e., the courts should look at the social policy directing the Act. This has more recently become known as the 'Purposive approach'. This approach appeared to receive the blessing of the House of Lords in *Kammins*

Ballrooms v Zenith Investments (1971) AC 850. Quite simply the courts in cases of ambiguity should look to:

(i) The subject-matter of the Act under interpretation;

(ii) The object parliament sought to achieve;

(iii) The part the section the section in question was designed to play

On the face of it, it may seem a good thing that the above approached is employed. However, critics have pointed out that judges have used this approach to cloak their distaste for the Act. Lord Denning for example in the Court of Appeal in the 1970's narrowly interpreted various Acts designed to protect trade unions. It is argued that by using this approach he single-handely frustrated the then Labour Government's industrial relations legislative programme. Many commentators favour the strict demarcation between the legislative, enacting laws, and the judiciary simply declaring it.

However, despite reservations about the social policy approach the *Law Commission in 1969* and the *Renton Committee 1975* both favoured it. Both bodies criticised the inflexibility of the attitudes of some judges. The Commission recommended that the courts should be able to rely on such documents as White Papers and reports of Parliamentary Committees.

In Parliamentary Session 1980-81 a Bill called the Interpretation of Legislation Bill was introduced in the House of Lords by Lord Scarman. However, the Government of the day refused to give it due support fearing that its proposals would go too far.

No recommendations have been put into effect as yet. However, the methods used in the European Court of Justice with respect to interpretation are very flexible and it is widely believed that the United Kingdom membership of the E.E.C. will eventually bring about a change of attitude on the part of the judiciary in the long run.

43. AIDS TO INTERPRETATION AND CONSTRUCTION

43.1 Rules of interpretation and construction

(a)   The statute must be read as a whole;

(b)   the *ejusdem generis* rule;

(c)   penal provisions construed narrowly;

(d)   the *Interpretation Act 1978.*

43.2 The statute must be read as a whole

Every section must be read in the light of every other section, especially in the light of an interpretation (definition) section, and schedules, if incorporated into the body of the Act must be read with the Act. For example, in the case of *Beswick v Beswick (1967) 2 All ER 1197* which concerned the question of the application of the rule of privity of contract in *s.56 Law of Property Act 1925.* Had Parliament by this section inadvertently abrogated the Common Law rule that a person cannot sue on a contract to which he is not a party? It was argued that the combined effect of these provisions was to enable a stranger to a contract to enforce the contract. This argument prevailed in the Court of Appeal but was rejected by the House of Lords. Their Lordships pointed out that *s.56* is one of 25 sections in the Act grouped under the heading 'Conveyances and other instruments', and in those circumstances held that the contract did require the word 'property' to be limited in its effect to real property.

The Long title and the Short Title, being part of the enactment, must, strictly speaking, be consulted in interpreting any part of the Act though in practice courts will only refer to the Long Title to resolve an ambiguity and do not regard the Short Title as an aid to interpretation at all.

Headings, marginal notes, punctuation and schedules which are not expressly incorporated into the text, are not part of the enactment and are not aids to interpretation.

43.3 The ejusdem generis rule

This rule is a particular aspect of section 43.2. General words which follow two or more particular words in an act must be confined to a meaning of the same kind *(ejusdem generis)* as the particular words. So in a reference to 'asses, goats, sheep, horses and other animals', the last three words would be limited in their application to animals of the livestock type and would not be extended to cover animals such as lions and tigers.

In *Gregory v Fearn (1953) 1 WLR 974* the court was concerned with a provision of the *Lord's Day Observance Act 1677* which stated that 'no tradesman, artificer, workman, labourer or other person whatsoever shall do any work on the Lord's day'. The court considered that the words 'or other person whatsoever' were confined to the general category of manual workers and did not apply to professional men (here estate agents).

Application of this rule was used in the case of *Powell v Kempton Park Race Course Co (1889) AC 143* to *s.1 Betting Act 1853.* This Act prohibited the keeping of a 'house, office, room or other place' for betting with persons resorting thereto.

The question was whether Tattersall's Ring at a racecourse was an 'other place' within the meaning of the Act. The House of Lords held that it was not, since the words 'house, office, room' created a class of indoor places within which a racecourse, being outdoor, did not fall. (Tattersall's Ring is an open-air enclosure on the racecourse.)

In *Roe v Hemmings (1951) 1 KB 676* the statute referred to 'quay or other place'. The court held that the words 'or other place' must be interpreted literally since no class of words was created by the one word 'quay'.

43.4 *Penal provisions construed narrowly*

Statutes imposing criminal penalties or tax obligations are, in the event of

ambiguity, to be construed in favour of the individual. See *R v Hallam (1957) 1 All ER 665* where the offence of 'knowingly possessing explosives' was held to be committed only if D knew that he possessed something, *and* he knew that what he possessed was explosive.

43.5 *The Interpretation Act 1978*

This Act prescribes definitions of certain words and phrases which are commonly encountered in statutes and applies to all Acts (except private Acts) passed since 1850, unless a special definition is given in the relevant Act.

(a) Words importing the masculine gender include the feminine, and *vice versa*, except in obvious cases, e.g. statutes regarding sexual offences.

(b) Words in the singular shall include the plural and *vice versa.*

(c) 'Month' shall mean calendar month.

(d) If an Act repeals a repealing statute, it shall not be construed as reviving any statute previously repealed unless words are added reviving that enactment, e.g.

$$\text{Act 1} \longrightarrow \underset{\text{repeals 1}}{\text{Act 2}} \longrightarrow \underset{\text{repeals 2}}{\text{Act 3}}$$

Act 3 does not therefore automatically revive Act 1.

However, if the words are added in Act 3 reviving Act 1, then Act 1 will be an Act again.

(e) 'Persons' shall include corporate or incorporate.

(f) 'Writing' shall include printing, lithography, photography and other modes of representing or reproducing words in a visible form.

43.6 *Presumptions and interpretations*

Where parts of the statute are not clear the court may be assisted by certain presumptions, though these sometimes conflict with each other.

The main presumptions are:

(a) against fundamental changes in the Common Law by mere implication. In *Leach v R (1912) 7 Cr App Rep 172* a wife who was competent to testify against her husband was thereby made compellable;

(b) against the imposition of criminal liability without fault. Courts are reluctant to hold that no *mens rea* is required unless the statute is expressly worded so as to make liability absolute, as modern statutes frequently are, e.g. many provisions of the *Factories Act 1961*. See also *Sweet v Parsley (1968) 2 WLR 470;*

(c)   against confiscating vested rights in the absence of express provision, interference with property will generally be minimised;,

(d)   against ousting courts' jurisdiction – although Parliament has the power to exclude any matter from competence of the courts, the courts are naturally slow to imply such exclusion;

(e)   against arbitrary conduct and abuse of power;

(f)   that the Crown is not bound by statute unless named in it;

(g)   against the operation of a statute outside the United Kingdom;

(h)   against allowing a wrongdoer to benefit from his wrong, e.g. in *Re Sigsworth (1935) Ch 89* the court refused to allow a man to inherit from his mother's estate, since he had murdered her;

(i)   against the imposition of taxation;

(j)   against the retrospective effect of a statute. In *Yew Bon Tew v Mara (1983) 1 AC 553* P was injured through the negligence of D's bus company. The limitation period was 12 months, and that period expired without P making a claim. Then a new Act came into force which provided for a three year limitation period, and P then filed a claim. The court held that the new Act did not operate retrospectively, since its effect would be to deprive D of his right not to be sued. D should be able to assume, once the existing limitation period expired, that he could not be sued, and in the absence of an express provision in the new Act any subsequent legislation would not operate retrospectively.

43.7   *Expression unius exclusio alterius*

'Express mention of one thing implies the exclusion of another'. This rule is connected to the Ejusdem generis rule. Where an Act lists specified matters which are not followed by general words then only those matters actually mentioned are caught by the Act. For example, if an Act specifically refers to 'lorries, trucks and vans', it will not apply to other vehicles, such as cars or coaches.

43.8   *Noscitur a Sociis*

'A word is known by the company it keeps'. The words in a section must be read in their context and the Act must be read as a whole. It is often found that words or a section are explained or modified in another part of the Act.

44. CONSTRUCTION OF STATUTES

44.1 Aids to construction

All Acts require interpretation but only statutes whose provisions are ambiguous or uncertain in extent require construction, though processes of interpretation and construction are inextricably interrelated. Judges frequently make no attempt to distinguish between the processes of interpretation and construction. The distinction is relevant because not all aids to construction are legitimate aids to interpretation. So the aids to construction which do not form part of the enactment may only be consulted where the process of interpretation has disclosed an uncertainty or an ambiguity.

There are two types of aids: internal and external.

44.2 Internal aids

These are aids to be found within the Queen's Printer's copy of the statute itself. Those parts of the Act which are not strictly part of the enactment, i.e. punctuation, headings, marginal notes, are only used as aids in cases of ambiguity.

Different parts of the statute:.

(a) *Long Title* – sets out the reasons for the legislation and the objects which it is intended to serve, e.g. the Act whose Short Title is the *Occupiers' Liability Act 1957* has the Long Title *An Act to amend the law of England and Wales as to the liability of occupiers and others for injury or damage resulting to persons or goods lawfully on any land or other property from dangers due to the state of the property or to things done or omitted to be done there, to make provision as to the operation in relation to the Crown of laws made by the Parliament of Northern Ireland for similar purposes or otherwise amending the law of tort, and for purposes connected therewith.*

It might be supposed that the insertion of a Long Title would afford Parliament an opportunity of stating its general intention in passing the Act, but in fact Long Titles tend to be succinct rather than explanatory and generally do little more than identify the subject-matter of the Act. Insertion of a Long Title is based on tradition rather than on utilitarian grounds.

The Long Title will not prevail over express provisions within the Act.

(b) *Short Title* – the title by which the Act is commonly and properly cited. Theoretically the Short Title is a valid aid both to interpretation and to construction, but there appears to be no reported case in which the Short Title has been used to determine a point of construction, though reference has sometimes been made to it. Sometimes the Short Title of a certain Act does not reflect the content of the Act accurately, e.g. the *Criminal Procedure Act 1865* applies to both civil and criminal proceedings. The *Unfair Contract Terms Act 1977* applies both to contract and negligence.

(c) *Headings* – these are sometimes consulted where enactment is uncertain or ambiguous. In *DPP v Schildkamp (1970) 2 WLR 279* Lord Upjohn was in favour of according greater weight to headings than the other law lords.

(d) *Marginal notes* – these are used for convenience or reference, and are not used even in the event of ambiguity. Nevertheless there have been cases in which the court has clearly adverted to the marginal note in constructing a section. In the light of *DPP v Schildkamp* it now appears that the court is entitled to look at marginal notes in cases of ambiguity, though they clearly carry little weight and certainly cannot displace a meaning which appears from the enactment proper.

(e) *Definition sections.*

(f) *Schedules* – form part of an Act if they are expressly incorporated by a section in the Act itself. They are used to list matters of detail and for amendments and repeals of previous Acts. They cannot be regarded as altering or enlarging the ordinary meaning of words used in the Act.

(g) *Preamble* – sets out the general purpose of the Act, but most modern Acts do not have a preamble and, if there is one, it is usually too vague to be of assistance.

44.3 *External aids*

These are aids which are not to be found in the Act.

(a) *Dictionaries* – words in statutes are presumed to bear their ordinary and natural meaning and it is legitimate to consult a dictionary to determine the meaning of the words which have no particular legal meaning. Therefore, in *Re Ripon (Highfield) Housing Confirmation Order (1939) 2 KB 838* the court adopted the *Oxford English Dictionary* definition of 'park'. Nevertheless dictionaries bear only slight weight and, in context, the dictionary meaning may not be the one which Parliament intended.

(b) *Reports of committees* – Reports of Law Commissions, the Law Reform Committee and similar bodies are legitimate aids to discovering the state of pre-existing law and mischief which the statute was passed to remedy.

(c) *Reports of Proceedings in Parliament (Hansard)* – in *Davis v Johnson (1978) 1 All ER 841* Lord Denning in the Court of Appeal referred to proceedings in Parliament in construing a provision of the *Domestic Violence and Matrimonial Proceedings Act 1976.* However, in the same case in the House of Lords, Lords Diplock and Scarman and Viscount Dilhorne disagreed with this practice. It has since been held that it is not permissible to use *Hansard* since to do so would be to question proceedings of Parliament in the courts, which is constitutionally unacceptable since the *Act of Settlement 1701.*

44.4 *Judicial precedents of interpretation*

The doctrine of precedent applies to the interpretation of statutes. The decision of a superior court on the interpretation of a statute is binding on a court inferior to the hierarchy which is called upon to interpret the same or a corresponding statutory provision.

44.5 *Conclusion*

Judges differ enormously in their approach to interpreting statutes, and the imprecise nature of the rules gives considerable leeway for the exercise of judicial discretion. Those judges who favour the use of the Literal Rule would deny vehemently the role of the judge in forming or altering statute law; whilst those judges who favour a more inventive construction of legislation would argue that they are merely giving effect to Parliament's intention, albeit expressed somewhat differently in the statute!

45. JUDICIAL PRECEDENT

45.1 *When is a precedent binding?*

Courts in countries other than England may also tend to follow their earlier decisions but they are not in general *bound* to do so. However, the English court system (despite the attacks of Lord Denning) is peculiar in that if the court which decided a precedent stands in a certain relation to the court hearing the present case, that precedent is not merely persuasive (i.e. available for use if so desired) but positively binding and must be applied to the case in hand, regardless of the wishes of the judges deciding the present case.

A precedent is binding and must be applied in a parallel case when:.

(a)   The precedent was decided by a higher court than the court hearing the present case:

Civil system

(i)   County Court judges are bound by parallel decisions of:

High Court judge sitting alone;

Divisional Courts of the High Court (usually three judges);

Court of Appeal;

House of Lords.

(ii)   A High Court judge sitting alone is bound by a parallel decision of:

Divisional Court of the same High Court Division (i.e. one QBD judge sitting alone will be bound by a decision of Divisional Court of QBD, but not a judge of the Chancery Division sitting alone);

Court of Appeal;

House of Lords.

(iii)   Divisional Court of High Court is bound by a parallel decision of:

Court of Appeal;

House of Lords.

(iv)   Court of Appeal (Civil Division) is bound by a parallel decision of the House of Lords.

(v)   The House of Lords is not bound by decisions of any other court because there is no court higher than the House of Lords (except the European Court of Justice on matters of EEC law only).

Criminal system

(i)   Magistrates are bound by parallel decisions of:

The High Court;

Court of Appeal;

House of Lords.

Note: The magistrates are *not* bound by parallel decisions of the Crown Court.

(ii)   A Crown Court judge is bound by parallel decisions of:

   The High Court;

   Court of Appeal;

   House of Lords.

(iii)   The Queen's Bench Division is bound by parallel decisions of: Court of Appeal;

   House of Lords.

(iv)   The Court of Appeal (Criminal Division) is bound by parallel decisions of the House of Lords.

(v)   The House of Lords is not bound by the decisions of any other court.

(b)   Some courts are bound by previous decisions of the same court:

Civil system

(i)   Divisional Court regards itself as bound by earlier Divisional Court decisions.

(ii)   Court of Appeal (Civil Division) is bound by previous decisions of that Division – see *Young v Bristol Aeroplane Co (1944) 2 All ER 293* – unless the previous decision is expressly or impliedly overruled by the House of Lords. Recently in *Davis v Johnson (1978) (supra)* the Court of Appeal purported to vary the earlier rule of precedent in *Young's case*, Lord Denning considering it a rule of practice, not one of law that the Court of Appeal was bound by its own decisions. In the House of Lords, however, their Lordships made it clear that they still considered the rule as stated in *Young's case* to be binding on the Court of Appeal. The Court of Appeal is not bound to follow its own decision if there are two conflicting decisions, when it can choose between the two. It is also not bound if its decision is *per incuriam* of a House of Lords' decision.

(iii)   House of Lords – Until 1966 it was also bound by its own decisions but now, if a point of public importance is involved, the House of Lords will not follow a previous House of Lords decision which the court regards as undesirable (see *1966 Practice Statement*).

Note: County Court and High Court judges sitting alone are not bound by their own previous decisions.

Criminal systems

(i)   The High Court (QBD) is bound by its own decisions except where it decides that it misapplied or misdirected itself as to the law and an individual's liberty is at stake: *R v Taylor (1950)*.

(ii)   The Court of Appeal (Criminal Division) is bound by decisions of its predecessor, the Court of Criminal Appeal, but it is not bound by its own decisions if it would cause injustice to the appellant since justice is to be done, even at the expense of certainty: *R v Gould (1964)*.

   In *R v Newsome and Brown (1970)* it was held that a five member court may depart from the decision of a three member court, but note that this does not apply to the Civil Division, and has been disputed.

45.2 *Precedents which are not binding – ways in which doctrine can retain its flexibility*

These are:

(a)   precedents which have to be overruled;

(b)   precedents which can be distinguished;

(c)   two conflicting decisions of the Court of Appeal;

(d)   statements of law made *per incuriam;*

(e)   persuasive authorities.

45.3 *Precedents overruled*

A decision may be overruled either by statute or by a higher court. If it is overruled by a higher court, the earlier decision is deemed to have been based on a misunderstanding of the law. The earlier rule of law is deemed never to have existed. This is the *declaratory theory* of the Common Law, i. e. Common Law is never changed – it is merely restated correctly.

Judicial overruling operates retrospectively and therefore the courts do not overrule earlier precedents unless there is good reason.

45.4 *Distinguishing*

A court can avoid following a decision which is apparently applicable to the case in hand, but of which it disapproves by *distinguishing* the precedent from the case in hand. Distinguishing is a process whereby a court actually and in theory finds that the material facts of the two cases involved differ so that the precedent need not be followed. An example of how fine a distinction may be drawn can be seen in two cases concerning the tort of conversion: *England v Cowley (1873) LR 8 Exch 126* and *Oakley v Lyster (1931) 1 KB 148.*

In *England v Cowley* the defendant refused to allow the plaintiff to remove goods from his (the defendant's) premises. It was held not to be conversion since there was no absolute denial of ownership. This case was distinguished by the Court of Appeal in *Oakley v Lyster* in which the defendant refused to allow the plaintiff to remove material from his (the defendant's) land and, in addition, asserted his own ownership to the material. It was held to be an act of conversion, the assertion of ownership apparently making the denial of ownership absolute.

If distinguishing cases is taken to extremes it can lead to uncertainty in the law.

45.5 *Two conflicting decisions of the Court of Appeal (Civil Division)*

Here the Court of Appeal may choose which it will follow – the decision not followed being deemed to be overruled. So in *Tiverton Estates Ltd v Wearwell Ltd (1975) Ch 146* the Court of Appeal was able to avoid following its own recent decision in the controversial case of *Law v Jones (1974) Ch 112* (to the effect that it was unnecessary for a memorandum under *s.40 Law of Property Act 1925* to acknowledge the existence of a contract) because it was in conflict with earlier decisions of the court.

45.6 *Per incuriam*

The Court of Appeal in *Young v Bristol Aeroplane Co (1944)* established the principle that the Court of Appeal was not bound to follow its own earlier decision if satisfied that the decision in question was reached *per incuriam* (through lack of care).

This means that some relevant statutory provision or precedent, which might have affected the decision, was not brought to the court's attention. This principle of *per incuriam* has been applied to other courts.

In *Baker v Queen (1975) 3 All ER 55* Lord Diplock said that a court could only use the *per incuriam* rule if it was applying it to its own decision. It was not able to use the rule in relation to the decision of a higher court, unless the court was the Court of Appeal applying *per incuriam* to a decision of the House of Lords. In *Duke v Reliance Systems (1987) 2 All ER 858* the Court of Appeal stated that the Per Incuriam rule could only apply where it could be shown that the inclusion of the omitted authority *definitely* would have altered the decision in question.

45.7   *Conflicting decisions of higher courts*

In *Miliangos v George Frank (1975)* Lord Simon said that, where a court at first instance was faced with conflicting decisions of courts above it in the hierarchy, it should follow the later decision of the court immediately above it in the hierarchy.

For example, in 1974 the House of Lords decided a case, the *ratio* of which was X. In 1979 the Court of Appeal decided a parallel case, the *ratio* of which was Y. In 1984 the High Court faced with a parallel case should follow the Court of Appeal and decide it according to Y.

The recent case of *Colchester Estates v Carlton Industries (1984) 2 All ER 601* held that, where a High Court judge was faced with two conflicting decisions of a court of coordinate jurisdiction, he should apply the later decision, since he should assume that the later judge had correctly applied or distinguished the earlier case.

For example, in 1974 a High Court judge decides a case, the *ratio* of which is X. In 1979 a High Court judge decides a similar case, the *ratio* of which is Y. In 1984, strictly speaking, a High Court judge could choose between the decisions, but in practice he should apply the later decision, Y.

45.8   *The House of Lords*

Decisions of the House of Lords are binding on itself and on all lower courts. So, for example, if a case was decided in a certain way in 1932 and similar facts come before the Court of Appeal in 1988 they would have to follow that previous decision. However, in the Practice Statement (Judicial Precedent) (1966) 1 WLR 1234, the Lord Chancellor announced that in future the House of Lords could depart from its own previous decisions when 'it appeared right to them to do so'. However they would have to bear in mind the following:-

(a)   the danger of disturbing retrospective financial arrangement;

(b)   rights in property; and

(c)   the special need to preserve certainty in the criminal law.

The House has availed itself of this power a few times since then. The House recently demonstrated in R.V. Shivpuri (1987) AC 1 that it was not afraid to use the power to overrule recent House of Lords decisions (in that case Anderton v Ryan (1985) AC 560). It reviewed the arguments for not exercising that right, the fact that the decision in Anderton v Ryan (Supra) had only been recently taken, and the need for certainty in the criminal law, but as Lord Bridge stated: 'The 1966 Practice Statement is an effective abandonment of our pretension to infallibility. If a serious error embodied in a decision of this house has distorted the law, the sooner it is corrected the better.'

46. JUDICIAL INVENTIVENESS

From time to time cases arise for which there is no precedent, but the judge cannot sit back and do nothing.

The judge can seek to draw an analogy with existing law, as in *Buckle v H Holmes (1926) 2 KB 125* where liability for a cat's misbehaviour was determined by reference to authority on liability for dogs.

Alternatively, he can try to fill the gaps by reference to some residual power, as in *DPP v Shaw (1961) 2 All ER 446*, the case of the Prostitutes' Directory.

However, there are those who would strongly argue, as did Lord Reid in *DPP v Shaw*, that any gaps must not be filled by the judges, but must be left to Parliament.

LLB

ENGLISH LEGAL SYSTEM

LESSON 5 (REVISION)

51. *REVIEW OF LESSONS 1-4*

    51. **SUMMARY OF PROBLEMS DEALT WITH**

52. *REVISION QUESTIONS*

NOTE.   THIS LESSON MUST BE WORKED BEFORE PROCEEDING TO LESSON 6.

51. REVIEW OF LESSONS 1-4

51.1 *Summary of problems dealt with*

This point in the manual is approximately one-third of the way through it. To consolidate what you have so far learned, you should read through each section again, pausing at the end of each to recall what you have just read. If you cannot recall it adequately and in detail, read and check your knowledge until you are satisfied.

When you have completed this, test your knowledge further by answering (in your head) the following revision questions.

52. *REVISION QUESTIONS*

1.   What are the differences between a crime and a tort?

2.   What are the differences between a plaintiff's claim in tort and contract?

3.   What was the most important source of law? Is the position different today?

4.   What sources of law does a court use today?

5.   How important to English law is an accurate and speedy system of law reporting?

6.   What types of legislation are there?

7.   What are the advantages of the different types of legislation?

8.   What is the justification for a doctrine of binding precedent?

9.   How do you determine the binding part of a judgment?

10.   When will custom be recognised by the court?

11.   What effect has Britain's membership of the EEC had?

12.   Explain the difference between Common Law and Equity.

13.   In which court would the following actions take place:

  (a)   an action in tort for a large amount of damages;

  (b)   an investigation into a suspicious death;

  (c)   an adoption application;

  (d)   a trial for a serious offence;

  (e)   an appeal on a point of law from the Queen's Bench Division;

  (f)   an action concerning the validity of a will;

  (g)   an action for unfair dismissal;

  (h)   an appeal from the Employment Appeal Tribunal;

  (i)   an application for a licence?

14.   What rules do the courts use to interpret statutes?

15.   When may a court not follow:

  (a)   the decision of a higher court;

  (b)   its own decision?

16.   Under what circumstances may the House of Lords depart from its own previous decisions? Has the House overruled its previous decisions fearlessly?

LLB

ENGLISH LEGAL SYSTEM

LESSON 6 (STUDY)

61. *THE JUDICIARY*

    61.1   INTRODUCTION
    61.2   APPOINTMENT
    61.3   THE MAGISTRATES' COURT
    61.4   THE CROWN COURT
    61.5   THE COUNTY COURT
    61.6   THE HIGH COURT
    61.7   THE COURT OF APPEAL
    61.8   THE JUDICIAL COMMITTEE OF THE HOUSE OF LORDS
    61.9   THE JUDICIAL COMMITTEE OF THE PRIVY COUNCIL
    61.10 TENURE
    61.11 QUALIFICATION
    61.12 TRAINING
    61.13 PROMOTION
    61.14 DISCIPLINE
    61.15 THE ROLE OF THE JUDGE

62. *THE MAGISTRACY*

    62.1   COMPOSITION OF THE BENCH
    62.2   THE MAGISTRATES' CLERK
    62.3   APPOINTMENT
    62.4   QUALIFICATION AND TRAINING
    62.5   TENURE
    62.6   CRITICISMS
    62.7   PROPOSALS FOR REFORM

61. *THE JUDICIARY*

61.1 *Introduction*

A distinguishing characteristic of the English judicial system is that there is no separate judicial profession as a branch of the public service, but the judges (other than lay magistrates) are selected from among the leading members of the Bar. This also accounts for the fact that the professional education of barristers and the organisation of the Bar are controlled by the profession itself and are not on a statutory basis.

It is from the ranks of QCs that judges of the Supreme Court are usually selected. There is no formal system of promotion in the judicial hierarchy, so that a barrister of the requisite number of years' standing may be appointed a Lord of Appeal in Ordinary without having been a *puisne* judge or a Lord Justice of Appeal. County Court and Circuit judges have occasionally been made judges of the High Court.

It has always been assumed that the judiciary is impartial and independent in its task of applying the law. Yet today many would argue that they are aged, conservative, and out of touch with reality, often making new law, rather than simply applying pre-existing rules.

The existence of a 'career judiciary' whereby a young lawyer elects to join the judicial service and work and gain experience in a judicial capacity is a favourite examination issue. The advantages of such a system are that the young 'judge-to-be' receives a training and experience that relates directly to his position as a judge. He learns to be a listener and an independent arbitrator; whereas in England our judges are chosen from the ranks of practising lawyers: arguably a 'talker' rather than a 'listener'. The qualities that make a good advocate are not always those that make a good judge, although both require quick intelligent minds and an ability to seize upon and develop the relevant and discard the irrelevant.

A career judiciary exists in many European countries and in the USA, and promotion is similar to that in the armed services: a progression from rank to rank. In England there is no such natural progression. A recently appointed judge could sit in the High Court straight away; in theory he could also begin in the Court of Appeal! There is a tendency for judges to be promoted from the High Court to the Court of Appeal, but it is only occasionally that a judge will be promoted from the Circuit bench.

It is also difficult to see on what basis promotion is granted. Consideration of candidates is a secretive process and, since the gift of higher judicial office is in practice in the hands of the politician, it is often argued that promotion may be conditional on having the appropriate views or political inclination. Judges who are in the judicial doldrums when one political party is in power, may find that a change of government results in a revival of their judicial career.

61.2 *Appointment*

The old theory that the Monarch is the 'fountain of justice' is still nominally effective; the courts are the Queen's courts, and the judges remain Her Majesty's judges. In practice, however, judicial appointments are made upon the advice of the government of the day.

The Queen appoints the Lord Chancellor, the Lord Chief Justice, the Master of the Rolls, the President of the Family Division, the Lords of Appeal in Ordinary and the Lords Justices of Appeal; she does so by convention on the advice of the Prime Minister who consults the Lord Chancellor. She appoints the *puisne* judges of the High Court, Circuit judges and Recorders and stipendiary magistrates on the recommendation of the Lord Chancellor.

61.3 *The Magistrates' Court*

(a) *Lay magistrates* – appointed by the Lord Chancellor on the advice of local advisory committees. They are not usually legally qualified, but are respected members of the local community.

(b) *Stipendiary magistrate* – appointed by the Queen on the recommendation of the Lord Chancellor. A stipendiary magistrate is usually a barrister or solicitor of seven years' standing, who is full-time, salaried and who usually sits alone.

61.4 *The Crown Court*

Generally the Lord Chancellor is responsible for deciding the number of judges who will be available in the Circuits and the places where the courts are to sit.

The Lord Chief Justice with the presiding judges of each Circuit is responsible for the allocation of work within the Circuits and the selection of individual judges for various types of work.

(a) *Circuit judges* – are full time judges and are appointed by the Crown on the recommendation of the Lord Chancellor to serve in the Crown Court and also in the County Courts, and to carry out such other judicial functions as may be conferred on them. They must be barristers of at least ten years' standing or Recorders who have held office for at least three years. They must be in satisfactory health when appointed and retire at the end of the completed year of service in which they reach the age of 72, although the Lord Chancellor may retain the services of a Circuit judge until he is 75. The Lord Chancellor may remove a Circuit judge on the ground of incapacity or misbehaviour and they do not enjoy the same degree of security as do the judges of the High Court, Court of Appeal and House of Lords: the *Courts Act 1971*. He is addressed in court as 'Your Honour'.

(b) *Recorders* – they are part-time judges of the Crown Court appointed by the Queen on the recommendation of the Lord Chancellor. They must be either barristers or solicitors of at least ten years' standing in each case. The Recorder is appointed for a specified term, and the frequency and duration of the occasions when he is required are defined in his appointment. The term of his appointment may be extended but he must retire, like a Circuit judge, at 72 and there is no provision for extending it beyond that age, and the appointment may be terminated for incapacity or misbehaviour. He is addressed in court as 'Your Honour'.

(c) *High Court judges* – they are full-time judges and exercise their jurisdiction in civil cases in the High Court (see later) and also sit in the Crown Court for trial, generally, of more serious criminal offences. The rules are flexible in so far as, if asked by the Lord Chancellor, a High Court judge will be able to sit not only in the High Court and Crown Court, but also in the Court of Appeal and, if he agrees, in a County Court. He is addressed in Court as 'My Lord'.

(d) *Court of Appeal judges* – a judge of this court (see later), if requested by the Lord Chancellor, may sit in the Crown Court or in a County Court, as well as in the High Court. He is addressed in court as 'My Lord'.

(e) *Magistrates* – if the Crown Court is hearing an appeal from the Magistrates' Court or is sentencing an offender committed to them by the magistrates, then at least two, and not more than four lay magistrates must sit with the judge. When magistrates sit in the Crown Court, they are not merely observers, they must play a full part in any decision, which is always by majority. In theory, therefore, it is possible for the magistrates to outvote the judge.

61.5 *The County Court*

(a) *Circuit judges* – the method of appointment is as discussed earlier. Every Circuit judge shall, by virtue of his office, be capable of sitting as a judge for any County Court district in England and Wales, and the Lord Chancellor shall assign one or more Circuit judges to each district and may from time to time vary the assignment of Circuit judges among the districts.

(b) *Registrars* – these may be solicitors of at least seven years' standing. They supervise most of the administrative work and deal with interlocutory matters (matters arising out of litigation before final judgment is given by a judge) and taxation of costs (settling the amount of costs to be paid by either party to the action). With leave of the judge, they may hear cases where the claim is admitted or where the defendant does not appear at the hearing. They can also hear defended claims up to £500 in value under the arbitration system in the small claims court within the County Court.

(c) *Other judges* – every Court of Appeal judge, every judge of the High Court and every Recorder shall, by virtue of his office, be capable of sitting as a judge for any County Court district in England and Wales and, if he consents to do so, shall sit as such a judge at such times and on such occasions as the Lord Chancellor considers desirable.

61.6 *The High Court*

(a) *High Court judges or puisne judges* – the maximum number of High Court judges is 85. They must be barristers of at least ten years' standing and are generally appointed from the ranks of Queen's Counsel. As well as sitting in the High Court they can sit in the Crown Court. High Court judges must, unless appointed before 1959, retire at 75.

(b) *Deputy High Court judges* – if it appears to the Lord Chancellor that it is expedient as a temporary measure to make an appointment in order to facilitate disposal of business in the High Court or Crown Court, he can appoint a person qualified for appointment as a High Court judge, or any person who has held office as a Court of Appeal or High Court judge to be a deputy High Court judge.

(c) *High Court outside London* – where it does not prove possible for High Court judges to keep abreast of work involved, it will be possible for them to release cases which are suitable for trial by a Circuit judge, so that it will be possible for a Circuit judge, or even a Recorder, to sit and hear such cases as a temporary High Court judge if he has been requested to do so by or on behalf of the Lord Chancellor.

(d) *Heads of Division* – a judge assigned to a particular Division of the High Court is appointed as head of that Division, so that there are in all three judges as heads for each of the three Divisions. The head of each Division is responsible for the organisation and management of the business of that Division. Heads of Divisions are:

Queen's Bench Division:	Lord Chief Justice
Family Division:	President
Chancery Division:	Vice-Chancellor

Her Majesty, on the recommendation of the Lord Chancellor, the Lord Chief Justice, the Master of the Rolls, the President of the Family Division and the Vice-Chancellor of the Chancery Division, can alter the number of High Court judges attached to any Division.

61.7 *The Court of Appeal*

(a) *Lord Justices of Appeal* – appointed by the Queen on the advice of the Prime Minister, who will be acting on the Lord Chancellor's recommendation. They must be judges of the High Court or barristers of at least 15 years' standing. The maximum number is 28. Retirement is at 75.

(b) *Lords of Appeal in Ordinary*, i.e. the Law Lords, may sit as judges in the Court of Appeal, but this is extremely rare.

(c) *Other ex officio judges* – the following judges can also sit in the Court of Appeal, but do so very rarely: the Lord Chancellor, the President of the Family Division, the Vice-Chancellor and former Lord Chancellors.

(d) *The Master of the Rolls* – the head of the Civil Division of the Court of Appeal; a very important and influential role. Appointed by the Queen on the recommendation of the Prime Minister.

(e) *The Lord Chief Justice* – the head of the Criminal Division of the Court of Appeal.

61.8 *The Judicial Committee of the House of Lords*

(a) *Lords of Appeal in Ordinary* commonly called the Law Lords. They must be holders of high judicial office for two years or barristers of 15 years' standing. They are usually appointed from the Court of Appeal by the Queen on the recommendation of the Prime Minister.

(b) *The Lord Chancellor* – the 500 strong judiciary is headed by the Lord Chancellor, who is appointed by the Prime Minister. Not only is he head of the judiciary, but he acts in effect as a minister of justice, and also heads the House of Lords, as well as sitting on the Judicial Committee of the House. As a political appointee he vacates office whenever there is a change of government.

(c) *Other peers who hold or who have held high judicial office* – this would be very rare.

61.9 *The Judicial Committee of the Privy Council*

(a) *The Lord Chancellor.*

(b) *The Lords of Appeal in Ordinary.*

(c) *Those members of the Privy Council who hold or who have held high judicial office* – very rarely sit.

(d) *The Lord President and ex-Lord Presidents of the Council* – very rarely sit.

61.10 *Tenure*

In days pas t when judges were appointed directly by the Crown they were capable of being dismissed at any time by the Monarch. After the Civil War the *Act of Settlement 1700* provided that judges should hold office 'whilst of good behaviour'. Thus they can only be removed after a request to that effect has been made by both Houses of Parliament. It has never proved necessary to use this procedure.

These provisions apply only to the senior judges. Circuit judges and magistrates may be dismissed by the Lord Chancellor, usually for inability or misbehaviour, although in the case of magistrates the Lord Chancellor is not required to show cause for the dismissal. In 1983 Mr Justice Bruce Campbell was removed from office after being convicted of smuggling.

Until 1959 senior appointments were made for life, with the result that many judges were very aged and often infirm before they decided to retire of their own accord. The *Judicial Pensions Act 1981* now requires anyone appointed after 1959 to retire at the age of 75.

61.11 *Qualification*

It is a distinctive feature of the English courts to recruit judges from the ranks of practising barristers; in many continental countries, the judiciary is a separate cadre which young lawyers enter without much previous experience of legal practice.

The vast majority of judges are white, male and middle class. Over 80% of them went to public schools and either Oxford or Cambridge Universities. Although they are expected to be impartial, a great many of them were, before their appointment, involved in politics, usually as candidates for one of the main political parties.

Although the percentage of female lawyers has increased, there are very few women judges. The first woman in the High Court was appointed in 1965, and to date there are three High Court women judges, all of whom sit in the Family Division. Although as yet there are no women sitting as judges in the House of Lords, in 1988 the first women Court of Appeal Judge was appointed; Lord Justice Butler Sloss, as she is known.

Appointments to the Circuit bench are made on the recommendation of the Lord Chancellor. His office maintains records on candidates who may apply for the position. Appointment to the High Court bench is by invitation, and the Lord Chancellor will consult with fellow judges, benchers of the Inns of Court and senior members of the Bar. It is a secretive process, and criticism has been made of what is claimed to be 'the old boy network'.

61.12 *Training*

Recorders and assistant recorders receive a short period of compulsory training, but all other judicial appointees receive no such training; instead there is a voluntary scheme of conferences and seminars, with bulletins being sent at periodic intervals. Refresher courses are available, but the scheme has met with criticism from those who view it as half-hearted and inadequate.

61.13 *Promotion*

It has been argued that there is no formal system of promotion; this would ensure that judges' decisions were not influenced by their desire to make progress in their career. However, there is an increasing tendency to promote to higher judicial office those who have showed promise in the lower courts. As with all judicial appointments the process is secretive.

However, the requirement that judges of the High Court and above be drawn from the Bar has lead to the illogical position that a brilliant Circuit judge is denied promotion because he happens to have qualified as a solicitor.

61.14 *Discipline*

One of the criticisms of the English judicial system is the lack of any formal complaints procedure. JUSTICE have consistently argued for the establishing of such a system, since an aggrieved party has very little he can do to register his complaint.

It is possible to complain to the judge directly about his behaviour, or to bring the matter to the

Lord Chancellor's attention. The Lord Chancellor can then express his displeasure, but both methods depend upon the judge's willingness to reform.

Parliament can pass a motion of censure criticising a judge, and many Parliamentary debates feature criticisms.

Newspapers also criticise judges, although they must avoid 'scurrilous abuse' which can be contempt of court. However, much criticism in the popular press is ill-informed and misleading.

61.15 *The role of the judge*

On taking office the judge takes an oath that 'he will do right to all manner of people after the Laws and Usages of the Realm without fear or favour, affection or ill will'.

His functions in court are:

(a) to supervise the conduct of proceedings – rather like a referee ensuring that both parties observe the rules of evidence and procedure;

(b) to decide the outcome of civil proceedings – explaining and applying the relevant law to the facts of the case before him. He is the sole arbiter of all legal issues raised whether in civil or criminal cases;

(c) in criminal cases he sums up the issues involved and the evidence presented to the court to enable the jury to decide the question of guilt or innocence. If the jury find the defendant guilty, it will be up to the judge to decide the sentence to impose.

In the past judges have been discouraged from speaking on controversial issues in public. The so-called Kilmuir rules that restricted judges have now been abandoned by the Lord Chancellor, Lord MacKay.

61.16 *Reform*

Several ideas for reform have been put forward:

(a) Longer training programme;

(b) Academics could be appointed to the appeal courts dealing primarily with matters of law, i.e., the House of Lords and Court of Appeal;

(c) Solicitors should be appointed to the bench. This would serve to widen the class of person appointed to the bench; this view was supported by the Committee on the future of the Legal Profession (1988).

(d) A career judiciary. Possibly the most unrealistic. The idea, similar to some other countries, notably France and Germany, is that people train to be judges after, for example, their degree. Then they progress through the court hierarchy;

(e) An open and well advertised criteria of selection requirements; and

(f) The creation of a permanent Royal Commission exclusively given the right of selection, thereby taking selection out of the political arena, i.e., from the Prime Minister and the Lord Chancellor.

62. THE MAGISTRACY

Introduction

If the English criminal justice system depended on the professional judges it would ground to a halt. There are just not enough judges. There are only about 500 full-time judges. The system works by the support of more than 25,000 lay magistrates, who are part-time, unpaid and amateur volunteers. Incredibly, they deal with 98% of all criminal cases. They are, therefore, the mainstay of the criminal justice system.

62.1 *Composition of the Bench*

A Magistrates' Court is staffed either by Justices of the Peace, who are ordinary people, unpaid, unqualified legally, or by legally qualified paid persons called stipendiary magistrates. A stipendiary magistrate is a barrister or solicitor of at least seven years' standing.

In most cases two or three lay justices sit on the Bench to hear cases, with three being the usual number so as to avoid the Bench being equally divided as to the outcome of a case. A stipendiary magistrate usually sits alone, unless he is sitting in the Juvenile Court: *Justice of the Peace Act 1979.* The lay justice is a part-time magistrate, whereas the stipendiary is a full-time appointment.

If a stipendiary sits with lay justices, he acts as chairman but he has no greater powers than the others; he merely speaks for the Bench. Where lay magistrates sit, their chairman has usually been selected at an annual election, but may also be the most senior magistrate present.

Magistrates play a very important role in the administration of justice in England and Wales. They deal with well over 98% of all criminal cases, as well as with committal proceedings and civil actions. Lay magistrates also sit in Juvenile Courts and act as licensing justices.

62.2 *The magistrates' clerk*

He is a legally qualified barrister or solicitor of at least five years' standing. He supervises the court's procedure and he advises the magistrates on the law and their powers of sentence. He must not assist magistrates in reaching their verdict on the facts, e.g. by retiring with them. He is seated in front and below the magistrates' bench. A restatement of the functions of a magistrates' clerk may be found in the *Practice Direction (1981) 2 All ER 831.*

62.3 *Appointment*

Most magistrates hold office by virtue of having their names on the Commission of the Peace for the borough or county concerned.

They are appointed by the Lord Chancellor, normally acting on the advice of local advisory committees. In the counties, the Lord Lieutenant is usually the chairman but the rest of the members are selected by the Lord Chancellor without public consultation. There is a tendency for political parties to dominate these committees, and this, as well as the secrecy involved, leads to criticisms as to the appointment of magistrates.

62.4 *Qualification and training*

They are appointed to serve a particular county or borough, and are required to reside within 15 miles of that area. Although lay magistrates are legally unqualified, they do receive a few lectures after their appointment, and they visit prisons before taking up their post.

In theory lay magistrates are expected to represent a reasonable crosssection of the community in the administration of the legal system. In practice it has been said that most magistrates are middle aged, middle class and middle minded! It has been estimated that over 80% belong to the professional or managerial classes, many being ex-local politicians, resulting in the gross under-representation of women, blacks and ordinary workers.

The only other formal qualification is that the person be a British citizen.

They must also be: 'personally suitable in character, integrity and understanding ... and ... should generally be recognised as such by those among whom they live and work.'

They receive a little initial training, periodic refresher courses and guidelines.

62.5 *Tenure*

Magistrates are required to retire at 70 although they may be removed from office by the Lord Chancellor at any time. Most appointments that are terminated result from a refusal by the magistrate to apply a law with which he disagrees.

62.6 *Criticisms*

Although lay magistrates manage to deal with a large number of cases cheaply and quickly (magistrates being unpaid except for their expenses), many feel that the justice dispensed in the Magistrates' Courts is too quick and too rough-and-ready. In a study undertaken by Professor Zander some years ago, he estimated that the average case before the magistrates took only 3-4 minutes to hear. (This problem may have been slightly alleviated by the provision of duty solicitor schemes.)

It has also been alleged that many magistrates are prosecution-minded. As they sit in court on average for 3-4 days per month, they get to know the policemen who regularly appear before them and tend to believe their evidence when it is in conflict with that given by the defendant.

The result is that magistrates are reputed to be more conviction-minded. Yet the evidence on this is far from clear. One study suggests that, where the defendant pleads not guilty in a Magistrates' Court, he is likely to be found guilty in 75% of cases, as opposed to 50% before a jury in the Crown Court. On the other hand, a Home Office study conducted in 1978 suggests that in fact the acquittal rate for some offences is actually higher before the magistrates than in the Crown Court.

In addition, it is found that not only are magistrates unrepresentative of the community which they serve, but also that they tend to place too much importance upon the opinion of the magistrates' clerk. He should not play any role in the decision-making process, but in practice the magistrates may well rely too heavily upon his opinion.

It is also argued that the method of appointment leaves too much room for party politics.

There are those who argue that the training magistrates receive is inadequate and that there is too much room for personal bias to influence the behaviour of the Bench.

There is vast disparity in sentencing, and there is obvious discrepancy in the principles used in different areas of the country.

62.7 *Proposals for reform*

It has been suggested that the lay magistrates' system be abolished and their jurisdiction absorbed by the higher courts. Stipendiary magistrates could be retained to deal with committal proceedings and summary trial. However, this would lead to too much work for the other courts, resulting in delay, and it would be difficult to find enough suitably qualified people to act as stipendiaries.

The present view is that abolition is impractical and that, therefore, reform should be undertaken.

All magistrates are now compelled to undergo an initial course of training (three weeks) as well as periodic refresher courses. Sentencing guidelines are issued to try to avoid too great a disparity in sentencing.

LLB

ENGLISH LEGAL SYSTEM

LESSON 7 (STUDY)

71. *ARREST*

    71.1   INTRODUCTION
    71.2   POWERS OF ARREST
    71.3   ARREST WITH A WARRANT
    71.4   ARREST WITHOUT A WARRANT
    71.5   GROUNDS FOR ARREST
    71.6   REQUIREMENTS OF VALID ARREST
    71.7   EFFECT OF WRONGFUL ARREST

72. *POLICE POWERS OF ENTRY SEARCH AND SEIZURE*

    72.1   INTRODUCTION
    72.2   POWERS OF ENTRY PRIOR TO JANUARY 1986
    72.3   POWERS TO SEARCH AND SEIZE PRIOR TO JANUARY 1986
    72.4   POWERS OF ENTRY WITHOUT WARRANT FROM JANUARY 1986
    72.5   POWERS TO SEARCH AND SEIZE FROM JANUARY 1986
    72.6   RETENTION OF EVIDENCE, ACCESS AND COPYING

71. *ARREST*

71.1 *Introduction*

The law of arrest is clearly important as it defines the extent to which the police may interfere with the physical freedom of the individual. In addition from a legal point of view, it is important because it gives rise to questions of both criminal and civil liability depending on the lawfulness or otherwise of the arrest. In this respect, if the arrest is lawful a person will be guilty of assault if he resists arrest; if it is unlawful, the policeman who effects the arrest will be liable in tort for false imprisonment, and, if he has used force to effect the arrest, for assault.

Until 1986 the law in this field was based on the *Magistrates' Courts Act 1980*, the *Criminal Law Act 1967* and the Common Law. However, the controversial *Police and Criminal Evidence Act 1984*, which came into effect from 1 January 1986, has introduced certain changes to the law.

It is a fundamental concept of freedom that a person should not be improperly deprived of his liberty, and in English law there are limited circumstances in which detention is justified. These include a person coming within the definition of a mental patient under the *Mental Health Act 1883*, a child in need of care and control under the *Children and Young Persons Acts 1933-1969*, imprisonment for contempt of court or Parliament, detention under the *Immigration and Extradition Acts*, imprisonment imposed by a court after criminal conviction, imprisonment after charge without grant of bail.

In addition, there is the power of arrest.

71.2 *Powers of arrest*

Arrest may be with or without a warrant.

71.3 *Arrest with a warrant*

This area of law has not been altered by the *Police and Criminal Evidence Act 1984.*

Where the police suspect a person of serious crime, an indictable offence or one punishable with imprisonment, they should apply for a warrant for the person's arrest under *s.1 Magistrates' Courts Act 1980* which requires that before a warrant is issued any information must be laid in writing and substantiated on oath. The warrant must identify the person to be arrested. General warrants, i. e. not naming the person, are unlawful *Entick v Carrington (1765) 2 Wils 275).*

S. 125 Magistrates' Courts Act 1980 provides that an arrest warrant issued by a justice of the peace remains in force until it is executed or withdrawn. It may be executed anywhere in England and Wales by any person to whom it is directed or by any constable acting within his police area. A warrant to arrest a person charged with an offence may be executed by a constable even if it is not in his possession at the time; but if the arrested person so demands it must be shown to him as soon as practicable.

In *R v Purdy (1974) 3 All ER 465* the whereabouts of a warrant at the time of arrest was considered. The appellant had sought to show that his arrest for non-payment of fines was invalid because the constable did not have the warrant in his physical possession at the time of the arrest but the court held that its presence in the police car, some 60 yards away, was sufficient to make the arrest valid as it could be produced by the police on request.

If a policeman arrests in accordance with a warrant he receives the full protection of the law and, even if the detainee later proves to be innocent, no damages can be obtained for assault or wrongful imprisonment. This is provided in the *Constables Protection Act 1750.*

71.4 *Arrest without a warrant*

The situations in which arrest without a warrant are permissible are limited, and can vary according to whether the person making the arrest is an ordinary citizen or a police constable.

For there to be a valid arrest, there must be grounds for the arrest, and the requisite formalities must be complied with.

71.5 *Grounds for arrest*

(a) *Common Law arrest for breach of the peace*

Every citizen has a right, and a duty, to arrest without warrant any person responsible for a breach of the peace continuing in his presence or if there is a reasonable apprehension of its renewal:

This principle was recently reconsidered by the House of Lords in *Albert v Lavin (1981) 1 All ER 628* where it was said that every citizen could and should take reasonable steps to make the person who was breaking or threatening to break the peace refrain from doing so and those reasonable steps in appropriate circumstances included detaining him against his will.

In *R v Howell (1982) QB 416* the defendant had been causing a disturbance in the street and was asked by a PC to stop swearing or else he would be arrested. The defendant did not stop, so the PC told him that he was being arrested, and the defendant then hit the PC. He was charged with assaulting a PC and convicted. He then appealed to the Court of Appeal where the right to arrest at Common Law for breach of the peace was examined. It was held that PCs and members of the public have the right to arrest without warrant anyone committing a breach of the peace in their presence or threatening to commit or renew such a breach. A breach of the peace occurs whenever harm or violence is done or threatened, so as to be likely to a person or his property, or when a person is put in fear by reason of some assault, riot or affray. The conduct complained of must, however, relate to violence. In this case the conviction was upheld.

(b) *Statutory powers of arrest*

   (i) *Arrest without warrant for arrestable offences: s.24 PCEA 1984*

   The powers of arrest vary according to when the arrest is made, and who is making the arrest.

   Definition of arrestable offence

   S.24 provides that an arrestable offence is one:

   (1) where the penalty is fixed by law (e.g. murder and treason);

   (2) where the penalty is five or more years of imprisonment (this is wider than the *Criminal Law Act 1967*, which only applied to statutory offences – the *PCEA 1984* covers Common Law crimes as well);

   (3) contained in *sub-s.2* (which includes certain Customs & Excise offences, *Official Secrets Act* offences, *Sexual Offences Act* offences such as indecent assault on a

woman, offences under *s.12* (taking a conveyance) and *s. 25 Theft Act* (going equipped) and offences under *s.1 Public Bodies Corrupt Practices Act);*

(4)   conspiring, attempting, aiding, abetting, counselling or procuring any arrestable offence.

Arrest taking place

(1)   *Before the commission of an offence*

Only a police officer may arrest someone before an offence has been committed. He may arrest anyone:

(A)   who is about to commit an arrestable offence; or

(B)   whom he has reasonable grounds to suspect may be about to commit an arrestable offence: *s.24(7).*

The ordinary citizen has *no* power of arrest in such a situation.

(2)   *During the commission of an offence*

Both the police officer and citizen have a power of arrest in respect of:

(A)   anyone who is in the act of committing an arrestable offence; or

(B)   anyone whom he has reasonable grounds for suspecting to be committing such an offence: *s.24(4).*

(3)   *After the commission of an offence*

A police officer may arrest:

(A)   anyone who is guilty of the offence; or

(B)   where he has reasonable grounds for suspecting that an arrestable offence has been committed, he may arrest anyone he reasonably suspects to be guilty of the offence. This is notwithstanding the fact that no offence may have been committed: *s.24(5) & (6).*

A citizen may arrest:

(A)   anyone who is guilty of the offence; or

(B)   anyone whom he has reasonable grounds for suspecting to be guilty of it: *s.24(5).*

However, it is important to note that an arrestable offence must have been committed, preserving the rule in *Walters v WH Smith & Son (1914) 1 KB 595* where the plaintiff was arrested by the defendant, who honestly but mistakenly believed the plaintiff to have stolen some books. In fact the books had been stolen by a third person and the plaintiff sued for damages for false imprisonment and malicious prosecution. The action for malicious prosecution failed because there was not an absence of reasonable and probable cause for the prosecution. In considering the action for false imprisonment, the court held that a private person is justified in arresting another on suspicion of having committed a felony if, and only if, he can show that the particular felony had in fact been committed and that he had reasonable and probable cause for suspecting the plaintiff of having committed it.

(iii) *Arrest without warrant for other offences*

Various statutes conferred powers of arrest and these have now been abolished by the *PCEA 1984.*

However, certain powers have been retained by *Sch.2*, e.g. the power to arrest a driver who is apparently unfit to drive through drink or drugs.

Other powers have not been affected, e.g. the power to arrest for making off without payment.

(iv) *Arrest by virtue of the general arrest conditions: s.25 PCEA 1984*

A police officer has an additional power of arrest under *s.25*. This new power is extensive:

(1) a police officer may arrest anyone whom he reasonably suspects to be attempting or committing any offence, or who has attempted or committed any offence; and

(2) it appears to him that the service of a summons is impractical or inappropriate because 'any of the general arrest conditions is satisfied'.

The general arrest conditions are as follows:

(1) the police officer does not know, nor can he ascertain the person's real name;

(2) the police officer has reasonable grounds to suspect that:

(A) the name given is not the real name;

(B) there is no satisfactory address for service;

(C) the address given is false;

(D) the arrest is necessary to:

– stop the person harming himself or another;

– stop the person suffering injury;

– stop the person damaging or losing property;

– preventing the person committing an offence against public decency;

– preventing the person unlawfully obstructing the highway;

(E) the arrest is necessary to protect a child or vulnerable person from the relevant person.

Note: The student must watch for precedents because the law under *s.25* is not entirely clear.

Who, for example, is a vulnerable person? Presumably the very elderly, the infirm or handicapped do qualify; does a pregnant woman?

Where valid grounds exist for the arrest, the arrest does not become unlawful because of the motive of the policeman.

In *Mohammed-Holgate v Duke (1984) 1 AC 437* a woman was arrested by a PC who suspected that the woman had stolen jewellery. She was taken to the police station, detained for six hours and then released without being charged. She brought an action for wrongful arrest. The judge found that the officer had reasonable grounds for suspecting that she had committed an offence, but that part of his reason for the arrest and detention was to obtain a confession, which was a wrongful exercise of his power of arrest. It was held (allowing the police appeal) that the *bona fide* arrest on reasonable grounds is not rendered unlawful because the police officer's motive for the arrest is to try to get a confession.

71.6 *Requirements of valid arrest*

(a) *The fact of arrest and the reason for it must be communicated*

In *Christie v Leachinsky (1947) AC 573* the accused was arrested on suspicion of being in unlawful possession of a bale of cloth. Lord Simon laid down the following principles:

1. If a policeman arrests without warrant upon reasonable suspicion of felony, or of other crime of a sort which does not require a warrant, he must in ordinary circumstances inform the person arrested of the true ground of arrest. He is not entitled to keep the reason to himself or to give a reason which is not the true reason. In other words, a citizen is entitled to know on what charge or on suspicion of what crime he is seized.

2. If the citizen is not so informed, but is nevertheless seized, the policeman, apart from certain exceptions, is liable for false imprisonment.

3. The requirement that the person arrested shall be informed of the reason why he is seized naturally does not exist if the circumstances are such that he must know the general nature of the alleged offence for which he is detained.

4. The requirement that he should be so informed does not mean that technical or precise language need be used. The matter is one of substance, and turns on the elementary proposition that in this country a person is, *prima facie*, entitled to his freedom and is only required to submit to restraint on his freedom if he knows in substance the reason why it is claimed that restraint should be imposed.

5. The person arrested cannot complain that he has not been supplied with the above information as and when he should be, if he himself produces the situation which makes it practically impossible to inform him, e.g. by immediate counter-attack or by running away.

These propositions equally apply to a private person who arrests on suspicion.

This principle has been incorporated into *s.28 PCEA 1984*, which provides that, where a person is arrested other than by being informed he is under arrest, he must as soon as practicable afterwards be informed:

(i)   of the fact he is under arrest; and

(ii)   the reason for it.

However, the duty on the police constable making the arrest is more onerous than under the old law, in that *s.28* requires the fact and reason to be communicated even if obvious. There is no need for this if the person escapes before this could practicably be done: *s.28 (5)*.

The law before 1986 merely required the arresting person to do what was reasonable in the circumstances of the case.

In *Tims v John Lewis & Co Ltd (1952) AC 676* a woman who was slightly deaf and her daughter were arrested by store detectives on suspicion of having stolen goods from the defendants' store. They were taken back into the store and made to wait in an office until the managing director arrived and decided whether to call the police. It was held that, although an arrested person must be brought before justices or bailed as quickly as possible, the detention in the office was lawful. When arresting a person the constable or private citizen must do what a reasonable person would do to inform the arrested person that he is being taken into custody. There is no need for an ear-trumpet when arresting a deaf man!

Where a constable is arresting someone who cannot speak English, however, he is not obliged to find an interpreter: *Wheatley v Lodge (1971) 1 All ER 173.*

It is not clear how far *s.28* alters this position. For example, what is to be done when arresting a drunk, or someone who is incapable of understanding what is happening?

(b)   *If arrest is other than at a police station, the arrested person must be taken to a police station as soon as practicable: s.30*

This section reiterates the rule in *Tims v John Lewis.*

If the person is detained longer than necessary, the detention will be unlawful.

(c)   *Reasonable force may be used to effect an arrest: s.117*

This also applies to the exercise of other powers under the Act. It is a question of fact in each case whether the force used was reasonable (see cases on *s.3 CLA 1967* for discussion of 'reasonable').

In *Farrell v Secretary of State for Defence (1980) 1 All ER 116* a suspected terrorist in Northern Ireland was shot dead by an army patrol and his widow was claiming damages for his death. The House of Lords held that *s.3* of the 1967 Act provided a defence of reasonable force only for a person accused of a crime or a person sued in tort. In each case when such a defence was put forward the question to be determined was whether the person who was accused or sued had used force as was reasonable in the circumstances in which he was placed in bringing about the lawful arrest of an offender or suspected offender. It followed, therefore, that the only circumstances which were relevant for the purpose of *s.3(1)* were the immediate circumstances in which the force was used.

71.7   *Effect of wrongful arrest*

If the arrest is unlawful, then any detention is *prima facie* imprisonment, a tort for which the arrested person may seek compensation.

Any bodily restraint or use of force will amount to the tort of battery and, as well as seeking a civil remedy through the courts, the arrested person may make a complaint to the Police Complaints Authority (see later).

72. POLICE POWERS OF ENTRY SEARCH AND SEIZURE

72.1 *Introduction*

The powers of the police to enter and search premises and seize items are governed by the *Police and Criminal Evidence Act 1984.* However, in order to fully understand the present law, it must be discussed in relation to the old law. This will enable the student to examine whether the *PCEA 1984* remedies the earlier defects, and whether it extends the powers of the police whilst providing the necessary safeguards for the individual.

72.2 *Powers of entry prior to January 1986*

In *Entick v Carrington (1765)* Lord Camden said:

> ... by the laws of England, every invasion of private property, be it ever so minute, is a trespass. No man can set foot upon my ground without my licence but he is liable to an action though the damage be nothing.

This statement soon became inaccurate. In 1976 there were some 188 statutes on the statute book giving powers of entry to a wide variety of officials such as Customs & Excise officials, the Department of Health and Social Security, midwives, sheriffs, etc. These cannot be studied in detail but the position so far as the police are concerned was as follows:

(a) The police were empowered under many statutes to search premises with a warrant. Examples included the power under *s. 23 (3) Misuse of Drugs Act 1971* to search premises where a justice of the peace was satisfied that there were reasonable grounds for suspecting that controlled drugs were kept in contravention of the Act, and *s.20 (c) Taxes Management Act 1970* which provided that a Circuit judge may issue a warrant to the police to search premises if there were reasonable grounds for belief that a tax fraud had been committed and there were incriminating documents on the premises.

(b) Under *s.2(6) Criminal Law Act 1967* the police could enter premises, by force if need be, in order to effect an arrest for an arrested offence when they knew or had reasonable grounds to suspect that the person to be arrested was present in the premises. Force which includes pushing open a partially closed door or window may only be used if necessary. In *Swales v Cox (1981) QB 489* the suspect was pursued into the house of his neighbour, who then helped him to resist arrest. When the neighbour was convicted of obstruction of the police he appealed arguing that the arrest of the suspect was unlawful because unnecessary force had been used by the police in pushing open and entering the front door. The case was remitted to the lower court to hear evidence to ascertain the necessity for using force.

(c) Police officers had an implied licence to enter premises to make enquiries from a householder, but once the householder revoked that licence the police must within a reasonable time leave the premises or they became trespassers and were liable to be ejected: *Robson v Hallett (1967) 2 QB 939.*

(d) If the police reasonably believed that a breach of the peace was occurring on private premises, or was imminent, they could enter to prevent it. In *Thomas v Sawkins (1935) 2 KB 249* leaders of a meeting to protest about the *Incitement to Disaffection Act 1934* held on private premises tried to eject police officers whom they considered were trespassers. The police satisfied the court that they were not trespassers since they had, at Common Law, the right to enter premises to prevent breaches of the peace. The *ratio* of the court was framed more widely in terms that the police could enter to prevent the commission of any offence but this has been doubted in later cases.

(e)   In *Swales v Cox (1981)* the circumstances in which, at *Common Law*, a police officer might enter private property were outlined:

    (i)   to prevent murder;

    (ii)   if a felony had been committed and the felon had been followed to a house;

    (iii) if a felony was about to be committed and would be committed unless prevented; or

    (iv)   following an offender running away from an affray.

In *McLorie v Oxford (1982) QB 1290* the court refused to extend these categories. The defendant's brother had been charged with attempted murder. The murder weapon was a car. The police called at the house to get the car. The father refused to allow the police access. Later the police returned and forced an entry. The defendant resisted the entry and was convicted of obstruction. The court decided that the police were acting unlawfully and the conviction was therefore quashed.

(f)   In *Finnigan v Sandiford (1981) 2 All ER 267* it was established that, even if a statute conferred a power of arrest without warrant, there could not be implied a power to enter premises where none had been expressly provided by the statute.

72.3 *Powers to search and seize prior to January 1986*

Despite the undeniable importance of this area of law, it is surprising how uncertain the law was.

Search of premises and seizure of items discovered

(a)   Searches under a valid search warrant must first be considered. One of the most important statutory powers to search with a warrant was that under *s.26 Theft Act 1968.* The section empowered the seizure of all goods reasonably believed to be stolen. The same view was taken at Common Law in *Chic Fashions (West Wales) v Jones (1968) 1 All ER 229* where the police, while executing a search warrant for particular stolen goods, also seized other goods which they found on the premises and which were reasonably believed to be stolen. The seizure was held to be lawful. Salmon LJ commented that:

> ... if the preservation of law and order requires that a policeman shall have the power to arrest a man whom he receiver, it is difficult to understand why the policeman should not have the power to seize goods on the man's premises which the policeman believes on reasonable grounds that he has stolen or received. If the man's person is not sacrosanct in the eyes of the law, how can the goods which he is reasonably suspected of having stolen or received be sacrosanct.

(b)   Where a lawful arrest took place the premises on which it occurred could validly be searched. The police could seize items which were evidence of any crime committed by the individual arrested and items which were evidence of a crime of a similar nature to that for which the arrest was effected, against other individuals. The decision in *Elias v Pasmore (1934) 2 KB 164* that, when a search followed a lawful arrest, any items found could be seized which were evidence of 'any crime by anyone', has now been discredited.

The reasoning of the trial judge that such a seizure was necessary in the interests of the state was criticised by the Court of Appeal in *Ghani v Jones (1970) 1 QB 693*, in which the Court of Appeal made it clear that it considered only evidence of a 'similar' crime involving other individuals could be seized.

(c)   A 'fishing expedition' search was unlawful. In *Jeffrey v Black (1978) QB 490* the Divisional Court affirmed the general principle to emerge from *Entick v Carrington (supra)* that general searches of a house without a warrant are unlawful unless they are incidental to a lawful arrest in that house, and general 'fishing' searches were also unlawful. Thus, in *Jeffrey v Black* it was held that a police officer who arrested a suspect for an offence at one place had no authority without a warrant or the consent of the suspect to search his house at another place where the house bore no relation to the offence with which he was initially charged.

The facts were that the suspect had been arrested for stealing a sandwich from a public house but his flat was later searched and he was prosecuted for unlawful possession of drugs upon the evidence found there. Despite the fact that the court held that the police had unlawfully obtained the evidence used in the prosecution, the court refused to exclude it.

(d)   Searches without a warrant must then be considered. If entry was lawful, being, for example, by consent, the rules on what may be seized are set out by the Court of Appeal in *Ghani v Jones (1970)*. In that case the police had searched 'without warrant' but with their consent the house of close relatives of a murder victim. They had confiscated passports and other documents. The Court of Appeal held that the documents and passports must be returned since the police had not been able to show that they were material evidence in solving the crime. The court laid down certain principles for the taking by police of private property. It was said that the police could seize the instrument of a crime, the fruit of a crime or material evidence of its commission, but that they must not hold the items longer than was reasonably necessary and the person from whom they were taken must either be implicated in the crime or must have been unreasonable in failing to consent to the police seizure.

This decision appears to justify seizure of:

(i)   goods on the person of the arrested person; and

(ii)   evidence in his house of the crime mentioned in the warrant.

To reconcile *Ghani v Jones (1969)* with *McLorie v Oxford (1982)* one has to take the view that in the latter the court was concerned only with entry to premises whereas in *Ghani v Jones* the point at stake was seizure once access had lawfully been gained by consent.

72.4   *Powers of entry without warrant from January 1986*

S. 17 PCEA 1984 governs entry and search without a warrant. It preserves the right of a police officer to enter to arrest for an arrestable offence and the Common Law right of an officer to enter private premises to deal with or to prevent a breach of the peace but all the other rules of Common Law allowing entry, set out in *Swales v Cox (1981)* and *McLorie v Oxford (1983)* are repealed but replaced and added to by statutory provision. *S.17* provides that, without prejudice to other enactments, a constable may enter and search premises:

(a)   to execute a warrant of arrest arising out of criminal proceedings or a warrant of commitment under *s. 76 Magistrates' Courts Act 1980;*

(b)   to arrest for an arrestable offence;

(c)   to arrest for offences under *ss.1 & 4 Public Order Act 1936* and when in uniform for offences under *ss.6-8 & 10 Criminal Law Act 1977;*

(d)   to capture someone unlawfully at large he is pursuing;

(e)   to save life or limb to prevent serious damage to property.

Unless the constable acts under (e) he must have reasonable grounds to believe that the person he seeks is present on the premises. The search allowed is only such as is reasonable for the purpose for which the entry took place.

As far as the Common Law powers of entry of a citizen are concerned, they may still enter to save life or limb or prevent serious damage to property.

72.5 Powers to search and seize from January 1986

Personal searches are considered in Lesson 8.

The *PCEA 1984* has changed the law relating to search and seizure in several respects. It has sought to clarify some of the uncertain parts of the law mentioned above, it has provided an extra power for the police to obtain from magistrates a search warrant where they need to search premises when a serious arrestable offence has been committed and it has provided that the police should apply for *all* search warrants under any statute whatsoever and execute *all* search warrants according to a set of conditions which were designed to protect the civil liberties of the population.

(a)   *Conditions applicable to all search warrants: ss.15 & 16*

Every search warrant must now be obtained by following a standardised procedure and, if the conditions of application or execution are not met, then any search carried out under the warrant is an unlawful one. In summary the sections require that the constable:

(i)   states the grounds of the application;

(ii)   states the enactment under which the warrant is sought;

(iii) specifies the premises to be searched; and

(iv)   identifies as far as possible what or whom is sought.

The procedure also requires the information in writing and that the constable support it by answering the magistrates on oath. Any warrant issued must indicate when it was issued, to whom, under what enactment and which premises are to be searched and it may only be executed on one occasion.

A search warrant must now be used within *one month* of issue and it is provided by *s.16(4)* that searches should take place at a reasonable hour unless such timing would frustrate the purpose of the search. There are further requirements placed by *s.16:* a constable searching must produce identification to the person who owns or appears to be in charge of the property if he is not in uniform, and must show him the warrant and leave a certified copy. If the premises searched are unoccupied, then a certified copy must be left in a prominent place on the premises. The warrant only authorises search to the extent required to carry out the purpose of the warrant and, once executed, the constable must endorse on the warrant details of anything or anyone found and details of anything seized which was not mentioned in the original warrant. Once this has been done, or if the search warrant was never used, the warrant must be returned to the clerk of the issuing court where it is retained for 12 months and is available for inspection by the occupier of the premises searched.

(b)   *The new search power under s.8 PCEA 1984*

In *Ghani v Jones (1970)* Lord Denning pointed out in his judgment that the police were hampered in searches for evidence in very serious criminal investigations by gaps in their powers to obtain search warrants. *S.8* is an attempt to remedy this situation. It provides that, upon application by a constable, a justice of the peace may grant a warrant to enter and search premises if he is satisfied there are reasonable grounds for believing:

(i)   a serious arrestable offence has been committed;

(ii)   material on the premises will be of substantial value to the investigation;

(iii)   that it will be admissible;

(iv)   that the evidence is not subject to legal privilege, excluded or special procedure material; and

(v)   *EITHER* it is not practicable to communicate with a person who could allow police on the premises or give them access to the evidence *OR* entry would not be granted unless the warrant is produced *OR* the search would be frustrated or hampered seriously if the police could not gain immediate entry.

One of the preconditions to obtaining a warrant is that a 'serious arrestable offence should have been committed'. These are defined in *Sch.5* of the Act and fall into two classes: those arrestable offences such as murder or manslaughter or some sexual or firearms offences which are always serious arrestable offences and all other arrestable offences such as theft, etc. which are serious arrestable offences only if their commission has the effect or is likely to have the effect of seriously harming the security of the state or public order or serious interfering with the administration of justice or causing death or serious injury or substantial financial gain or serious financial loss.

Unfortunately, therefore, there is an element of uncertainty for the police in deciding whether a given theft, for example, constitutes a serious arrestable offence. This is made worse because the Act provides that whether an offence is one which will cause serious financial loss is determined by its effect on the victim. A millionaire from whom a piece of jewellery worth £10,000 was stolen might not be considered by a court to have suffered serious financial loss so no serious arrestable offence would be established to allow application for a search warrant under *s.8*, but a woman whose only as set was jewellery of a similar value would have suffered serious financial loss by virtue of such a theft and a search warrant might therefore be available under *s.8*. This is surely not a very desirable state of affairs.

Items which are subject to legal privilege cannot be included under a search warrant and these are defined by *s.10* of the 1984 Act. Anything held with the intention of furthering a criminal purpose is not an 'item subject to legal privilege'. Those documents which are encompassed within the definition are client-lawyer communications or communications between a legal adviser and a representative of his client or any other person made in connection with or in contemplation of legal proceedings and for the purpose of those proceedings and enclosures subject to similar provisions. These items only remain privileged while in the hands of the person entitled to them.

'Excluded material' is defined by *s.11* of the Act and in summary it amounts to material of specially defined sorts which is held *in confidence;* this means held subject to an express or implied undertaking or to a statutory duty to keep it confidential and the information held by a journalist is only considered confidential if throughout the period it has been held by him it has been required to be so treated. The special sorts of material which, subject to the confidentiality requirement qualify as excluded material are:

(i)   personal identifiable records about the physical, mental, moral or spiritual well-being of a person, alive or dead, which are held for the purposes of a trade, business profession or paid or unpaid office;

(ii) human tissue or tissue fluid held for diagnosis or medical treatment; and

(iii) documents or records held by a journalist which were acquired or created for the purposes of journalism.

To obtain access to excluded material a constable has to make a special application in accordance with *Sch.1* of the Act to a Circuit judge who may order production of such evidence and failing production is sue a search warrant if a statute other than the *PCEA 1984* would have allowed access to the items and the issue of a warrant under that other enactment would have been appropriate.

'Special procedure material' is defined by *s.14* of the Act as material held in the course of a trade, undertaking, business or profession, or for a paid or unpaid office which is confidential, but which does not fall within the restricted types of material which are excluded material under *s.11* and journalistic material which is not excluded material. This type of evidence may be ordered to be produced to the police and, failing production, included in a search warrant if an application is made to a Circuit judge who considers that an enactment other than the *PCEA 1984* would formerly have authorised access and that would be appropriate or, alternatively, that access would be in the public interest because of the benefit to the investigation and the circumstances under which the evidence is held.

Note: No orders would be made by a Circuit judge for production of excluded material or special procedure material unless the usual conditions in *s.8* were complied with.

(c) *Searches of premises after arrest*

(i) By *s.32(2) (b)* a power is given to a constable to enter and search any premises, where the arrested person was arrested or where he was immediately before arrest, for evidence relating to the offence for which the arrest took place. However, such a search may only take place if the constable has reasonable grounds for believing that evidence is on those premises, and the search is restricted by *sub-s. (3)* to a search to the extent 'reasonably required' to find such evidence. If the premises where the arrest took place include several dwellings the power to search is restricted to the place where the arrested person was, or was immediately prior to arrest and the parts of the block used in common with other occupiers.

(ii) By *s.18* if a person is under arrest for an arrestable offence a constable may enter and search premises occupied or controlled by the arrested person with reasonable grounds for suspecting evidence relating to that offence or some other arrestable of fence connected with or similar to that offence is on the premises.

This clarifies the position from 1986 for, under cases such as *Jeffrey v Black (1977)* and *McLorie v Oxford (1982)*, the exact extent of police powers to search on arrest were unclear. Indeed, under the old law it was probably in order for the police to seize evidence of *any* offence committed by the arrested person. The civil liberties of the individual are clearer under the new law.

(d) *Powers to seize evidence*

By *s.19* a constable *lawfully* on premises may seize anything if he has reasonable grounds for believing:

(i)

it was obtained in consequence of the commission of an offence; and

(ii)   it is necessary to seize it to prevent it being concealed, lost, altered or destroyed;

OR

(i)   it is evidence in relation to an offence he is investigating or any other offence; and

(ii)   it is necessary to seize it to prevent it being concealed, lost, altered or destroyed.

This is an additional power to other statutory powers he may have.

72.6 *Retention of evidence, access and copying*

In summary *ss.21 & 22* of the Act provide that a person who occupied premises on which evidence was seized or under whose custody or control evidence was, before it was seized, may by request to the police obtain a copy (and such copies must be produced within a reasonable time) or obtain access under a constable's supervision. If access to, or copying of evidence would prejudice an investigation it may be refused.

Evidence may be retained so long as it is necessary in the circumstances.

Further reading

Part II & Sch. 1 Police and Criminal Evidence Act 1984.
Wade and Bradley, *Constitutional and Administrative Law* (10th edn), pp.485-489. de Smith, *Constitutional and Administrative Law* (5th edn), pp. 476-480 TC Walters and MA O'Connell, *A Guide to the Police and Criminal Evidence Act 1984*, Chapter 2.

LLB

ENGLISH LEGAL SYSTEM

LESSON 8 (STUDY)

81. *SEARCH OF THE PERSON*

    81.1   **PRIOR TO 1986**
    81.2   **POLICE POWERS TO STOP AND SEARCH**
    81.3   **SEARCH OTHER THAN AT A POLICE STATION**
    81.4   **SEARCH AT A POLICE STATION**

82. *DETENTION AND INTERROGATION*

    82.1   **INTRODUCTION**
    82.2   **CUSTODY OFFICERS AND DESIGNATED POLICE STATIONS**
    82.3   **LIMITS ON DETENTION**
    82.4   **TREATMENT OF DETAINEES**
    82.5   **CAUTIONS AND INTERVIEWS**

83. *THE CODES OF PRACTICE*

84. *THE ADMISSIBILITY OF EVIDENCE*

    84.1   **PRIOR TO 1986**
    84.2   **FROM JANUARY 1986**

85. *HABEAS CORPUS AND OTHER REMEDIES*

86. *THE POLICE*

    86.1   **INTRODUCTION**
    86.2   **THE POLICE AUTHORITIES**
    86.3   **THE POWERS OF THE HOME SECRETARY**
    86.4   **THE CHIEF CONSTABLE**
    86.5   **CONTROL OF THE POLICE BY THE COURTS**
    86.6   **LEGAL STATUS OF A POLICE OFFICER**
    86.7   **COMPLAINTS AGAINST THE POLICE**

87. *ADMISSIBILITY OF STATEMENTS – CONFESSIONS*

    87.1   **HEARSAY**
    87.2   **CONFESSION**

81.   SEARCH OF THE PERSON

81.1   *Prior to 1986*

(a)   Some statutes authorised search without or before arrest. For example, *s.23 Misuse of Drugs Act 1971* provided that a person may be searched on reasonable suspicion of unlawful possession of drugs. There was no general power to stop and search.

(b)   An arrested person could lawfully be searched and property in his possession, relevant to the charge for which he was arrested, could be detained. However, it was established in *Lindley v Rutter (1981) QB 128* that personal clothing and effects must not be removed unless it was necessary to do so to prevent injury or escape or to preserve evidence.

81.2   *Police powers to stop and search*

There is no general Common Law power given to a police officer to permit him to stop and search individuals without arrest. However, certain statutes incorporate powers to stop and search an individual without arrest, e.g. *s.23 Misuse of Drugs Act 1971* permits a search of a person where he is reasonably suspected to be in unlawful possession of controlled drugs; many local Acts of Parliament gave constables powers to stop and search individuals believed to be in possession of stolen goods.

The *Police and Criminal Evidence Act 1984* has retained certain statutory powers to stop and search without arrest, e.g. *s. 23 Misuse of Drugs Act 1971* and various powers under statutes designed to conserve wildlife, whilst abolishing those under old local Acts and replacing these by a general power to stop and search provided that certain conditions are met.

A constable may stop and search a person or a vehicle in a public place and may detain the person or vehicle while he carries out the search, but the search may only be undertaken if the constable reasonably suspects that the person or vehicle has on or in them articles which are stolen or prohibited. If in the course of such a search a constable finds an item he reasonably believes to be stolen or prohibited he may seize it.

This general summary requires further explanation:

(a)   The search may take place only in a public place. This means a place to which the public or a section of the public have access whether by payment or not and whether they have express or implied permission to be there or are there as of right or any other place to which at the time of the search the public have ready access, provided it is not a dwelling. If a person or vehicle is in a garden or yard attached to a dwelling a search would only be permissible if the constable did not believe that the individual to be searched resided in the property or was there with the owner's consent and a vehicle could only be searched if it did not belong to the owner of the property and was on his premises without his consent.

(b)   The constable must only act if he reasonably suspects that the person or vehicle has or contains stolen or prohibited articles. This means that the officer must be acting on more than a hunch and must have objective grounds for his belief, not simply based on the grounds of an individual's colour or clothing.

(c)   Stolen articles would include not only those obtained by theft but others dishonestly obtained as well. Prohibited articles include offensive weapons, which are those designed or adapted to cause physical injury or which are intended to be used by the carrier or another for such a purpose. Prohibited articles are also those which are made or adapted for or intended for use in burglary, theft, taking a conveyance or obtaining property by deception.

(d)   A vehicle which may be searched includes not only motor cars, but hovercraft, ships, aircraft, etc.

A constable is not required, having detained a person or vehicle to search it, to carry out such a search if he is subsequently satisfied that the search is unnecessary, and the initial detention will remain unlawful.

If a constable wishes to search under *s.1 PCEA 1984* and he is not in uniform, he must first provide documentary evidence of his position and any policeman, whether in uniform or not, is required to inform the person to be searched or person in charge of the vehicle to be searched of his name, police station, the reason for the search and the grounds for the search. If he fails to provide the information the search will be unlawful. The detention for search must, by *s.2(8)* of the Act, be no longer than is reasonably required to enable the search to be carried out. If an unattended vehicle is searched a notice must be left, preferably inside the vehicle, giving similar details of the constable's name, station, etc.

Unless it is not practicable to do so (perhaps in a public order case), a constable must make a note in writing as soon as possible detailing a name or description of a person searched together with the object and grounds for the search, when and where it was made, what was found and what injury or damage, if any, resulted from the search. A person who has been searched or had his vehicle searched may ask for a copy of this notice within one year from the date of search.

Finally, note that the usual rules on personal searches, that a person may not be required to remove more than coat or jacket and gloves in public, apply and that a person searched is not required, under these sections of the *PCEA 1984*, to give his name. Note that the requirements to give information and record searches apply to the retained statutory powers to stop and search and not just to searches under *s.1 PCEA 1984*.

81.3 *Search other than at a police station*

Where an arrest takes place other than at a police station a constable has under *s. 32 PCEA 1984* the following powers to search the person of the arrested individual:

(a)   if he has reasonable grounds to believe the arrested person is a danger to himself or to others;

(b)   so far as is reasonable to:

(i)   search for means of escape secreted on the arrested person;

(ii)   anything may be searched for on the arrested person which might be evidence relating to an offence.

The power to search extends only so far as is reasonable for the purpose for which the search is undertaken. As for the powers to stop and search a restriction is place on what a person can be required to remove in public. He can only be asked to remove coat or jacket and gloves.

81.4 *Search at a police station*

Once an arrested person reaches a police station or if a person is arrested at a police station, the rules relating to searches of the person are set out in *Part V* of the Act. *S.54* provides that the custody officer must ascertain what a person has with him on arrival and keep a record of the items and a search is allowed to establish this. *Sub-s. (4)* only allows seizure of clothing and personal effects if the custody officer either believes on reasonable grounds they may be evidence relating to an offence or that the arrested person may use them to inflict physical injury on himself or another, cause damage to property, escape or destroy evidence.

A constable of the same sex will carry out any search under *s.54*, which does not authorise intimate searches, i. e. searches of a person's body orifices.

S.55 provides the procedure for intimate searches and they are subject to stringent conditions. An officer of at least the rank of superintendent must authorise such a search and then only if he has reasonable grounds to believe that a person arrested and in police detention may have concealed on him something which he could use to cause physical injury to himself or to others while in police detention or under the custody of the court or, alternatively, reasonable grounds to believe the arrested person may have a Class A drug hidden on him which he had in his possession with criminal intent before arrest.

Intimate searches are regarded as a last resort and must be ordered in writing or a written confirmation of an oral order must be given. They should generally be carried out by a doctor or nurse and only if a superintendent considers this impracticable by a constable of the same sex. The only places where they can occur are at a hospital, surgery, place used for medical purposes or police station and drugs searches are not permitted at police stations. Details of the findings of an intimate search must be recorded in the custody record of an individual as soon as practicable after the search and items found during the search can be retained if it is reasonably believed they would otherwise be used to cause physical injury, damage to property, to assist escape or destroy evidence of an offence or if they may be evidence of an offence.

Chief constables' annual reports must contain information about the number of intimate searches, by whom they were carried out and what was found. This should ensure that powers to search in this way are not abused.

82.   DETENTION AND INTERROGATION

82.1 *Introduction*

Until 1986 the position of an individual detained by the police and his treatment and interrogation were governed largely by the *Judges' Rules*. The Rules dealt with such matters as cautions, access to solicitors, etc. Since the Rules did not have the force of law, the judge retained a discretion as to whether or not evidence obtained in breach of the Rules should be admitted. Some statutory protection of an arrested individual came, however, to be considered desirable and *s.62 Criminal Law Act 1977* provided that a person arrested had the right to have someone informed by the police. However, no obligations were placed on the police to inform a person of his rights.

As a *quid pro quo* for the extension of police powers to stop and search, arrest and search and seize, it was admitted that the civil liberties of a person in police custody should be strengthened and this is dealt with in *Parts IV & V* of the Act and in *Code of Practice C*.

82.2 *Custody officers and designated police stations*

Under the Act those arrested must usually be incarcerated in a specially designated police station where a 'custody officer' (a new position created under the Act) will be responsible for supervising their welfare and treatment and keeping a detailed record of this.

The idea of designated police stations is to ensure that detainees are kept in hygienic surroundings with proper access to rest facilities, etc. By having a special custody officer, who is independent of the investigation of the offence for which arrest took place, the position of the detainee is safeguarded from, for example, having improper pressure brought to bear upon him.

If an individual is first taken to a police station, which is not a designated one, so that there is no custody officer, the Act still requires by *s.36* that if possible an officer who is not investigating the offence for which arrest took place should be responsible for the welfare and treatment of the detainee. If this is not possible, an inspector at a designated police station must be informed as soon as is practicable.

82.3 *Limits on detention*

The *PCEA 1984* places strict time limits on the length of detention without charge. There is a limit of 24 hours generally but even within this time an individual's case should be reviewed six hours after arrest and again at nine-hourly intervals thereafter. If no charge has been brought an inspector reviews the case to see if there are grounds to continue detention. If a charge has been brought the custody officer must consider whether detention is still required or whether bail could be given. Reviews may only be postponed if questioning is proceeding and the review would prejudice the investigation or if no reviewing officer is readily available. On all reviews the person detained should be allowed to make representations and this could take place orally, in writing or by a legal representative. After 24 hours have elapsed a detainee should be released unless charged or unless a superintendent has authorised continued detention up to a maximum of 36 hours. The grounds on which a superintendent may authorise such an extension are severely limited. It is only permissible if it is necessary to secure or preserve or obtain evidence in a case where the offence involved is a serious arrestable one and where the police have been carrying out the investigation diligently and expeditiously. If after 36 hours the police desire a longer period of detention they must make an application to the magistrates. This will be heard privately by two magistrates and the detainee must be present and is allowed legal representation. At the hearing full details of the offence, evidence and grounds for seeking continued detention must be given. If satisfied of the police case the magistrates can order further 36 hour periods of detention up to 96 hours from arrest.

When an arrested individual is brought into the police station one of the first duties of the custody officer is to decide whether there is enough evidence to charge the individual. If so, he may detain the individual while this process is carried out. If he decides that there is insufficient evidence he may detain to question or release without charge, telling the individual that charges may later be brought. He should order release unless detention is necessary to preserve or obtain evidence. The grounds for detention must be given by the custody officer to the detainee and recorded in the custody record unless the detainee is incapable of understanding, violent or likely to become so or in need of medical attention, when they may simply be recorded.

Once charged a person should be released unless the name and address given cannot be verified or it is necessary for the individual's protection or to prevent physical injury to the detainee or another, to prevent damage to property or the detainee is likely to fail to answer bail or to interfere with witnesses or obstruct the course of justice. These grounds accord with those in the *Bail Act 1976* which makes a presumption in favour of bail.

Once an individual has been charged he must be brought before a court as soon as practicable to the first available court sitting.

82.4 *Treatment of detainees*

As noted above, when a custody officer decides to detain an individual he must usually explain the grounds for this. At the same time the custody officer must both orally impart certain information to the detainee and give him a notice recording the same information. The detainee acknowledges receipt of the notice by signing the custody record. The information to be given is as follows:

(a)   He is entitled on request to have a friend or relative or someone whom he knows who is likely to be interested in his welfare told of the arrest and the place of detention as soon as practicable. If the first person is unobtainable, the police must try up to two alternatives. This is provided by *s.56.*

   The contacting of the designated person may be delayed by the police for up to 36 hours but such delay is only permissible where it is authorised by an officer of at least the rank of superintendent, confirmed in writing, on one of the following grounds that giving the information would:

   (i)   lead to interference with or harm to evidence of a serious arrestable offence or physical injury to other people;

   (ii)   would alert suspects who were not yet arrested; or

   (iii) would hinder recovery of property obtained by one of these offences.

   If delay is allowed the detainee must be told that informing the contact is to be delayed and why and this is noted on the custody record.

(b)   By *s.58* he is entitled upon request to consult a solicitor privately at any time. The time of such a request is noted and usually once such a request is made questioning is suspended pending arrival of the solicitor. Again, a superintendent may allow a delay of up to 36 hours in contacting a solicitor if a serious arrestable offence is involved. The superintendent's grounds for allowing the delay are the same as under *s.56* set out in (a) above.

(c)   He is entitled to copies of the *Codes of Practice* applicable to the police.

   Those detained must be allowed writing materials and to speak on the telephone to someone in addition to the right to have a person informed of his arrest. However, all letters and calls may be monitored by the police unless they are to a solicitor.

82.5 *Cautions and interviews*

Where a person is suspected of an offence he must be cautioned before any questions or further questions are put to him which may provide evidence for a prosecution and, if he is not under arrest, he must be told he is free to leave or to obtain legal advice. If he is under arrest he must be cautioned on arrest unless that is impracticable because of his condition or behaviour or he has been cautioned immediately prior to arrest. The modern wording under the *Code of Practice* for a caution is now: 'You do not have to say anything unless you wish to do so, but what you say may be given in evidence', but the wording given does not have to be exact. If there are breaks in interviews it should be made plain the person questioned is still under caution or the caution should be readministered. Records are made of cautions.

Interviews must be conducted without the use of oppression and police officers must not indicate, unless asked, what the police are likely to do in given circumstances. When an officer believes he has sufficient evidence for a prosecution to succeed he must immediately cease questioning. Any interview must have a record giving details of its commencement and termination, breaks and those present and they are to be made contemporaneously unless this is not practicable. The person writing such a record should sign it. There are limits on the length of interviews in that a detained person must be allowed an uninterrupted 8 hours a day rest with no questioning, normally at night. However, if a rest period would delay release, prejudice the investigation or cause physical risk of harm or serious loss or damage to property, it may be delayed or interrupted.

The Code also deals with meal breaks, the location of interviews, etc. Special provisions are inserted to cope with the cases of juveniles, the mentally handicapped, the deaf or foreigners.

83. *THE CODES OF PRACTICE*

There are four *Codes of Practice* on the exercise of statutory powers to stop and search, the search and seizure of items found on persons and premises, the detention, questioning and treatment of persons by police officers and the identification of persons by police officers. The main points of the first three have been dealt with in the foregoing lessons. It should be noted that an officer who fails to comply with a provision in one of the Codes, which came into force from midnight on 31 December 1985, is under *s.67(8)* liable to disciplinary proceedings in respect of the failure. The Codes are by *s.67(11)* admissible evidence in all criminal and civil proceedings.

84. THE ADMISSIBILITY OF EVIDENCE

84.1 *Prior to 1986*

The courts had a discretion to admit or reject any evidence obtained illegally, such as in breach of the *Judges' Rules*, or contrary to statute or Common Law: In *Jeffrey v Black (supra)* Lord Widgery CJ expressed the view that, even where evidence was unlawfully obtained, the courts should use their discretion to rule it inadmissible only where the police were guilty of trickery, oppressive, unfair, or morally reprehensible behaviour. This view contrasts starkly with United States law, where unlawfully obtained evidence is excluded. In *R v Sang (1980) AC 402* the accused sought to establish that he had been trapped into a conspiracy to utter forged bank notes as a result of a police informer's activities and that without this encouragement no such offence would have been committed. On this basis he wished the trial judge to rule the prosecution's evidence inadmissible. The House of Lords held:

(a)   to ensure that an accused has a fair criminal trial, the judge had a discretion to refuse to admit evidence if in his opinion its prejudicial effect outweighed its probative value;

(b)   due to the fact that the court's only consideration was how evidence is used at the trial and not how it was obtained, except with regard to evidence obtained from the accused after the commission of an offence and to admissions and confessions, a judge had no discretion to refuse to admit relevant admissible evidence on the ground that it was obtained by improper or unfair means; and

(c)   it was no ground for the exercise of the discretion that the evidence was obtained as a result of the activities of an *agent provocateur*. No defence of entrapment exists in English law.

84.2 *From January 1986*

S.78 PCEA 1984 now provides:

(a)   In any proceedings the court may refuse to allow evidence on which the prosecution proposes to rely to be given if it appears to the court that, having regard to all the circumstances, including the circumstances in which the evidence was obtained, the admission of the evidence would have such an adverse effect on the fairness of the proceedings that the court ought not to admit it.

(b)   Nothing in this section shall prejudice any rule of law requiring a court to exclude evidence.

In *R. v Mason (Carl) (1987) The Times, 23 May,* the Court of Appeal considered the application of section 78 to confessions. It confirmed that the section gave the court the discretion to exclude confessions, but the court stated that section 78 merely restates the power of a judge at common law before the 1984 Act. Further, in *R v H (1987) Crim LR 47*, D was accused of raping his girlfriend. He pleaded consent. D objected to the admission of the recording. Gatehouse J. held that the tapes were a trap and would have an adverse effect on the proceedings, and that in all the circumstances it should not be admitted.

Finally in *R. v O'Connor (1987) Crim LR 260* and *R. v Robertson (1987) The Times, 11 June*, it was held that evidence of a Co-accused's previous conviction, where the effect is to implicate the accused, obtained under section 74(1) of the 1984 Act, should be excluded under the trial judges discretion under section 78.

85.   *HABEAS CORPUS AND OTHER REMEDIES*

A person unlawfully deprived of his liberty, whether as a result of criminal conviction or charge or, for instance, pending deportation or extradition, may test the legality of this detention by the writ of *habeas corpus*. The writ is available to anyone, including an alien, who is within the jurisdiction and who can make out a *prima facie* case. It is not a discretionary remedy and cannot be refused on the ground that some other remedy would be more appropriate.

Habeas corpus is available only where the detention is unlawful. Thus it will clearly issue where, for instance, an action was *ultra vires;* but it is not certain whether the court will go further and examine the facts of a case in deciding unlawfulness.

Application for *habeas corpus* is made initially to the Divisional Court of the Queen's Bench Division and such an application takes precedence over all the Court's other business. Appeal may be made by either side to the Court of Appeal and the House of Lords in civil cases and direct to the House of Lords in criminal cases. In practice there are very few applications, few of which are successful.

Other remedies for unlawful detention include actions in tort for assault and for false imprisonment (see, for example, *Broome v Cassell (1972) 1 All ER 801)*, self-help (see, for example, *R v Fennell (1971) 1 QB 428)*, or the police complaints machinery under the *PCEA 1984*.

86. THE POLICE

86.1 *Introduction*

In the nineteenth century much of the rural population of the United Kingdom migrated to urban areas and this, together with population growth, necessitated a more efficient means of preserving law and order. The origins of the modern police can be seen from this time. At first small local forces were set up in urban areas, like Sir Robert Peel's force in London in 1829, and these forces spread. Today, although the number of police forces has diminished with amalgamations, they are still locally organised with local accountability. There is no unified nationally and centrally organised force although the Criminal Investigation Department exists as a nationwide service and certain central records are maintained.

In 1962 a Royal Commission examined the question of whether a national and centrally governed police force was needed. The majority of its members, with one dissenter, concluded that the adoption of such a force would not lead Britain to become a totalitarian state (as opponents of the proposal feared), but that such a step was not needed provided certain recommendations were carried out. Many were incorporated in the *Police Act 1964*, which has been subsequently amended by the *Police Act 1976* and the *Police and Criminal Evidence Act 1984*.

A police force is maintained by every county council except where a combined force has been constituted after an amalgamation. In London there are two police forces: the Metropolitan Police and the City of London Police. The Metropolitan area extends over a circle with a radius of 15 miles from Charing Cross, except for the City. The Metropolitan force is headed by the Metropolitan Police Commissioner who is appointed by the Crown on the advice of the Home Secretary and who wields more power than any chief constable elsewhere in the UK. The Commissioner has very considerable powers for the governance of his force, although any general orders he makes are subject to the Home Secretary's approval.

86.2 *The police authorities*

Each police force has its own police authority. These authorities are established under the *Police Act 1964*. The general composition of such an authority is that it is made up as to two-thirds by elected councillors from the county council concerned and as to one-third of lay magistrates. If the force is an amalgamated one, two-thirds of the committee are councillors from the respective county councils and one-third magistrates within the combined area. In London the police authority for the Metropolitan Police is the Home Secretary himself and the police authority for the City is the Court of Common Council.

By *s.4(1) Police Act 1964* it is the duty of a police authority to maintain for its area an adequate and efficient police force. The police authority selects the chief constable for its area and his assistant and deputies but such appointments are subject to the approval of the Home Secretary. The police authority is entitled to receive from the chief constable an annual report on the policing of the area and may from time to time request other reports, but it cannot take operational decisions despite its powers, subject to the Home Secretary's direction, to decide on the size and the establishment of the force. In reporting to a police authority a chief constable may withhold information if the Home Secretary agrees it is unnecessary for the authority to receive it or contrary to the public interest that it should. The police authority may, with the concurrence of the Home Secretary, compulsorily retire a chief constable, deputy or assistant in the interests of efficiency. The Home Secretary himself may direct the appropriate police authority to take such a step. In the former case the Home Secretary may, and in the latter he must, appoint someone to inquire into the matter and hear the officer's representations, if any.

86.3 *The powers of the Home Secretary*

Although each force is funded as to about 50% by precepts from local rates, the remaining funding comes from central government. This, together with the powers conferred on the Home Secretary by the *Police Act 1964*, gives him much influence over police forces on a national basis. Each year as a condition of receiving central government finance a police force requires the Home Secretary's certificate of efficiency showing that it is properly administered. The Home Secretary may at any time set up an inquiry into the policing of a particular area and his approval is necessary when a police authority appoints or dismisses a chief constable or his deputy or assistant.

The Home Secretary has wide powers under the *Police Act 1964* to make general regulations for all the police forces subject to consultation with the Police Advisory Board for England and Wales or for Scotland. The regulations will deal with such matters as promotion, pay, discipline, equipment, clothing and allowances.

Contrary to the recommendations of the 1962 Royal Commission on the police, the Home Secretary has no general duty to ensure the efficiency of the police although *s.28 Police Act 1964* does require him to exercise all his statutory powers under the Act in such a way as will best promote the efficiency of the police. Before 1964 the Home Secretary was only directly accountable to Parliament as regards his administration of the Metropolitan force. Parliamentary control over other forces was slight as the Home Secretary's responsibilities did not extend much to them. Now that the Home Secretary has overall responsibility to promote the efficiency of all police forces (s. *28 Police Act 1964*), as well as having numerous specific powers over police authorities, he can be questioned in Parliament about the operation of any police force. He is still not fully accountable, however, for much power remains in the hands of police authorities and he has, anyway, a discretion not to reveal to Parliament any matter which he considers should not be publicly disclosed.

86.4 *The chief constable*

The chief constable is at the pinnacle of the police hierarchy and he makes the operational decisions for his force. He also appoints, promotes and dismisses any police officer below the rank of assistant chief constable. His powers are therefore considerable although the police authority does have a supervisory role in that the chief constable is under a statutory duty to make an annual report to them and to report on other matters as they so require and, furthermore, the authority can, in the interests of efficiency and with the concurrence of the Home Secretary, dismiss a chief constable. The chief constable's duties in respect of complaints against the police are set out in section 86.7 and he is, of course, the individual who is sued in respect of wrongdoings by the police. If damages are awarded against him, the police fund pays the sum.

86.5 *Control of the police by the courts*

The extent to which police authorities are subject to the control of the courts had always been in doubt. In *R v Metropolitan Police Commissioner, ex p Blackburn (1968) 1 All ER 763* the matter arose for direct consideration. Under the *Betting, Gaming and Lotteries Act 1963* certain forms of gaming had been made illegal. The Act proved difficult to enforce, and the Commissioner had therefore instructed his senior officers that no proceedings should be taken for certain breaches of the law unless cheating was involved or the establishment in breach was the haunt of criminals. Blackburn sought to compel the commissioner to enforce the law. The Court of Appeal held that every chief constable owed a duty to the public to enforce the law and that duty would be enforced by the court. Although chief constables had a wide discretion in deciding when to prosecute, the court would intervene to ensure that the chief constable was not simply following a fixed rule of policy. The police commissioner had, by then, altered his policy so that no order by the court was necessary. However, the principle of judicial intervention in the actions of police forces was established. However, in *R v Metropolitan Police Commissioner, ex p Blackburn (1979)* Blackburn sought *mandamus* to force the Metropolitan Police to enforce the law relating to obscene publications after he had purchased a pornographic magazine openly displayed for sale in the City. In considering Blackburn's appeal from the refusal of the Divisional Court to order *mandamus*, the Court of Appeal said that the courts had no jurisdiction to tell the Metropolitan Police Commissioner how to perform his duties although they could intervene if no attempt was made to enforce the law.

In *R v Chief Constable for Devon and Cornwall, ex p CEGB (1982)* the CEGB sought *mandamus* to compel the Cornish police to remove protesters demonstrating against, and disrupting, a survey of land to ascertain its suitability as a site for a nuclear power station. The police had declined to act because they considered there was no likelihood that there would be breaches of the peace or unlawful assembly. In refusing the *mandamus* sought the Court of Appeal explained that the view of the law taken by the police was erroneous but nevertheless the court could not tell the police how and when their powers should be exercised.

86.6 *Legal status of a police officer*

At Common Law a police officer can personally be sued for any wrongful or unlawful act he commits, even if he was ordered by a superior officer so to act: *Christie v Leachinsky (1947)*. By *s.48 Police Act 1964* a chief constable is made vicariously liable for the torts committed by his officers in the performance of their functions under his direction and control. Any damages awarded against the chief constable will be paid by the police authority, which may also, in its discretion, meet any claims made against police officers personally.

Although chief constables may be vicariously liable for their officers' actions, this does not mean that the relationship is an employer/employee one. Police constables (and every officer is a constable) hold a public office which is governed, not by contracts of employment, but by statute.

A police constable is, by statute, restricted in a way that no ordinary employee would be. He cannot join a trade union or take part in politics and he must:

> at all times abstain from any activity which is likely to give rise to the impression amongst members of the public that he may so interfere (Police Regulations).

86.7 *Complaints against the police*

Complaints by the public against the police have traditionally been investigated internally. Under the *Police Act 1964* a chief constable was required to arrange investigation of any complaint received. The investigation would generally be carried out by a member of another force and the resulting report would be sent to the Director of Public Prosecutions unless it was clear that no criminal offence had been committed.

Following many years of discussion an independent element was introduced into the investigation of complaints. By the *Police Act 1976* a *Police Complaints Board*, appointed by the Prime Minister from amongst people who had not been in the police, was set up. The reports of all investigations into complaints were sent by chief constables to the Board. The Board could recommend or direct that disciplinary charges be brought against a constable, and could require a disciplinary hearing to be before a tribunal consisting of the chief constable and two members of the Board, rather than (as was usual) before the chief constable alone.

Under the *PCEA 1984* the Police Complaints Board was abolished and replaced by a Police Complaints Authority with somewhat enhanced powers. The Authority has nine members, none of whom may be former policemen, each member is appointed for a three year term and is removable by the Home Secretary within that period for bankruptcy, incompetence or criminal conviction. The purpose of the Authority is to introduce that element of independent investigation into complaints against the police, the lack of which has been a source of discontent to civil rights campaigners for many years.

A chief constable is under a duty to record complaints against members of his force and to pass on to the relevant chief officer any complaints against members of another force.

If the officer against whom the complaint is made is of the rank of chief superintendent or above, the complaint must be referred to the relevant police authority and not to the chief constable.

A chief constable must investigate complaints against members of his own force and take steps to preserve any evidence. There are three categories of investigation, where a minor complaint is made, an intermediate class and the most serious complaints which must always now be referred to the Police Complaints Authority.

(a)   If the complaint made against an officer is such that it is obvious that the officer complained of has committed no criminal or disciplinary offence *and* the complainant agrees, the chief constable may appoint an officer to investigate and try to reach an informal resolution of the complaint. Failing this being possible, the procedure under (b) below is used.

(b)   If the complainant will not agree or the offence is more serious in nature or no informal resolution proves possible under (a), then the chief constable must appoint a different officer to investigate and the investigating officer must be of at least the rank of chief inspector and of equivalent or higher rank to the officer investigated. The chief constable may call in an officer from another force to carry out the investigation. Once the report is complete it must be forwarded to the chief constable unless the Police Complaints Authority is supervising the investigation. If the officer against whom the complaint was made is a senior officer, the report goes to the police authority or to the Police Complaints Authority if the latter is supervising the investigation.

(c)   The most serious complaints alleging conduct resulting in death or serious injury must be referred to the Police Complaints Authority who will supervise the investigation. Serious injury means fractures, damage to internal organs, deep cuts or laceration or impairment of bodily function.

Note that the Police Complaints Authority may call in any complaint made against the police to supervise its investigation and that, even where no serious complaint has been made, if the circumstances would appear to warrant it, the matter must still be referred to the Police Complaints Authority.

In these serious cases the Police Complaints Authority are likely to make the appointment of the investigating officer subject to their approval and they must be sent a copy of his report as well as this being sent to the chief constable or police authority as appropriate. On receipt of the report the Police Complaints Authority must indicate to the chief constable or police authority whether they consider the investigation satisfactory and, if not, why not.

After an investigation has been completed in one of the three above mentioned ways, the chief constable must consider the report and decide whether he considers a criminal offence has been committed and he should prosecute or whether charges should be brought under the police disciplinary code. He must send details of his conclusions to the Police Complaints Authority, together with the original complaint and report if the investigation has not been supervised by the

Authority. If the Authority disagrees with the chief constable's chosen course of action, it may direct him to send the papers to the Director of Public Prosecutions or to bring disciplinary charges.

The future of the new complaints procedure

Under the *PCEA 1984* the Police Complaints Authority is under a duty to make an annual report and triennial review for the Home Secretary. Copies of these documents must be sent to the police authorities and must be published and laid before Parliament. This will, of course, allow the efficacy of the new system to be considered by MPs. Since the procedure has been in operation for a short time, its final contribution cannot be assessed but it is, of course, still open to criticism in that the police themselves investigate complaints against fellow officers, albeit subject to independent supervision by the Police Complaints Authority.

As is clear from the above, the main criticism of the Police Complaints Authority is in its relative lack of independence, for, although an investigation is under the supervision of an independant person, the investigation is itself done by the police, albeit often by a member of another force. It is perhaps too early to say how successful it has been. However, even a majority of Chief Constables – a recent survey shows – are in favour – in order to improve public confidence – of making the Authority wholly independent. One notable success in recent times was the announcement in April 1988 that the Police Complaints Authority had recommended the prosecution of about a dozen police officers involved in the 'Wapping Strike' of 1986. The Wapping investigation was headed by a retired Merchant Sea Captain.

87. *ADMISSIBILITY OF STATEMENTS – CONFESSIONS*

87.1 *Hearsay*

A hearsay statement is:

(i)   a statement made by a person out of court, which is;

(ii)   now sought to be admitted in court by another person; and

(iii)   the purpose of which is to prove the truth of the statement: *Myers v D.P.P. (1965) AC 1001 (H.L.).*

It is a fundamental proposition of English law that a hearsay statement is inadmissible in a proceeding as a general rule. However, this general rule is subject to a number of well recognised exceptions.

87.2 *Confessions*

One such exception at common law arises when a confession is sought to be admitted: *Ibrahim v R. (1914) A.C. 599.* Section 82(1) of the P.C.E.A. 1984 defines a 'confession' as including 'any statement wholly or partly adverse to the person who made it, whether made to a person in authority or not, whether made in words or otherwise'. Hence, a confession is a technical term and does not only refer to the popular meaning of the word, i.e., 'I did it'.

However, although a confession overcomes the hearsay hurdle, to be admissible it must fulfil the provisions of section 76 of the P.C.E.A. 1984, which Provides:

'76(1) In any proceedings a confession made by an accused person may be given in evidence against him in so far as it is relevant to any matter in issue in the proceedings and is not excluded by the court in pursuance of this section.

(2)   If, in any proceedings where the prosecution proposes to give in evidence a confession made by an accused person, it is represented to the court that the confession was or may have been obtained –

(a)   by oppression of the person who made it; or

(b)   in consequence of anything said or done which was likely, in the circumstances existing at the time, to render unreliable any confession which might be made by him in consequence thereof, the court shall not allow the confession to be given in evidence against except in so far as the prosecution proves to the court beyond reasonable doubt that the confession (notwithstanding that it may be true) was not obtained as aforesaid.

It is most important to note that the confession itself need not be unreliable, provided it may possibly lead to the 'likelihood of unreliability' that is sufficient to make it inadmissible.

Section 76(8) defines 'oppression' as including 'torture, inhuman or degrading treatment, and the use or threat of violence (whether or not amounting to torture)'.

An example of oppression would include prolonged and continuous interrogation which tends to sap the freewill of the accused: *See R. v Prager (1972) 1 All ER 1114* and *R. v Fulling (1987) 1 WLR 923.*

An example of something which may lead to a likelihood of unreliability would arise where a police officer promises to go easy on the accused or his family if he confesses: *R. v Rennie (1982) All ER 385*. Another would arise where an officer threatens to implicate loved ones unless a confession is made.

Further reading

Codes of Practice A, B & C is sued under *s. 66 Police and Criminal Evidence Act 1984.*
Parts IV, V & VI Police and Criminal Evidence Act 1984.
TC Walters and MA O' Connell, *A Guide to the Police and Criminal Evidence Act 1984*, Chapters 4, 5 & 6.

LLB

ENGLISH LEGAL SYSTEM

LESSON 9 (STUDY)

91.   PROSECUTION OF OFFENCES

91.1   *The decision to prosecute*

The initial decision whether to prosecute a person is one of the most important decisions to be made. A wrong decision can have disastrous consequences and it is therefore vital that proper consideration be given to all the circumstances of the case, e.g. the nature and gravity of the offence, the age and health of the offender, whether it is a first offence, whether a caution would be sufficient, the political consequences of a prosecution.

The decision is made by the police although certain prosecutions require the consent of the Attorney-General or Director of Public Prosecutions.

The decision of the police can be challenged in the courts but in practice judges are unwilling to interfere with the discretion unless the police have acted improperly or are neglecting their duty to enforce the law: *R v Metropolitan Police Commissioner, ex p Blackburn (1966)*.

It has been argued that the decision should not be left to the police: their involvement with the case and their desire to improve the crime figures could lead to them taking a less than balanced view of the case. However, there really is little alternative since the police are often the only people in a position to judge. To refer every single case to an independent party would be time-consuming and expensive.

The recommendations of the *Royal Commission on Criminal Procedure (1981)* led to the *Prosecution of Offences Act 1985* which retains police discretion, but if the police decide to prosecute, that decision can be reviewed by the Crown Prosecution Service.

91.2   *Conduct of the prosecution*

Before 1986 there was no uniform approach to the conduct of prosecutions. In some police areas the prosecution was handled in the Magistrates' Courts by the police themselves, whereas in other areas a solicitor would handle the case. This lead to the following criticisms:

(a)   lack of uniformity;

(b)   police bias would be carried over from the investigation to the prosecution;

(c)   the police lacked the ability to be objective and therefore too many weak cases went to court;

(d)   the police were not experienced advocates, and owed no ethical duty to the court;

(e)   where solicitors were used, there was a conflict between their duty to the court and the duty to their client, the police.

91.3   *Proposals for reform*

The main proposal for reform by the Royal Commission was the establishing of an independent prosecution service. This service would be staffed by lawyers who would conduct the prosecution of the case in the Magistrates' Court.

91.4   *Advantages and disadvantages of a public prosecution system*

(a)   *Advantages*

    (i)   *Impartiality* – the decision to prosecute would not be taken by those in charge of investigations, whose mind is likely to be prejudiced by the investigation.

(ii)   *Uniformity of procedure* – it would be a system with general policy guidelines.

(iii) *Economic use of resources* – fewer cases would go to trial with insufficient evidence.

(iv)   *Specialisation and expertise* – the system would be manned by lawyers who would be able to assess the evidence as well as weigh up policy considerations.

(b) *Disadvantages*

(i)   *Expensive* – the state would have to pay police to investigate and a separate body to prosecute.

(ii)   *Bureaucratic*.

(iii) *Delay*, too much 'red tape' may cause delays, especially if there is rigid insistence on rules and form-filling.

(iv)   *Political bias*.

To counter the criticism that the system would be open to abuse by political intervention, the Royal Commission recommended that it be organised on a local rather than national basis.

91.5   *The Prosecution of Offences Act 1985*

This Act was fully in force by October 1986 and provided for the setting up of an independent prosecution service for England and Wales (one already existed in Scotland).

However, the system is organised on a national basis, rather than the local system envisaged by the Royal Commission. The Director of Public Prosecutions has overall control, and he is answerable to the Attorney-General.

The decision to prosecute rests with the police, although the consent of the Attorney-General or the Director of Public Prosecutions is required in some cases. However, the Director of Public Prosecutions can take over a case where the police have decided to prosecute and offer no evidence. Guidelines will be issued, although it will not be possible for the Director of Public Prosecutions to intervene and prosecute in most cases if the police have decided not to. The right of private prosecution is retained subject to the Director of Public Prosecutions being able to take over the case if he sees fit.

Once the decision to prosecute has been taken the conduct of the case will pass to the Crown Prosecutor. He will review the evidence and decide if the case should continue.

The persons who will make up the staff of the prosecution service will be civil servants in status, although they will be qualified lawyers. They will have the same rights of audience as solicitors, and they will be responsible for the presentation of the case in court.

The legal profession is also concerned that, although in the short term there are more jobs available, in the long term the system could prove disadvantageous. It has emerged that many of the new posts will be offered to lawyers already employed in the civil service.

The rates of remuneration are comparatively low, and it is proving difficult to attract the necessary personnel. As a result those who have taken up posts find themselves overworked and unable to cope with the vast volume of work. Consequently, there have been delays and instances of cases collapsing through bad preparation, which has invoked criticism from magistrates.

The new Act has been criticised by those who welcome the separation of the decision to prosecute and the conduct of the case, but who are worried by the establishment of a national system. The present government was committed to localised decision-making and it appears inconsistent to establish a national, centralised system. It is worrying that the impression of government involvement in sensitive cases, e.g. violent strikers, will be given, even if there is in fact no such involvement.

This 'nationalised' service has been criticised as being expensive, bureaucratic and cumbersome. To combat allegations that there will be more delay, the Home Secretary is proposing to introduce time limits on criminal procedure so that failure to complete stages of the case within a certain time will result in the accused being entitled to bail: *The Criminal Justice Bill.* A more radical proposal which would result in the case being dropped has not been implemented. Some sources have expressed concern that the government is not really aware of the costs involved and that it might be tempted to cut corners, which would result in a worse situation than exists presently.

The profession is also worried about inequality of bargaining power, since the instructing of counsel will be done by the prosecution service who may be in a position to fix low rates. The Act also gives the Lord Chancellor the power to increase the rights of audience of the new prosecutor as he sees fit. The Bar have sought reassurances that this will not be used when the prosecution system is fully established, to grant rights of audience in the Crown Court which up until now has been the exclusive domain of the Bar.

91.6 *The working of the Crown Prosecution Service*

The power and responsibilities of prosecution still remains with the Director of Public Prosecutions. They include commencing and conducting prosecutions in any case which seem to be of exceptional importance or difficulty and advising the police on criminal matters in general. He is now head of the Crown Prosecution Service. The country is divided into a number of areas each under a Chief Crown Prosecutor. Under him will come the salaried Crown Prosecutors who are qualified barristers or solicitors. There are also salaried Law Clerks who do preparatory work. These are in turn backed by support staff.

However, the power of charging a person still remains with the police, the Crown Prosecution Service then decides whether to continue or discontinue a prosecution. Further, the task of gathering evidence against a suspect is for the police, and not the service. It is also true that most Crown Prosecutors were members of the solicitors' department of the police forces, although now their relationship has changed from legal adviser and client to one of independent prosecutors – nevertheless it is likely that the police will have considerable influence over prosecutions.

A final criticism of the Service lies in the fact that there is no general duty on the Service to conduct prosecutions commenced by private individuals or organisations other than the police.

Note in conclusion that in this 1988/99 period the Crown Prosecution Service is understaffed by about 75,000 legal personnel.

92. BAIL

92.1 Introduction

In English law the accused is presumed innocent until proven guilty. Therefore, in principle, his liberty should not be curtailed. However, that is to ignore the reality of the situation, which often requires that suspected criminals be kept in custody once apprehended, for their own safety or the safety of others. To allow a man his liberty merely to commit further offences is undesirable, yet detention in all cases pending conviction would be a serious infringement of human rights, especially when conviction itself might not lead to a custodial sentence.

Bail is the procedure whereby a person accused of a crime is allowed his liberty subject to the condition that he must surrender to custody at a specified time and place. Bail may be granted by the police, the Magistrates' Court, the Crown Court, the High Court or the Court of Appeal, but, the principles to be applied are common to all these courts.

This area is governed by the *Bail Act 1976* which was enacted in response to criticisms about the working of bail.

92.2 Police bail

If the accused has been arrested without a warrant, the warrant will specify whether bail is to be granted. The decision of whether to grant bail is made by the court; the police merely enforce that decision.

It is in the case of an accused arrested without warrant that the police must consider the question of bail.

The custody officer is given the responsibility for granting bail and the principles to be applied are as follows:

(a) *The accused who has not yet been charged*

The custody officer must consider whether there is enough evidence to charge the accused. If so, the accused may be detained in order to effect the charge: *s.37 (1) PCEA 1984*. If not, the accused should be released, either with or without bail unless the detention is necessary:

(i) to secure or preserve evidence relating to the offence for which he was arrested; or

(ii) to obtain such evidence by questioning: *s.37(2) PCEA 1984*.

The grounds for detention must be given to the accused and recorded in the custody record.

(b) *The accused who has been charged*

The custody officer must order the release of the accused unless:

(i) *If the accused is adult*:

(1) his name and address cannot be ascertained or the custody officer has reasonable grounds for believing that any name or address is false;

(2) reasonable grounds for believing that detention necessary for protection of accused or to prevent him causing physical injury to other persons or property;

(3) reasonable grounds for believing that the accused will fail to answer his bail;

(4) reasonable grounds for believing that detention necessary to prevent interference with the administration of justice or investigation of offences.

(ii) *If the accused is a juvenile:*

Paragraphs (i) (1)-(4) apply.

(5) the custody officer has reasonable grounds for believing he ought to be detained in his own interest.

If the accused is released on bail he will be required to appear back at the police station at a certain time. If he is detained, he must be brought before the court as soon as practicable.

The accused may be required to find a person or persons who will act as sureties, i. e. someone willing to promise to pay a sum of money to the Crown if the accused fails to comply with the conditions of bail, i. e. enter into a recognisance. The amount of money payable is determined by the police and they can object to persons they consider to be unsuitable acting as sureties. Reference is made to the surety's character, resources, previous convictions and relationship to the accused: *s.8(2) Bail Act 1976.* There is an appeal against this decision.

About 80% of those charged are granted bail by the police. Those refused bail tend to be those charged with serious offences, e.g. robbery, burglary, rape.

92.3 *Bail granted by the court*

S.4 Bail Act 1976 applies to persons accused of an offence when they appear before the court, or apply to the court for bail. It also applies to persons remanded for reports after conviction and persons appearing before the court charged for breaching a probation or community service order.

Right to bail

S.4 gives the accused a right to bail, subject to certain exceptions.

The court must be presented with information about the accused and their reasons for refusing bail must be given to allow the accused to appeal.

Exceptions

These are contained in *Sch.1 Bail Act 1976.*

(a) *Persons accused or convicted of offences punishable by imprisonment*

The court can refuse bail if it is satisfied that substantial grounds for believing that if bail was granted the accused would:

(i) refuse to surrender to custody; or

(ii) commit an offence; or

(iii) interfere with witnesses; or

(iv) obstruct the course of justice.

The court can also refuse bail if it lacks sufficient information on which to base its decision.

The information that should be available is the nature of the offence, its seriousness, probable punishment, character and antecedents of the defendant, the defendant's ties with the community, his previous bail record, the strength of evidence against him.

(b) *Persons accused/convicted of non-imprisonable offences*

The court can refuse bail only if:

(i)   the accused has previously failed to surrender to bail; *AND*

(ii)   the court believes he would again fail to surrender to custody.

Note that in both cases a refusal may only be made if there are substantial grounds, this requires more than merely the balance of probabilities.

Conditions

Bail must be unconditional, or the court may impose conditions. Such conditions can include the duty to report regularly to a police station, to avoid certain places or to surrender a passport.

92.4   *The courts*

(a) *The Magistrates' Court*

If the accused has not been granted bail by warrant or the police, his first opportunity to request bail will be at his appearance in the Magistrates' Court. The court will then consider the question of bail. Either the accused must be remanded in custody for no more than eight days or bailed to appear at a later date.

If it is not possible to have trial after eight days, the magistrates will need to remand for a number of eight day periods.

Technically the accused can request bail at each remand hearing but it is possible to remand an accused in his absence for a maximum of three successive remand hearings if he consents and is legally represented: *s.59 Criminal Justice Act 1982.* This avoids the need to bring the accused to court.

If the accused does not consent, then at the first hearing the magistrates consider the question of bail; likewise at a second hearing. After that they will not consider matters previously before the court, only if there are new developments can an application be made: *R v Nottingham Justices, ex p Davies (1981) QB 38.* The Criminal Justice Bill propose to make judges give reasons for allowing bail when the prosecution objects. It also proposes to reverse the effect of *R v Nottingham Justices ex parte Davies* by requiring the question of bail to be considered at every court appearance.

Appeal lies to the Crown Court where the magistrates have refused bail: *s.60 Criminal Justice Act 1982.* Legal Aid is available. There is also the possibility of applying to the High Court. Application is by summons to a judge in Chambers with affidavit or by giving written notice to the judge. However, such an application rarely attracts Legal Aid and applicants without lawyers must use the Official Solicitor, who merely makes written representation, which hardly ever succeeds.

(b) *The Crown Court*

The Crown Court can consider an application for bail from anyone whose case is to be heard or has been heard by the Crown Court.

The application may be made orally to the court or in writing.

The Crown Court judge will consider the case on its merits and is not bound by decisions of the Magistrates' Court or High Court in the matter.

The accused can only apply once unless the circumstances of the case alter drastically.

92.5 *Consequences of breach*

If the accused breaches the conditions of his bail he may be found guilty of the offence of failing to surrender to custody without reasonable cause. It is not possible under the present law for the accused to give a personal recognisance unless he is likely to leave Great Britain. In such a case, this recognisance will be forfeited. In all cases the court has the power to order that the sums of money promised by the sureties be forfeited, either in full or in part.

93. THE CRIMINAL PROCESS

93.1 Introduction

Once the decision to prosecute has been taken, the accused will either be charged with the offence or, if it is a minor offence, a summons will be issued. This is done by the laying of an information before a magistrate.

The summons must be served on the accused and it must state the offence charged and brief particulars. If the accused was charged with the offence, he will either be bailed to appear in court or remanded in custody.

93.2 Appearance in court

It is usual for the accused to appear in court; failure to do so will lead to the issue of a warrant for his arrest. However, it is possible for an accused to be tried in his absence in the Magistrates' Court. *S.12 MCA 1980* allows the accused to plead 'guilty' by post to certain offences, and *ss.11 & 13* gives magistrates the power to continue a case in the absence of the accused if he has not pleaded 'guilty' by post. In most cases, though, the accused will appear.

93.3 Classification of offences

Where the accused appears in the Magistrates' Court for the first time, the whole course of proceedings depends upon the type of offence he has committed.

(a) *An indictable offence* – defined in *Sch.1 Interpretation Act 1978* as:

> an offence which if committed by an adult is triable on indictment, whether it is exclusively so triable, or triable either way.

An indictable offence is usually one of the major, more serious offences, such as murder, rape, robbery or causing grievous bodily harm.

(b) *A summary offence* – defined by the *Interpretation Act 1978* as:

> an offence which if committed by an adult is triable only summarily.

These are the minor offences, which may only be tried in the Magistrates' Court, such as traffic offences, drunkenness, assaulting a police officer in the execution of his duty.

They are mainly statutory offences.

(c) *Offences triable either way* – defined by the *Interpretation Act 1978:*

> An offence which if committed by an adult is triable either on indictment or summarily.

These include most of the *Theft Act* offences.

It is important to determine the classification of the offence.

93.4 Determining the mode of trial

If the offence is one which is triable either way then, before any evidence is heard, there must be a preliminary hearing before the magistrates to determine the mode of trial: *s. 18 Magistrates' Courts Act 1980*. There needs to be one lay justice, but in practice two usually sit.

The clerk reads the charge to the accused, and the prosecution and defence have the opportunity to make representations as to the most appropriate form of trial: *s.19(2) (b) MCA 1980*.

The magistrates then consider whether trial on indictment in the Crown Court or summary trial in the Magistrates' Court would be more appropriate. They must bear in mind any representations made by the prosecution and defence, but the nature of the case and their punishment powers are the most important considerations. The magistrates assume that the accused is of good character, then they look at the particulars of the offence – if it is serious, they then consider whether their powers of punishment would be sufficient (£2,000 fine, six months' imprisonment for each offence, with maximum of 12 months). If there are not sufficient powers, they will commit to the Crown Court for trial, even if the accused would prefer trial in the Magistrates' Court. If, however, they opt for summary trial, the accused is asked if he consents. If he does not consent, he has the right to be tried by jury in the Crown Court, and the magistrates will hold committal proceedings: *s.20 MCA 1980.*

If he does consent, the magistrates will proceed with summary trial. If the plea is 'not guilty', then at any time before the close of the prosecution case, if the magistrates decide that trial on indictment would be more suitable, they can stop the trial and hold committal proceedings: *s.25(2) MCA 1980.*

If after summary trial the evidence is such that the magistrates' powers of sentencing are inadequate, the accused can, if found guilty, be committed to the Crown Court for sentencing: *s.38 MCA 1980.*

In cases involving criminal damage special rules apply in determining the mode of trial. If the value involved in the offence is less than £400, summary trial is *compulsory.* If the amount is more than £400, then the offence is triable either way. There are proposals in the Criminal Justice Bill to increase this limit to £2,000.

93.5 *Summary trial*

The magistrates sit without a jury and therefore combine the function of judge and jury. After listening to the evidence the magistrates come to a decision on the facts, but are advised on points of law by the clerk, unless the magistrate is a stipendiary.

Legal representation

Both barristers and solicitors have the right of audience although they are not robed. The accused can also defend himself, although he would be wise to take advantage of the Duty Solicitor Scheme.

Course of trial

The clerk puts the information to the accused and he is asked whether he pleads 'guilty' or 'not guilty'. If he pleads 'guilty', the magistrates proceed to sentence him, usually after consideration of any reports. If he pleads 'not guilty', then the issue proceeds to trial, and if his plea is ambiguous, he is asked to clarify it, and if it is still unclear a plea of 'not guilty' is entered.

The prosecution then begin to present their case calling their evidence. At the end of the prosecution's case, the defence may make a submission of no case to answer, i.e. that there is not sufficient evidence on which a reasonable man could convict. This is very difficult to succeed, and it is only in the rare situation when the prosecution's witnesses have been so discredited or the prosecution has failed to bring evidence as to a vital element of the crime, that such a submission will be made.

If the submission succeeds, the accused is found 'not guilty'. If the submission fails, the defence goes on to present their case. It is not necessary for the defence to call any witnesses or argue a case since it is for the prosecution to prove the guilt of the accused beyond reasonable doubt, but usually the defence calls witnesses.

The prosecution does not have the right to a closing speech, but the defence does.

At the end of the case the decision of the magistrates is announced. A stipendiary usually announces his decision straight away, but lay justices retire and reach a majority verdict.

If the verdict is 'not guilty', the accused is free to leave. If the verdict is 'guilty', the magistrates then sentence the accused.

Sentencing

After the verdict the prosecution will sum up the case against the accused and give the accused's antecedents (age and background) and any previous convictions. The defence makes a plea in mitigation, in an attempt to excuse or explain the accused's behaviour. Any relevant social enquiry or medical reports will also be given to the court.

Powers of sentencing are governed by the statute creating the offence and the *MCA 1980*.

If the statute provides for imprisonment of more than six months, *s.31 (1) MCA 1980* reduces that to six months, unless the statute expressly states that *s.31* is not to apply.

If the offence was a summary offence, the maximum prison sentence is six months for each offence. If there is more than one offence the sentences can run concurrently (at the same time) or consecutively (one after the other). However, *s.133 MCA 1980* provides that the total sentence must not exceed six months.

Therefore, there can be two six months concurrent
                    but two three months consecutively

The maximum fine was increased to £2,000 in May 1984.

The magistrates can also give a conditional or absolute discharge, community service orders, youth custody, detention centre, suspended sentence or probation.

If the offence was one that was triable either way and, after hearing evidence of antecedents and character, the magistrates powers are inadequate, *s.38 MCA 1980* allows the accused to be committed to the Crown Court for sentencing.

The powers of sentencing for offences triable either way depend on whether the offence is listed in *Sch.I* or if it is an offence created by statute.

If it is a *Sch.I* offence:

    Maximum imprisonment = six months

    Maximum fine   = £2,000

If two or more offences, the total sum of imprisonment must not exceed 12 months.

If the offence was created by statute:

>   Maximum imprisonment   =   six months or amount in statute, whichever is *less*
>
>   Maximum fine   =   £2,000 or amount in statute, whichever is *more*

Advantages and disadvantages of summary trial

(a)   Less expensive and quicker than trial on indictment;

(b)   sentencing powers of magistrates are less than those of the Crown Court;

(c)   however, higher rate of acquittal if trial by jury.

93.6 *Committal proceedings*

Trial on indictment takes place in the Crown Court but is usually preceded by committal proceedings in the Magistrates' Court. These committal proceedings are designed to identify weak prosecution cases and the magistrates are required to decide if a *prima facie* case has been made out against the accused. A *prima facie* case is merely that there is evidence on which a reasonable jury could convict.

Most committal proceedings end in a committal for trial because of the low standard of proof for the prosecution.

93.7 *Committal with consideration of evidence*

This is an old-fashioned committal, and is now governed by *s.6 (1) MCA 1980*.

Procedure

The prosecution open the case, outlining evidence and the charges against the accused.

Then they produce their evidence, either in the form of written depositions under *s. 102 MCA 1980* or oral witness evidence. The defence has the opportunity to cross-examine. At the end of the prosecution's case, the defence will make a submission of no case to answer, and the *Practice Note 1962* says that submission should be upheld:

(a)   where there is no evidence to prove an essential element of the alleged offence;

(b)   where the prosecution's evidence has been so discredited by cross examination or is so manifestly unreliable that no reasonable tribunal could safely convict on it.

The defence may then present a case but they are unlikely to do so, since that would reveal how they are intending to present their case.

Then the magistrates must decide on all the evidence whether or not to commit. If the submission fails, the charges are read to the accused and he is given the alibi warning.

If they do not commit the accused is free to leave, but it does not amount to an acquittal. If they decide that there is a case to answer, then the accused is committed for trial at the Crown Court.

93.8 *Committal without consideration of evidence*

This alternative was introduced by *s.1 Criminal Justice Act 1967* and is now governed by *s.6(2) MCA 1980.*

The defence can agree to the examining justices committing for trial without consideration of evidence.

A *s.6(2)* committal can only take place if:

(a)   all the evidence is in the form of *s.102* statements;

(b)   the accused is legally represented;

(c)   there is no desire to make a submission of no case to answer.

Procedure

The clerk reads the charge to the accused and the *s.102* statements are handed to the clerk. The defence are asked if they object to the *s.102* statements and if they wish to submit that there is no case. Provided the answer is 'no' to both questions, the magistrates will commit for trial.

93.9 *Other orders and applications*

(a)   *Publicity*

Until recently an accused at a committal hearing could insist on reporting restrictions being lifted and this could work hardship on any co-accused who objected to publicity. To remove this difficulty the *Criminal Justice (Amendment) Act 1981* now provides that, where there are co-accused and one or more of them requests publicity, it is at the discretion of the magistrates to grant such a request depending on what they believe 'the interests of justice' demand. Further, the magistrates have an additional power to restrict publicity, including the power to make an order banning *all* reporting of the case, under *s.4 (2) Contempt of Court Act 1981* which states:

> where it appears to be necessary for avoiding a substantial risk of prejudice to the administration of justice in those proceedings, or in any other proceedings pending or imminent.

(b)   *Witness orders*

If the accused is committed for trial on indictment and pleads 'not guilty', it will be necessary to call as witnesses at the Crown Court some or all of those who contributed evidence at the committal proceedings. To ensure their attendance at the Crown Court, the examining justices must make a witness order in respect of each person who testified or made a written statement at the committal stage.

Witness orders may be full or conditional.

A *full order* requires the subject to attend and give evidence at the Crown Court.

A *conditional order* requires him to do so only if notice is subsequently given to him to that effect.

(c)   *Alibi warning*

When the accused raises an alibi, i.e. that he was elsewhere at the material time and place when the offence was alleged to have been committed, a lack of advance warning might unfairly hamper the prosecution's attempts to test the strength of the defence. Accordingly, *s.11 Criminal Justice Act 1967* provides that, unless the accused gives advance notice of particulars of his alibi, he may not adduce alibi evidence at the trial on indictment as of right but must apply to the judge for leave to adduce the same.

The alibi notice must be given in court either during or at the end of the committal proceedings or in writing to the prosecution not later than seven days before the close of the committal proceedings. As such the Magistrates' Court at the committal proceedings is required to warn the accused of the effect of *s.11 CJA 1967*.

(d) *Bail.*

(e) *Legal Aid.*

93.10 *Committal for trial*

The Magistrates' Court committing someone for trial at the Crown Court must specify the *place of trial* and in doing so have regard to the convenience of the defence, the prosecution and witnesses, the expediting of the trial and any directions given by or on behalf of the Lord Chief Justice: *s.7 MCA 1980.* Without prejudice to this provision, the Crown Court can at any time alter the place of trial and, if the defendant or prosecution is dissatisfied with the place of trial fixed by the Magistrates' Court (e.g. for reasons of local prejudice), he can apply to a High Court judge for a direction.

They should commit the accused to the nearest Crown Court with facilities to deal with that type of case.

This will depend upon the class of offence.

Classes of criminal offences tried in the Crown Court

For the purposes of trial on indictment in the Crown Court criminal offences are classified into the following four classes:

Class 1   Offences to be tried by a High Court judge only:.

(a)   any offences for which a person may be sentenced to death;

(b)   misprision of treason;

(c)   murder;

(d)   genocide;

(e)   an offence under *s.1 Official Secrets Act 1911;*

(f)   incitement, attempt or conspiracy to commit any of the above offences.

Class 2   Offences to be tried only by a High Court judge unless a presiding judge (High Court judge responsible for a particular Circuit) directs otherwise:

(a)   manslaughter;

(b)   infanticide;

(c) child destruction;

(d) abortion;

(e) rape;

(f) sexual intercourse with a girl under 13;

(g) incest with a girl under 13;

(h) sedition;

(i) an offence under *s.1 Geneva Conventions Act 1957.*

(j) mutiny;

(k) piracy;

(l) incitement, attempt or conspiracy to commit any of the above offences.

Class 3 All offences other than those in Class 1, 2 and 4, e.g. perjury, most cases of forgery, aggravated burglary, etc. to be tried either by a High Court judge unless released to a Circuit judge or Recorder.

Class 4 All offences which may, in appropriate circumstances, be tried either on indictment or summarily. They include:

(a) offences which may be tried either way;

(b) conspiracy to commit any of the above offences;

(c) the following offences:

(i) a person who causes death of another person by driving a motor vehicle on a road recklessly;

(ii) burglary;

(iii) forgery offences not triable summarily;

(iv) incitement, attempt or conspiracy to commit any of the above offences.

(d) any offence in Class 3, if included in Class 4 in accordance with directions given by a presiding judge or on his authority.

When tried on indictment offences in Class 4 may be tried by a High Court judge, Circuit judge or Recorder, but will normally be listed for trial by a Circuit judge or Recorder.

93.11 *Trial on indictment*

Once the accused has been committed for trial, he will come before the Crown Court.

The arraignment

The counts on the indictment are read to the accused and he must plead 'guilty' or 'not guilty' to each count. If he pleads 'guilty' the judge will proceed to sentence.

If he pleads 'not guilty' the prosecution must prove their case and the jury must be empanelled.

Opening speeches

Once the jury has been empanelled, the prosecution open their case, outlining the evidence and charges against the accused. The defence can also have an opening speech if they call witnesses other than the accused and character witnesses.

The prosecution's case

The prosecution then begins to call witnesses to give evidence. The defence has the opportunity to cross-examine and the prosecution will then get the opportunity to re-examine with regard to any new issues raised by the cross-examination.

Submission of no case

At the end of the prosecution's case, the defence can make a submission of no case to answer and the judge will decide this in the absence of the jury. If he finds that there is no case, the jury will be called back and told to acquit. If there is a case to answer, the trial will continue.

The defence case

The defence does not have to bring evidence since it is for the prosecution to prove its case, but they usually will.

If the accused gives evidence, he will do so first of all, and then the other witnesses will follow.

Closing speeches

The prosecution makes the first closing speech. The defence makes the last closing speech.

Summing up

The judge then sums up the case, explaining to the jury their role, the burden and standard of proof, the offence and its elements, points of evidence.

He then tells the jury to retire and consider their verdict.

The verdict

Initially the jury must try to reach a unanimous verdict but if, after at least two hours ten minutes, they have not, they are recalled and the judge directs them that he will accept a majority verdict

If there are 12 jurors at least 10 must agree
If there are 11 jurors at least 10 must agree
If there are 10 jurors at least 9 must agree
If there are 9 jurors all 9 must agree

When the jury announce their verdict, if the accused has been found guilty, the judge will proceed with sentencing the accused.

93.12 *Plea bargaining*

This is an imprecise phrase which may be used to mean:

(a) an agreement between the judge and the accused that, if he pleads guilty to some or all of the offences charged against him, the sentence will or will not take a certain form. In *R v Turner (1970) 2 QB 321* it was held that a judge should never indicate the sentence that he is minded to impose unless he can say that whatever happens, whether the accused pleads 'guilty' or 'not guilty', the sentence will or will not take a particular form, e.g. a probation order, fine or custodial sentence;

(b) an undertaking by the prosecution that, if the accused will admit to certain charges, they will refrain from putting more serious charges into the indictment or will ask the judge to impose a relatively light sentence. This form of plea bargaining is not possible under the English system as the prosecution draw up the indictment quite independently of the defence;

(c) the prosecution agreeing with the defence that, if the accused pleads 'guilty' to a lesser offence, they will accept the plea;

(d) the prosecution offering no evidence on one or more counts in the indictment against the accused if he will plead 'guilty' to the remainder.

Plea bargaining in the sense of (c) and (d) above is approved by the courts. It is in the public interest that court time and money should not be wasted.

The judge's consent to a plea of 'guilty' to a lesser offence is essential. Where the prosecution propose to offer no evidence on one count in exchange for a plea on another count, they normally ask for the judge's consent to this being done.

Such consent is not automatic *(R v Broad (1970) 68 CAR 28)* and in its absence the prosecution is obliged to call all the evidence.

93.13 *Choice of court*

In respect of offences triable either way there are various factors which operate, in the circumstances, to make a choice of one court as opposed to another more attractive.

In favour of the Crown Court:

1. There is a higher rate of acquittal in the crown court. The magistrates have become too case hardened in certain types of cases, e.g. shoplifting.

2. In cases involving difficult points of law it would appear better to go before the professional judge who can explain it better to the jury.

3. It is the practise of the Magistrates' Court to too often flout the rules of evidence and thus give rise to unjust convictions.

4. By going through the committal proceeding the defence can get to know the prosecutions case in advance.

In favour of the magistrates' court;

1. If the accused intends to plead guilty he is better off in the magistrates' court where the power of sentencing is less.

2. Magistrates' court proceedings are much quicker.

3. Because of the informality of the magistrates' court the accused person undergoes less stress as opposed finding himself in a busy crown court.

4. There is less press coverage of magistrates' court matters, whereas in the crown court the press is always lurking.

5. Trial at the magistrates' court is cheaper.

LLB

ENGLISH LEGAL SYSTEM

LESSON 10 (REVISION)

101. *REVIEW OF LESSONS 6-9*

    101.1 SUMMARY OF PROBLEMS DEALT WITH

102. *REVISION QUESTIONS*

NOTE: THIS LESSON MUST BE WORKED BEFORE PROCEEDING TO LESSON 11.

101. *REVIEW OF LESSONS 6-9*

101.1 *Summary of problems dealt with*

This point in the manual is approximately two-thirds of the way through it. As in Lesson 5, consolidate what you have so far learned by reading through each section again, pausing at the end of each to recall what you have just read. If you cannot recall it adequately and in detail, read and check your knowledge until you are satisfied.

When you have completed this task, test your knowledge by answering (in your head) the following revision questions.

102. *REVISION QUESTIONS*

1. Who may be appointed as a judge?

2. Who may become a magistrate? What criticisms can you make of the appointment of lay magistrates?

3. When may a police constable arrest someone? Does a private citizen have the same powers?

4. Is an Englishman's home his castle?

5. What may police lawfully seize whilst searching premises? Can items unlawfully seized be used in evidence?

6. What searches may be made of a person?

7. What safeguards are there for the person detained in police custody?

8. Contrast and compare the roles and influence of the chief constable, the police authority, the Home Secretary and the Police Complaints Authority.

9. On what basis is the decision to prosecute made?

10. What changes does the *Prosecution of Offences Act 1985* introduce?

11. On what basis may bail be obtained?

12. What are the court procedures where a person is charged with murder?

13. What is meant by 'committal proceedings'?

14. Describe the role of the Magistrates' Court in criminal proceedings.

15. What is meant by 'plea bargaining'?

LLB

ENGLISH LEGAL SYSTEM

LESSON 11 (STUDY)

111. *JURIES*

112. *SENTENCING*

113. *AIMS OF PUNISHMENT*

111. *JURIES*

111.1 *Trial by jury*

Trial by jury in its modern form is a means of ascertaining the facts in issue in a judicial proceeding according to evidence adduced in court.

111.2 *Criminal juries*

A jury traditionally consists of 12 persons, but the *Juries Act 1974* provides that, where in the course of a criminal trial any member of the jury dies or is discharged because of illness or otherwise, the trial may continue, provided the number of jurors is not reduced below nine.

A criminal jury sits in the Crown Court where trial is by indictment and the accused pleads 'not guilty'. Where the plea is 'not guilty' a jury of 12 must be sworn in, each juror being sworn separately. Before the jury is sworn in it is selected by ballot in open court from the panel (approximately 15) summoned to attend at the time and place in question. Either side can challenge a member of the jury for cause i.e. if there is good reason why he should not sit, e.g. bias, disqualification. The defendant is allowed three peremptory challenges of the jurors, i.e. he can object to three jurors without providing a reason. The prosecution may ask any number of jurors to 'stand by', in which case they will not serve unless the jury panel is exhausted. There are proposals in the Criminal Justice Bill to remove the right of random challenge, and to limit the use of requiring jurors to 'stand by'.

After the closing speeches of counsel for the prosecution and defence, the judge sums up the evidence for the jury's guidance, and directs them upon the law and certain rules of evidence. The jury must be directed separately on each count. After the judge has finished summing up, the jury retires to consider its verdict. The jury must at first attempt to reach a unanimous verdict and, if they find difficulty in agreeing, the judge may try to help them, although he must not try to speed up their verdict by threatening them. If the jury cannot reach a *unanimous verdict* after two hours or such longer period as the court thinks reasonable, they may return a *majority verdict*, i. e. 10 out of 12 must agree. If the verdict is 'not guilty', the jury will not be asked whether it was unanimous, but if it is 'guilty', they must be asked the numbers who agreed with or dissented from it.

111.3 *Civil juries*

By the *Administration of Justice (Miscellaneous Provisions) Act 1933* a civil court should have discretion as to whether or not a jury should be summoned; except that a jury must be ordered on the application of either party in cases of defamation, malicious prosecution or false imprisonment, or on the application of a party of whom fraud is alleged, unless the court considers that the trial will involve a prolonged examination of documents or accounts, or a scientific or local investigation which cannot conveniently be made with a jury. Civil juries are now rarely used except for defamation cases in the Queen's Bench Division.

Where the court has discretion under the Act it must be exercised judicially, in the same way as any other discretion. Actions for personal injuries, which include the results of motor accidents, constitute 40% of the cases in the Queen' s Bench Division. The Court of Appeal has ruled in *Ward v James (1966) 1 QB 273* that these should be tried by the judge alone in the absence of special circumstances. Also the Faulks Committee has recommended that, where a jury is used in such cases, the function in the assessment of damages should be limited. Where, as is usual, a judge sits without a jury, he determines the facts as well as the law, and also assesses the damages. The number of jury trials in the Queen' s Bench Division (outside the Queen's Bench Division juries are hardly ever encountered in civil actions) is likely to be not much more than 1% in the future.

Rules governing the admissibility of majority verdicts are the same as with criminal juries.

111.4 *Jury service*

By the *Juries Act 1974*, in order to qualify for jury service a person must:

(a) be on a register of electors;

(b) be not less than 18 nor more than 65 years of age; (There are proposals in the Criminal Justice Bill to allow persons to sit on a jury until the age of 70)

(c) have been ordinarily resident in the UK for at least five years since the age of 13;

(d) not be ineligible. The list of those ineligible includes judges, barristers, solicitors, articled clerks, clergy and the mentally ill;

(e) not be disqualified. In response to criticism that too many persons were eligible to sit on the jury, the *Juries Disqualification Act 1984* was passed. This widened the categories of persons disqualified.

The following are by virtue of *s.1* disqualified:

(i)   anyone who within the previous ten years has been sentenced to imprisonment, suspended sentence, borstal, youth custody or detention centre, or community service order;

(ii) anyone who within the last five years has been placed on probation.

In addition, anyone who has been sentenced to more than five years' imprisonment is disqualified permanently from serving on a jury;

(f) not be excusable. The list of those excusable includes MPs, members of the Forces, medical and other professions.

The Lord Chancellor is responsible for summoning jurors in the Crown, High and County Courts, and he is to prepare lists (panels) of persons summoned as jurors.

A juror is entitled to an allowance for travelling and subsistence, and for consequential financial loss or loss of earnings. If a person summoned fails to attend, he is liable to a fine of up to £100.

Selection is on a random basis by computer.

111.5 *Criticisms of the jury system*

(a) The system of random selection is both inadequate and suspect.

It is possible to engage in jury vetting, whereby the prosecution, through the use of asking a juror to stand by for the Crown, selects a favourable jury.

(b) The use of random, peremptory challenges can lead to injustice.

The *Criminal Justice Bill 1987* proposes the abolition of random challenges.

(c) There is no test of a juror's literacy or intelligence.

(d) Juries tend to be defence-biased, but can also react against a judge or barrister by entering a verdict which seems to go against the evidence.

Recent evidence has shown that perverse verdicts and questionable verdicts form a much higher percentage of verdicts than had previously been thought.

(e) It is too easy for disqualified people to sit on juries.

(f) It is a very expensive and slow method of trial.

(g) It is argued that jury trial is available for too many cases, and the *Criminal Justice White Paper and Bill* proposed the limiting of jury trial by making certain triable either way offences summary offences.

(h) The jury can be confused by complex issues, and the Roskill Committee (1986) proposed to abolish the jury for fraud trials. However, the *Criminal Justice Act 1987* retains it, but reforms the way fraud trials are conducted.

Note

In 1986 the government introduced a *Criminal Justice White Paper* proposing a number of changes for the administration of criminal justice. This was incorporated in the *Criminal Justice Bill*. However, the General Election of June 1987 meant that the Bill could not be fully enacted, and only the part in relation to fraud trials became law, as the *Criminal Justice Act 1987*. The government has, however, reintroduced the Bill, which should become law in 1988.

111.6 *Advantages of having a jury*

(a) The jury brings with it a fresh mind to bear on the issue and is free from the hardened views naturally prevalent among professional judges and magistrates, whose views about suspects must reflect their daily acquaintance with them.

(b) Jurors are best placed, as a result of their experience with daily life to judge the accused as a 'peer'. At a time when women, working class and black professional judges and magistrates are only now beginning to surface, albeit is bits and patches, it is important to have this element of the cross-section of the community having an imput into the criminal justice system. Statistics, and the experience of practising lawyers, appear to suggest that a black accused is more likely to be acquitted if the jury is composed substantially of black jurors.

(c) As a consequence they sympathise more readily with defendants from varied backgrounds.

(d) From experience of other countries, arguably, one of the first signs that a country is heading down the road of tyranny is the abolition of the jury system. It is therefore truly a bulwark of this country's democracy and freedom.

112. SENTENCING

112.1 Procedure

Once the court convicts the accused, it is necessary for the judge or magistrates to consider the appropriate sentence. This may take place immediately or there may be an adjournment pending reports or the outcome of another trial.

Counsel for the prosecution sums up the facts of the case: how the offence was committed, how grave it was, whether there was violence, whether there was any breach of trust. He will also detail how much cooperation the accused gave, and should try to be as balanced as possible since he is a minister of justice.

A police officer will then give details of the accused's previous convictions, as well as general details of his background, age and education.

The judge is then given copies of any reports to read. These reports may be:

(a)   *Social enquiry reports* – prepared by probation officers after interviewing the offender. The report explains the offender's background and personal circumstances, and goes on to consider the best way to deal with him and his suitability for probation or other forms of sentence.

(b)   *Home Secretary's report* – made on behalf of the Home Secretary where the accused is being considered for youth custody.

(c)   *Medical and psychiatric reports* – made by a doctor on order of the court and are important if the health of the offender is relevant to the offence or punishment.

(d)   *Social worker's report* – may be presented to the court by the social worker working with a juvenile offender and family. It would cover the intelligence, behaviour and response of the juvenile.

The person who compiled the report can be called upon to give evidence.

112.2 Plea in mitigation

The defence then have the opportunity to make a plea in mitigation in order to lessen the gravity of the offence and to show the defendants remorse. Character witnesses may be called and give evidence on behalf of the defendant. The defendant can represent himself, but it is more usual for him to have a lawyer.

112.3 Taking other offences into consideration

It is customary for the police to prepare a list of unsolved crimes which resemble the crimes committed by the defendant. He is then asked to study the list and given the opportunity to have any offences that he might have committed taken into consideration. By admitting his guilt to these crimes the defendant will find that his sentence will be increased by the judge to punish him for his additional wrongdoing. However, the increase is usually only slight and in practice he will not be tried for those offences in the future. Thus the slate can be wiped clean and, once he has served his sentence, he can start afresh. It also serves to clear up unsolved crimes for the police.

112.4 Types of sentence available

The judge or magistrate has a number of options open to him when pas sing sentence.

112.5 *Immediate imprisonment*

The defendant cannot be sent to prison for the first time unless no other method of sentencing would be appropriate. The court should consider any reports and give the defendant the opportunity to be legally represented:. *s.20 Powers of Criminal Courts Act 1973.*

The maximum sentence in the Crown Court is life for a Common Law of fence or the maximum prescribed by the statute creating the offence. The magistrates' powers are more limited: a maximum of six months for an offence with the total not to exceed six months if summary offences or 12 months if triable either way offences.

The maximum period specified is to reflect the punishment appropriate for the worst offence of its kind. In reality this maximum is rarely applied, and the judge will 'scale down' the sentence accordingly. The judge will need to balance the need for the punishment to fit the crime with the need to achieve the best result for the offender. Often the two needs will conflict, and the judge can expect public outcry if he adopts an approach considered to be too lenient with the offender.

The sentencer will bear in mind the tariff for the offence, which is a notional scale of sentences to reflect the increasing severity of an offence. The judge will decide, hopefully on the basis of knowledge of current sentencing practices, what he considers the appropriate sentence for the offence. This may then be reduced by any mitigating factors. It might also be increased if the judge considers the accused to be more dangerous than the gravity of the offence would indicate.

However, at all times the judge must bear in mind the need to avoid custodial sentences where possible or, if they are needed, to keep them to a minimum length. This is because a prison sentence is at its most effective as a deterrent if it is a 'short, sharp shock', and also present levels of over-crowding in prisons are giving grave cause for concern.

A prisoner sentenced to more than one month will qualify for remission of one third if he behaves well. This helps the Prison Service maintain good discipline; remission will be lost if the prisoner misbehaves.

If a prisoner has been sentenced to more than 18 months, he will be eligible for parole after he has served 12 months, or at least one-third of his sentence, whichever is greater. The Home Secretary will issue a parole licence on recommendation from the Parole Board. If a prisoner is granted parole, he is released from jail, but can be re-imprisoned for misbehaviour during the period of parole.

The Home Secretary has in July 1987 used his powers under *s.32 Criminal Justice Act 1982* to order the release of 3,500 prisoners in order to overcome the problems of over-crowding. Those released had been convicted of petty non-violent crimes.

112.6 *Suspended sentences*

The court may decide that a period of imprisonment is appropriate, yet wish to give the defendant the opportunity to mend his ways. It may be unwise to decide upon a non-custodial sentence; yet immediate imprisonment may not be the solution. The court can then have recourse to the suspended sentence. This imposes a period of imprisonment, but wholly or partly suspends its operation for a period of time. If for that period the defendant is of good behaviour, he can avoid going to jail. If, however, he commits further offences punishable with imprisonment, he runs the risk of being sent to jail for the initial offence. The court can pass a suspended sentence only if it considers that otherwise a custodial sentence would be appropriate, and that sentence must be for two years or less and the period of suspension must be between one and two years.

112.7 *Partly suspended sentences*

If the court considers the possibility of a suspended sentence, but would nevertheless like the offender to serve a short deterrent spell in prison, it can since 1982 pass a partly suspended sentence. This is available for sentences between three months and two years, and ensures that a short time is served in j ail with the remainder being suspended.

112.8 *Youth custody and detention centres*

Imprisonment is not available for those offenders under the age of 21; it is desirous that young, easily influenced juveniles do not mix with older, more hardened criminals. *S. 1 (f) Criminal Justice Act 1982* provides that the court must not pas s a custodial sentence in respect of a young offender unless no other method is appropriate.

If it does pass a custodial sentence, then where it is served will be determined by the length of the sentence. If in excess of four months, it will usually be served as youth custody (the old Borstal training) and the offender should be given some training to equip him for his return to society.

If between three weeks and four months, the of fender will usually be sent to a detention centre where he will undergo a rigorous and highly disciplined regime, designed to give him the 'short sharp shock' he needs to reform himself.

112.9 *Mentally disordered offenders*

Someone who is mentally ill may be punished in the same manner as a sane offender. However, in order to try to pass the sentence best suited to the offender, the court has other additional powers at its disposal:

(a) *Hospital orders*

An offender convicted of an imprisonable offence may have a hospital order made in respect of him. This is a drastic step and only available if no other measures would be appropriate, and the offender must be suffering from a specified disorder. He is then confined to hospital for treatment, and released when fit. If, however, the public would be placed at risk by a dangerous offender, then a restricted order may be made, by which the patient cannot be released unless the Home Secretary or Mental Health Review Tribunal gives permission.

(b) *Guardianship order*

Under the *Mental Health Act 1983* the court has power to make a guardianship order, entrusting the offender who is over 16, suffering from a specified disorder and who has committed an imprisonable offence to the care and supervision of a guardian. That guardian can then direct where the offender should live, work and receive treatment.

This order should only be made in exceptional circumstances.

(c) *Probation and condition*

It is also possible for the court to attach a condition that the offender seeks psychiatric treatment to any grant of probation.

112.10 *Fines*

A fine, i.e. a financial penalty, is one of the most common sentences imposed. It is simple and does not cost much to enforce, in contrast with imprisonment which imposes a costly burden on the taxpayer.

The Crown Court can impose a fine of unlimited amount for any offence other than murder or treason. The magistrates' powers are limited by statute, and there is a scale of offences. Offences at the top end of the scale carry a maximum of £2,000 fine.

It is also possible for the court to order that the parents of a child offender pay any fine imposed.

112.11 *Probation*

A probation order may be made in respect of someone over 17, and it places him under the supervision of a probation officer. The offender must consent.

The probation officer should try to help and guide the offender and ensure that he does not commit further offences. The period of probation can be between six months and three years, and the court may impose conditions. If probation is breached, the offender can be fined or even become liable to punishment for the original offence.

Probation is not available for murder.

112.12 *Supervision orders*

This is the equivalent of probation for juveniles, and the supervising officer will work with the juvenile and his family in order to instil a sense of social responsibility and help remedy any problems that might have contributed to the commission of the offence.

The order can last for three years and can have conditions attached, e.g. that the juvenile's movements at night be restricted or that more stringent control be exercised, similar to a care order.

There is no need for the juvenile to consent.

112.13 *Care orders*

If it is thought necessary, having regard to the seriousness of the offence and the need for care and control that the juvenile would not otherwise receive, it is possible for the court to make a care order. This removes the right of control from the parents and responsibility for the juvenile then vests in the local authority. The juvenile might continue to live at home or he can be removed to live elsewhere.

112.14 *Discharge*

If the court considers punishment or probation inappropriate, it can discharge the offender, either conditionally or absolutely.

An absolute discharge is a method by which the court can acknowledge that an offence has been committed, yet indicate that they do not hold the offender to be at fault. The offender is entirely free to go without punishment.

A conditional discharge is not an immediate punishment. The offender is free to go. If, however, he commits another offence within the specified period, he can be sentenced for the original offence.

112.15 *Binding over*

An offender can be bound over to keep the peace and be of good behaviour. He is asked to give an undertaking, called a recognisance, and if he refuses he may be imprisoned. If he breaches his undertaking by behaving badly, he can be ordered to forfeit a sum of money. Binding over is only appropriate if the offender is likely to breach the peace in the future.

112.16 Community service order

An offender of 16 and above who had been convicted of an imprisonable offence may consent to the court making a community service order. This orders the offender to undertake work for the benefit of the community under the supervision of a probation officer. It may be for between 40 and 240 hours, all of which are unpaid. An order should be made after considering a social enquiry report, and one problem has been the lack of places on suitable schemes.

The work done will benefit the community whilst at the same time punishing and giving the offender the opportunity to make amends for his wrongdoing.

Failure to comply with the order can lead to a fine or to the offender being sentenced for the original offence.

112.17 *Attendance centres*

The court can order that an offender of over 21 convicted of an imprisonable offence who has not served a custodial sentence, should attend at an attendance centre for between 12 and 36 hours. This period is divided up into a number of shorter periods, during which time the supervisors try to instil some discipline and encourage new hobbies and interests.

A problem has been the lack of suitable centres.

112.18 *Endorsements and disqualifications*

In respect of *Road Traffic Act 1972* offences the court has powers to endorse the offender's licence and also to disqualify him from driving.

112.19 *Compensation*

An offender may be ordered to pay compensation for any injury or damage that he has caused. This order should only be made if liability is obvious and should reflect the means of the offender. Its aim is more to compensate the victim than punish the offender.

112.20 *Forfeiture or confiscation*

The *Powers of Criminal Courts Act 1973* provides that the court can in certain cases order that the offender forfeit property, and an important new development has taken place with respect to convicted drug dealers. The *Drug Trafficking Offences Act 1986* gives rise to a presumption that the assets of the offender have been acquired through the commission of offences, and thus liable to confiscation. It will be for the offender to show that the assets were lawfully acquired.

The *Criminal Justice Bill 1987* contains further powers in relation to confiscation orders.

113. *AIMS OF PUNISHMENT*

113.1 *The considerations that influence judges and legislators*

There are many different reasons given for the imposition of punishment upon offenders. Some are practical utilitarian reasons, and others are more abstract moral reasons. They include:

(a) *Individual deterrence*

The fact that D has been punished may deter him from criminal activity in future. For example, an offender convicted of possessing a 'soft drug' for his own use will probably be fined or given some other form of non-custodial sentence if he is a first offender. But if he offends again, he risks more serious punishment (see *R v Robinson-Coupar and Baxendale (1982)*).

(b) *General deterrence*

Other people, seeing D sentenced, may be deterred from criminal behaviour. For example, persons convicted of a crime involving the abuse of a position of trust are usually sent to prison, even if they are first offenders, e.g. managers, schoolteachers, civil servants or postmen. And punishments of the utmost severity are invariably passed on persons convicted of spying (see *R v Bingham (1972), R v Bettaney (1984)*).

(c) *Incapacitation*

Where an offender has carried out a particularly harmful crime or series of crimes, a long sentence is sometimes imposed to protect the public from him for a while. For example, although there is a general rule that a convicted defendant has the right to a determinate sentence in all crimes except murder, this does not apply to those crimes with a maximum punishment of life imprisonment where the defendant shows signs of violent mental instability. Such a person may legitimately be sentenced to 'life imprisonment' (see *R v Bryant and Mead (1983)*).

(d) *Reform of the offender*

It is fondly hoped that some forms of punishment – e.g. Borstal training – may lead to the reform of the offender. There is increasing scepticism as to whether such measures are every really reformative. However, some crimes, by their very nature, indicate that the defendant is in need of psychiatric help, e.g. bestiality (see *R v Higson (1984)*).

(e) *Retribution*

It is widely felt in society that wrongful behaviour must be punished simply because it is right that wrongful behaviour must be punished, whether or not the punishment be productive of any positive good. Whilst theorists do hot in general try to justify this notion, it is undoubtedly reflected in the attitudes of the courts to sentencing. For example, in *R v Wallis (1984)* a sentence of 12 months' imprisonment was described as 'extremely lenient' in the case of a youth convicted of aiding and abetting the suicide of a girl aged 17.

In *R v Roberts (1982)* the Court of Appeal considered the purposes of punishment in the crime of rape. The reasons given in that case are of general application:

(1)   to mark the gravity of the offence;

(2)   to emphasise public disapproval;

(3)   to serve as a warning to others;

(4)   to punish the offender; and

(5)   to protect women (or, in cases other than rape, 'to protect the public').

LLB

ENGLISH LEGAL SYSTEM

LESSON 12 (STUDY)

121. *THE CIVIL PROCESS*

    121.1 INTRODUCTION
    121.2 CONCILIATION

122. *CIVIL PROCEDURE*

    122.1 INTRODUCTION
    122.2 HIGH COURT (QUEEN'S BENCH DIVISION) PROCEDURE
    122.3 STAGES IN QUEEN'S BENCH PROCEDURE
    122.4 PROCEEDINGS IN THE COMMERCIAL COURT
    122.5 COUNTY COURT PROCEDURE
    122.6 STAGES IN COUNTY COURT PROCEDURE
    122.7 SMALL CLAIMS
    122.8 ENFORCEMENT

123. *ARBITRATION*

    123.1 INTRODUCTION
    123.2 ARBITRATION – AN ALTERNATIVE TO COURTS

124. *TRIBUNALS*

    124.1 ADMINISTRATIVE TRIBUNALS
    124.2 DOMESTIC TRIBUNALS

121. *THE CIVIL PROCESS*

121.1 *Introduction*

Although the Law Reports appear to be filled with disputes, in reality very few relationships deteriorate to the extent that they require intervention by the courts. Most transactions are completed without a hitch and, where problems are experienced, they are usually resolved amicably by the parties themselves.

However, in a tiny percentage of cases the parties need to look elsewhere for assistance, and such disputes may be resolved in one of three ways:

(a) conciliation;

(b) litigation;

(c) arbitration.

121.2 *Conciliation*

This is the most informal way of resolving disputes, and depends upon the intervention of a neutral third party to assist the parties to reach an amicable solution.

The third party tries to achieve a mutually acceptable compromise, but there is no power to make a binding decision. Obviously, the success of this method depends up on the willingness of the contracting parties to move from their individual demands and reach a compromise; and also the ability of the conciliator to reconcile and heal divisions.

122. CIVIL PROCEDURE

122.1 *Introduction*

Generally, the first step a person will take when considering enforcing a civil right is to consult a solicitor. However, he may decide to 'act for himself' (i.e. take the case through the courts without a legal representative). He is then referred to as a 'litigant in person' and has a 'right of audience', i.e. he can speak in any court, even the House of Lords, and present his case. However, a company which takes or defends legal proceedings must be represented by a solicitor or barrister. A 'litigant in person' is also entitled to have a friend in court with him to give advice and take notes. A person doing this is called a 'McKenzieman' – the name coming from the case of *McKenzie v McKenzie (1971)* where this right was established.

Before actually issuing court proceedings the solicitor or the individual himself will have written a *letter before action* warning the potential defendant that proceedings will be commenced unless he does what the prospective plaintiff requires him to do. There may then be a long period of negotiations before proceedings are actually instituted.

The court in which he brings his action will depend on the type of action (e.g. contract or family) and the remedy he is seeking. Contract disputes will be commenced in the County Court or the High Court (Queen's Bench Division). In deciding which court to commence his action the person *(litigant)* will have to consider:

(a)   the limits on the County Court jurisdiction (£5,000 maximum on claims in contract); and

(b)   the fact that proceedings in the High Court are usually more expensive and take longer.

A person may also consider *arbitration*. This is an informal method of settling disputes. Arbitration is used to mean either:

(a)   the settlement of disputes by an independent person (or persons) outside the court system; or

(b)   an informal procedure within the County Court system, or a special procedure of the High Court for certain technical matters to be tried by an official referee.

In this section we shall cover civil procedure within the court system *(litigation)* outlining the procedure in the High Court (Queen' Bench Division) and the County Court. In the next section arbitration will be covered.

122.2 *High Court (Queen's Bench Division) procedure*

The *Rules of the Supreme Court* govern the procedure in the whole of the Supreme Court (High Court and Court of Appeal). The procedure is different for each division of the High Court and we shall outline the procedure in the Queen's Bench Division. The detailed rules are contained in Orders, each order having a number of rules. Thus *RSC Order 53* has a number of sub-orders or rules. The rules are usually written *RSC 0.53 r.2.*

All the rules are contained in two volumes commonly called the 'White Book' (because it has a white cover). Every solicitor or barrister or 'litigant in person' will consult it in conducting cases in the High Court to ensure he is completing the proper documents in the correct manner.

The stages in the procedure are set out below. The number beside each stage indicates the paragraph explaining that stage. 'P' refers to the plaintiff (the person initiating the proceedings), 'D' refers to the defendant (the person against whom the proceedings are taken).

122.3 *Stages in Queens Bench procedure*

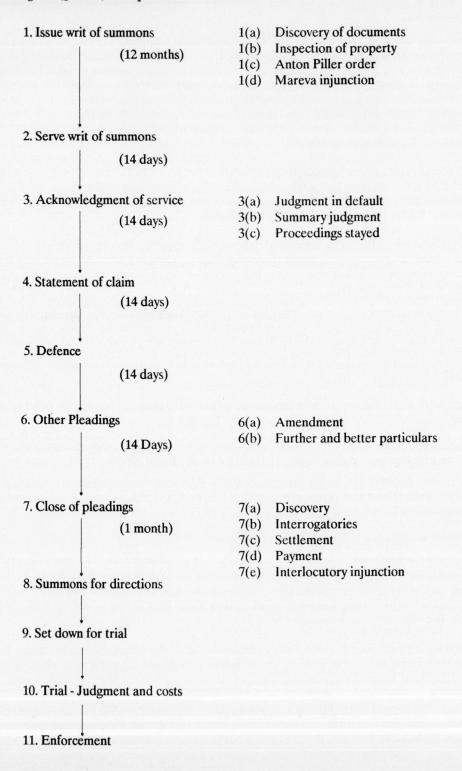

1. Issue writ of summons

    (12 months)

1(a)   Discovery of documents
1(b)   Inspection of property
1(c)   Anton Piller order
1(d)   Mareva injunction

2. Serve writ of summons

    (14 days)

3. Acknowledgment of service

    (14 days)

3(a)   Judgment in default
3(b)   Summary judgment
3(c)   Proceedings stayed

4. Statement of claim

    (14 days)

5. Defence

    (14 days)

6. Other Pleadings

    (14 Days)

6(a)   Amendment
6(b)   Further and better particulars

7. Close of pleadings

    (1 month)

7(a)   Discovery
7(b)   Interrogatories
7(c)   Settlement
7(d)   Payment
7(e)   Interlocutory injunction

8. Summons for directions

9. Set down for trial

10. Trial - Judgment and costs

11. Enforcement

1. *Issue of writ of summons*

Most proceedings are commenced by issuing a *writ of summons* which is an order by the court in a particular form. It contains details of the parties (plaintiff(s) and defendant(s)) and the court (i.e the Central Office in London or a district registry) where the action is started. It must also contain a brief summary of the P's case – a general indorsement. In many cases it will contain a more detailed account of P's case, his *statement of claim* (see 4), in the form of a special indorsement. The writ:

(i) notifies the D of the issue of the writ;

(ii) informs the D that he must satisfy the claim, particulars of which must be stated in the writ, or return an acknowledgment of service to the court indicating whether he intends to contest the proceedings; and

(iii) informs the D that if he fails to satisfy the claim or return the acknowledgment, judgment will be entered against him.

Anyone may issue a writ. This is done by taking (or sending) three copies of the completed writ to the Central Office (London) or a district registry (elsewhere) and paying a fee. The court officials give the writ a number and stamp it with the court seal *(seal it)*. One copy is kept as the court's record and the other two copies are returned to P. He keeps one for himself and serves the other on D.

A person may be declared by the court a 'vexatious litigant' (a person who regularly brings court actions to annoy opponents and which have no reasonable prospect of success); such a person must get leave of the court before he is allowed to issue a writ.

A writ must be issued within the limitation period as prescribed by the *Limitation Act 1980* which, in the case of breach of contract, is six years from the date of the breach.

(a) *Discovery of documents*

Even before an action is commenced it is possible to seek an order for discovery of documents if the documents would disclose that the applicant might have a plausible action. For example, medical records may be inspected to see if they disclose evidence of negligence. However, this power is only granted if the case involves personal injuries.

(b) *Inspection of property*

It is also possible to obtain an order from the court allowing inspection of any property that is likely to be the subject of a dispute. For example, if A has made a contract with B, providing for A's stallion to breed with B's mare, and the foal to be sold and the proceeds shared. If B refuses to hand over the money, A may want to inspect the foal to ensure that it is the foal of his stallion before incurring the expense of litigation.

(c) *Anton Piller order*

An Anton Piller order directs the defendant to allow the plaintiff to enter D's premises and inspect any of P's property that is there. It is not possible for P to insist on entry, but refusal by D will amount to contempt of court.

The order is applied for by the plaintiff *ex parte*, i.e. without giving notice to the defendant. This element of surprise ensures that D is unable to destroy the evidence or notify accomplices and is very effective in cases such as video pirating.

This order is so called after the decision of the Court of Appeal in *Anton Piller KG v Manufacturing Processes Ltd (1976)*, the case in which the order was created. The order can require D to grant entry to P to inspect and remove any documents; D can also be forced to provide details of anyone else involved in the illicit activities. The order may be obtained before an action is even commenced which preserves the surprise effect of the order.

(d) *Mareva injunction*

A Mareva injunction is a powerful new weapon that the courts have developed to prevent a defendant being able to defeat judgment by removing his as sets before the jurisdiction or in some way diminishing his assets.

Before a Mareva injunction was evolved the courts had decided that a defendant was free to use his assets as he saw fit until judgment went against him: *Lister v Stubbs (1890)*.

In *Mareva Compania Naviera SA v International Bulk Carriers SA (1975)* the Court of Appeal, in a case concerning foreign defendants, allowed an injunction preventing monies being removed from the country. There was no clear reasoning employed by the court, as Lord Denning pointed out in *Rasu Maritima v Perusahaan (1978)*, but the Vice-Chancellor, Sir Robert Megarry, extended the principle in *Barclay-Johnson v Yuill (1980)* to cover all defendants, not only foreign defendants. This decision was incorporated into statute by *s.37(3) Supreme Court Act 1981*.

Thus, a Mareva injunction will be granted if:

(i) P can show that he will have a good case at trial;

(ii) the English court has jurisdiction to hear the case;

(iii) D appears to have assets within the jurisdiction;

(iv) P can show that there is a risk that D will either transfer the assets out of the jurisdiction or dissipate them if the injunction is not granted;

(v) without the injunction D would not or could not satisfy P's claim;

(vi) the balance of convenience is in favour of granting the injunction.

The effect of a Mareva injunction is to freeze D's assets, although it does not give P any preferential rights over the assets. It is possible for D to apply to court to use his assets for everyday expenses, both personal and business.

2. *Service of writ*

The writ is valid for 12 months from date of issue, and must be served on D in one of the following alternative ways:

(i) personally handing it to D;

(ii) by first class post to D's last known address;

(iii) leaving it at D's last known address;

(iv) on D's solicitor if agreed;

(v)   by fixing the writ on any land that is the subject of dispute.

If none of these methods is possible, P may apply for an order for *substituted service*. The court will then grant permission for P to bring the writ to D's attention in an alternative way, e.g. newspaper advertisement.

3.   *Acknowledgment of service*

An acknowledgment of service is a formal document which is served on D with the writ. It informs D that he must return it to the court within 14 days if he does not wish to have judgment entered against him. On the acknowledgment of service D (or his solicitor) must state whether he intends to defend the proceedings and give his address (or his solicitor' s if he has instructed a solicitor).

(a)   *Judgment in default*

If D fails to acknowledge service within the time limit, P may apply to the court for judgment in default under *RSC 0.13*. This has the effect of giving judgment to P without D' s case being heard, although the judgment can be set aside if D can show good cause for not having acknowledged service.

(b)   *Summary judgment*

Once D has acknowledged service it is possible for P to apply by summons to the court for summary judgment under *RSC 0.14*. This application will be made when P alleges that D can have no defence to the action, and is merely delaying the action by putting in a defence. The parties appear before the *master* who is a judicial officer *(not a judge)* whose principal function is to decide 'interlocutory' matters which are points raised during the court proceedings which need to be settled before the case is finally heard by a judge. He will either allow the application, giving judgment for P, or dismiss the application and give D leave to defend. This permission to defend the action may be unconditional or it may have conditions attached, e.g. that D deposit a sum of money in court.

This procedure helps reduce delay and is often used, especially where the action concerns a dishonoured bill of exchange.

(c)   *Proceedings stayed*

If there is an arbitration clause in a contract, and one party commences litigation, then the other can apply to the court to have the proceedings stayed pending the result of arbitration. The proceedings can also be dismissed if they are frivolous, vexatious and an abuse of the process of court.

4.   *Statement of Claim*

P's first pleadings set out the facts on which P's case is based. The function of *pleadings* is to define the is sues involved in the case and it is not possible at trial to introduce new grounds which were not contained in the pleadings. The Statement of Claim must be served on D within 14 days of his acknowledging service.

5.   *Defence*

Within 14 days of receiving P's Statement of Claim, D must serve a defence, in which he must accept or deny each point in the Statement of Claim. He may also serve a counterclaim in which he counterattacks by claiming damages from P.

6. *Other pleadings*

It is possible for either party to issue a reply to the other's pleading.

The word 'pleadings' is used to describe all the documents prepared, usually by counsel, which contain the statements of the material facts in summary form on which the person claiming relies and includes:

(i)   Statement of Claim;

(ii) defence plus any counterclaim, which the defendant may have;

(iii) reply – plaintiff – further pleadings;

(iv) rejoinder – defendant – further defences.

Pleadings can continue though it is rare to go further than the reply stage.

(a) *Amendment*

The writ and pleadings may be amended once before close of pleadings without leave of the court. If further or later amendment is necessary, then this is only possible with leave of the court.

(b) *Further and better particulars*

If any part of the pleadings is unclear a party may request that clarification is given, i.e. that further and better particulars are provided. If this request is refused, a court order may be sought.

7. *Close of pleadings*

This is an arbitrary point, 14 days from the date of the last pleading. It signifies the end of the preliminary stage of defining issues, and the beginning of the stage which is preparatory for trial.

(a) *Discovery*

It is a feature of civil actions that the parties must declare, by making a list of documents, the existence of *all* important and relevant documents in their possession. The opportunity must then be given to the other party to inspect those documents which are not the subject of privilege. If a party wishes to see a document which the other side are withholding, then application may be made to the court for an order requiring discovery.

(b) *Interrogatories*

In certain circumstances it may be necessary to confine a party to a particular point of evidence. In such a situation it is possible to ask the court for permission to ask an interrogatory, which is a question answerable on oath about an evidential matter (rarely used).

(c) *Settlement*

It is possible to settle an action at any time; many settlements are reached at the court doors! This occurs when the parties agree to resolve their dispute, and the most common way of reaching a settlement is by the use of *without prejudice* offers. The defendant may make an offer, either verbally or in writing, which he stipulates is 'without prejudice'. This ensures that the offer cannot be drawn to the court's attention, and is therefore confidential, and does not stop him denying liability at trial. In many cases this procedure will lead to the conclusion of the case without the need to present arguments in court.

(d) *Payment into court*

Another way of trying to prompt a settlement is by paying a sum of money into court. This then forces the plaintiff to decide whether to accept the sum or continue with the action. If he accepts the sum this is in effect a settlement; if he continues with the action, then the fact that there has been a payment into court is not disclosed until after the judge has given his verdict. If the amount of damages awarded exceeds the payment in, then the plaintiff is unaffected but, if the amount is less than that paid in by D, then P is responsible for all of the costs incurred after the date of the payment in. This may run into thousands of pounds, especially if there has been an early payment in, and this will encourage the P to settle quickly if the payment is a realistic amount.

(e) *Interlocutory injunction*

In some commercial cases the D may be doing something that amounts to a breach of the parties' agreement. It may be possible to obtain an interlocutory injunction which prohibits D from carrying on that activity pending trial.

8. *Summons for directions*

The plaintiff must take out a summons for directions within one month of close of pleadings, and at the Summons for Directions the master will attempt to deal with all preliminary matters and confine the litigation to those issues which are in dispute.

9. *Setting down for trial*

At the Summons for Directions the master will specify a time limit within which P must set the action down for trial. This P does by taking two copies of all the pleadings to the court, and then the case will be placed on the case lists.

10. *Trial*

This is held in 'open court' – i.e. anyone may attend and listen. The steps in the trial are:

(i) Plaintiff's counsel opens the case; he outlines the facts and lays the issues before the court. The plaintiff may appear in person but it is more usual for him to be represented by counsel. A solicitor has no right of audience in the High Court.

Counsel may call witnesses whom he examines 'in chief'. They may then be cross-examined by the defence.

(ii) Defence's counsel (if there is oral evidence) produces his evidence and calls his witnesses; the plaintiff's counsel may cross-examine.

(iii) Defence's closing address.

(iv) Plaintiff's closing address.

(iii) and (iv) are reversed where the defence counsel has no oral evidence to argue.

(v)   Judge gives judgment though, if there is a jury, he only sums up the evidence, directs them as to the relevant law and leaves the determination of the issue on its facts to them.

The person who loses usually has costs 'awarded against him'. This means that he is ordered to pay the other person's legal costs of bringing the court action in addition to any damages awarded.

11.   *Enforcement*

It is a characteristic of English litigation that the successful party must enforce his own judgment; the court does not ensure automatically that he is paid.

122.4 *Proceedings in the Commercial Court*

The Commercial Court is a specialist court of the Queen's Bench Division, which is designed to provide a speedy, simple and expert resolution of commercial disputes. The judges have many years' experience in commercial matters, and often sit to hear actions outside normal court hours for the convenience of the parties. The sums involved are often considerable, and usually the cases involve a foreign party.

Initially a date is set for trial, unlike normal actions which have no fixed date, and pleadings are as brief and uncomplicated as is possible.

The judge has access to the Commercial Court Committee, which comprises experts of commercial matters who give advice on certain aspects of the dispute.

122.5 *County Court procedure*

The *County Court Rules 1981* govern procedure in the County Court. Recent changes in the rules have brought them more in line with the *Rules of the*

Supreme Court. They are also divided into orders, each of which have a number of sub-orders or rules – usually quoted as *CCR 0.10 r.6.* All the orders are contained in one book called the 'Green Book' (because it has a green cover). In County Court litigation it is consulted in the same way as the 'White Book' is in High Court litigation. Many steps in the procedure are to a large extent the same as those in the High Court (with different names in some cases).

A person issuing proceedings in the County Court must ensure that they are within its jurisdiction in value (maximum claim in contract £5,000) and locality (i.e. must issue proceedings in the area in which D lives or works or where 'the cause of action' arose). For example, if a person is hit by a car in Oxford driven by a person who lives in Cambridge, he will have to issue proceedings in Oxford or Cambridge County Court.

The procedure is set out below and again the numbers indicate the paragraph which explains that particular step.

122.6 *Stages in County Court procedure*

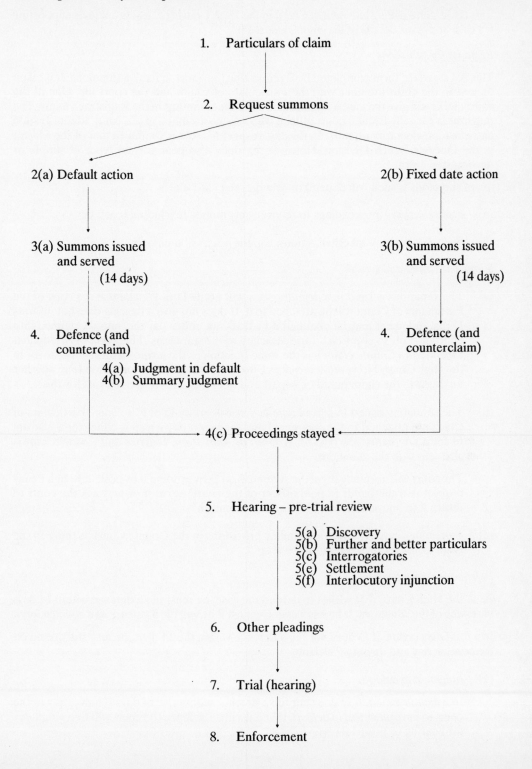

1. Particulars of claim

2. Request summons

2(a) Default action

2(b) Fixed date action

3(a) Summons issued
     and served
        (14 days)

3(b) Summons issued
     and served
        (14 days)

4. Defence (and
    counterclaim)

4. Defence (and
    counterclaim)

4(a) Judgment in default
4(b) Summary judgment

4(c) Proceedings stayed

5. Hearing – pre-trial review

5(a) Discovery
5(b) Further and better particulars
5(c) Interrogatories
5(e) Settlement
5(f) Interlocutory injunction

6. Other pleadings

7. Trial (hearing)

8. Enforcement

1. *Particulars of Claim*

   This is the same as P's *Statement of Claim* in the High Court (i.e. it sets out facts supporting P's case and gives details of his claim against D).

2. *Requests for summons*

   This is a standard form completed by P requesting the court to issue a summons. It is taken or sent to the court together with the Particulars of Claim and the court fee. One of the court clerks will give the case a number and issue the summons in the Registrar's name. The *Registrar* is a legally-trained court official who supervises much of the court administration and most interlocutory matters. In this last respect his role is similar to that of the Master in the Queen's Bench Division. However, he does also hear certain types of simple or uncontested cases.

The type of summons is sued will depend on whether the case is a:

(a) *default action* – proceedings to recover only money (excluding rent); or

(b) *fixed date action* – all other actions, e.g. for possession of land.

3. *Summons issued and served*

(a) The summons is sued in a *default action* will notify D of P's claim and a copy of the Particulars of Claim will be attached to it. It does not give a hearing date but informs D that judgment may be obtained if he does not either pay the amount claimed into court or reply to court on a form attached to the summons. This *Form of Admission, Defence and Counterclaim* has the same function as the *acknowledgment of service* in the High Court. However, it requires D to give a little more information (e.g. whether he disputes the claim in full or in part and, if he disputes it, the reasons for this).

(b) The summons issued in a *fixed date action* will notify D of P's claim (Particulars of Claim are attached to the summons) and the *return day* which is either for a hearing or for a *pre-trial review* (see 5). A *Form of Admission, Defence and Counterclaim* is also sent with the summons.

   The court will normally serve the summons on D by sending it by post, although P may request that the bailiff (a paid officer of the court) serve it or may ask the court to return it to him so that he (P) may serve it himself.

(c) *Proceedings stayed* There are similar provisions in the County Court as those in the High Court for proceedings to be stayed.

4. *Defence and counterclaim*

   As in the High Court, if D wishes to defend the case, he must file a defence within 14 days of service of the summons. If he has a claim against P he will file a *defence and counterclaim*.

   In a *fixed date action*, if D does not file a defence within the 14 days, he may still attend on the hearing day and dispute P's claim.

(a) *Judgment in default*

   In a *default action*, if D does not file a defence within the 14 days P may apply to the court to have *judgment in default*. If D does file a defence the court will fix a *return day* for hearing or pre-trial review.

(b) *Summary judgment*

If D files a defence and P's claim is for more than £500 P may apply for summary judgment on the ground that D has no real defence. This is the same procedure as summary judgment in the High Court except note that it is only available in County Court in default action where P claims more than £500 and D has failed a defence. (For claims under £500 see section 122.7).

5. *Hearing – Pre-trial review*

Unless the case is of a type where the return day is the actual hearing (e.g. actions for possession of land) it will be a *pretrial review*. This is a preliminary hearing before the Registrar and is similar to the summons for directions in the High Court. There are two important differences:

(i) it is held much earlier in the proceedings; and

(ii) if D fails to attend P may obtain judgment in certain circumstances.

The Registrar will give *directions for trial* which may include orders for:

(a) *Discovery* – same as High Court.

(b) *Further and better particulars* – same as High Court.

(c) *Interrogatories* – same as High Court (rarely used)

In addition he may fix a date for the full trial. More commonly, he does not, and the parties have to apply to the court for a date when they are ready.

(d) *Settlement.*

(e) *Payment into court*

(f) *Interlocutory injunction.*

all are possible as in High Court

6. *Other pleadings*

These are the same as in the High Court.

7. *Trial (hearing)*

This will be before a single *judge* in 'open court' (i.e. anyone may attend and listen). The conduct of the trial is similar to that in the High Court. However, solicitors have a right of audience. The judge will give judgment and usually award costs against the loser.

8. *Enforcement*

As in the High Court it is left to the winning party to enforce judgment (if the loser does not do as ordered). (See section 122.8).

122.7 *Small claims*

Arbitration within the *County Court* is a procedure for dealing with claims at informal hearings in private before the Registrar (usually) where the strict rules of evidence in court hearings do not apply. Generally it is used for 'small claims' (under £500) as all such claims which are defended are automatically referred to arbitration. However, either party may apply for the matter to be referred to arbitration even if the claim is more than £500.

There is usually an appointment for 'preliminary consideration' by the arbitrator of the dispute and the ways in which it may be resolved. A date is then set for the dispute to be heard. This hearing is in private and informal. The strict rules of evidence do not apply. The arbitrator may adopt any procedure he considers convenient and gives a fair and equal opportunity to each party to present his case. The arbitrator makes an award (i.e. decision in favour of one of the parties).

This procedure is used in commercial disputes, e.g. a faulty cooker where the oven does not work.

There is a 'no costs rule' on claims under £500 which discourages legal representation. The rule is that the arbitrator will not order that the winning party has any solicitors' charges paid by the loser (unless the arbitrator directs that there has been unreasonable conduct on the loser's part). Thus most such 'small claims' are agreed by 'litigant in person'.

122.8 *Enforcement*

Once judgment is obtained, it is for the winning party (judgment creditor) to ensure that he recovers the sum outstanding. The losing party (judgment debtor) may pay the award immediately, but if he does not, the following methods are available:

High Court	*County Court*
1. *Oral examination* – an order bringing the judgment debtor (D) before the *master* to be examined as to his means. Used to find out what assets/income he has to help creditor (P) decide how to enforce judgment.	1. *Oral examination* – same order to bring debtor before *Registrar.*
2. *Writ of fieri facias* – order to the *sheriff* to seize and sell such of D's property as to satisfy the judgment debt. Certain property is exempt – e.g. clothes, bedding.	2. *Warrant of Execution* – same order to the *bailiff.*
3. *Attachment of earnings order* – available in limited circumstances in High Court (see 8 below). below)	3. *Attachment of earnings order* – order to D's employers to deduct money from D's salary to pay to P.
4. *Garnishee proceeding* – procedure whereby debt owed by third party (bank) to D is transferred from D to P. *Ex parte* application on affidavit to *master*, who if satisfied grants garnishee order nisi, forbidding payment of debt to D. Then D, the garnishee, and P must appear before the master at a later date when the order will be made absolute if D has failed to pay.	4. Garnishee proceedings – also available in County Court.

High Court	*County Court*
5. *Charging order* – procedure whereby charge is registered against D's land or shares, which protects P should D try to sell the land. Order comes in two parts (nisi and absolute) and should be combined with the appointment of a receiver if protection is to be acquired in the event of D's bankruptcy. If after six months of the order being made absolute, D still has not paid P may apply to the court for an order for sale.	5. *Charging order* – also available in County Court
6. *Appointment of receiver* – an equitable method, only available if no other method will secure payment. Must file affidavit naming responsible person to act as receiver and stating that there has been no success at enforcing judgment by other methods. Can be used against rent, royalties, etc. Once application granted, receiver will administer D's assets (e.g. collect rents and pay debt).	6. *Appointment of receiver* – also available in County Court.
7. *Administration order* – *not* available in High Court	7. *Administration order* if judgment debts of not more than £5,000 court may make administration order, whereby court supervises payments of debts out of D's income (used for bad HP debts, etc.). Usually D will apply for this order to protect himself as, once the order has been made, any creditor whose debt has been notified to the court cannot take other action to recover the money without leave of the court.

The judgment creditor may want to enforce a High Court judgment in the County Court or *vice versa.* **Thus:**

8. *Registration in County Court* – High Court judgment may be registered in County Court and enforced as if judgment of that court, e.g. to get attachment of earnings order.	8. *Registration in High Court* – County Court judgments of more than £2,000 may be registered and enforced in the High Court. (Enables better enforcement by *sheriffs*).

In addition, as a last resort, P may apply to have D declared bankrupt. This is not really technically a method of enforcement as no judgment is required to make the application.

High court	*County Court*
9. *Bankruptcy* – P may apply to the court to have D declared bankrupt. Has the effect of freezing D's assets and the official receiver will administer D's property. Often the threat will be enough to make D pay. Can be expensive since P must pay for petition and a deposit.	9. *Bankruptcy* – same as in High Court.

Other types of enforcement

10. *Writ of possession* – after judgment for possession of land, it directs sheriff to enter land and let P have possession.	10. *Warrant of possession* – as for writ, but directed to bailiff.
11. *Writ of delivery* – orders possession of goods.	11. *Warrant of delivery.*
12. *Committal orders* – after judgments such as specific performance or an injunction where D fails to comply, P may apply to enforce by committal (i.e. order commits the person to prison).	12. *Committal orders* – available in County Court.

122.9 Choice of Court

As seen earlier, whereas the financial and geographic jurisdiction of the High Court is unlimited, the County Court's jurisdiction is limited in both respects. The bringing of an action, which is more appropriately dealt with in the County Court, in the High Court Act may lead to penalties in costs. By sections 19 and 20 of the County Courts Act 1984 where an action in tort or contract is commenced in the High court and the plaintiff:

1. recovers less than £3,000 he shall only be entitled to costs on a county court scale; and

2. recovers less than £600 he shall not be entitled to cost at all.

This is unless the High Court is either:

1. satisfied that there was reasonable ground for supposing the amount recoverable to be in excess of £5,000; or

2. satisfied that there was other sufficient reason for bringing the action in the High Court.

Note therefore that if the plaintiff recovers between £3,000 and £5,000 he is free from any penalty in cost.

In favour of the High Court:

Apart from the operation of sections 19 and 20, there are a number of tactical factors which make a High Court action more attractive:

1. There is more control of action in the High Court, especially in respect of issue and service of writ.

2. The High Court procedure is much more intimidating and can show the seriousness of the plaintiff.

3. The enforcement procedure in the High Court by the sheriff is much more efficient than by the county court bailiff. However, it must be noted that a county court judgement of more than £2,000 may now be enforced in the High Court.

4. The default action in the High Court is as efficient as in the county court, but there is the added advantage of a better enforcement procedure.

5. A High Court action may persuade an opponent to come up with a better settlement figure.

In favour of the county court:

1. The county court is geographically more convenient, especially in rural areas.

2. Some clients prefer the relative informality of the county court.

Proposals for Reform of Civil Procedure

1. A reduction in limitation periods to encourage earlier commencement of actions.

2. Introducing a new time limit from the time the consultation with the solicitor took place to the time when the writ is issued.

3. Closer supervision of time limits by the court.

4. Increasing the use of computers by the courts.

5. Specialist qualifications for solicitors dealing with personal injuries actions.

6. Possible alternative methods of resolving disputes, e.g. Paper Adjudication as in the Criminal Injuries Board.

7. More detailed disclosure of arguments and evidence.

8. More comprehensive pre-trial review.

9. Increasing the limit on arbitration in the small claims court.

10. Merging the divisions of the High Court.

11. Means of encouraging earlier settlement.

123. *ARBITRATION*

123.1 *Introduction*

'Arbitration' can mean either a process of settling disputes outside the court system governed by the *Arbitration Acts* or a procedure within the court structure (informal procedure in the County Court f or dealing mostly with *small claims* or a special procedure in the High Court for dealing with technical matters).

123.2 *Arbitration – An alternative to courts*

Arbitration as an alternative to court proceedings (litigation) is widely used in commercial disputes. Generally this will be an option chosen by the parties themselves (by agreement) although certain statutes provide for reference of particular types of dispute to arbitration, e.g. the *Agricultural Holdings Act 1948* requires disputes of tenancies of agricultural land to be submitted to arbitration. The rules governing both arbitration by agreement and by statute are largely the same (unless the particular statute makes special provisions).

Commercial contracts often contain clauses providing for reference of disputes to arbitration. These clauses may be specifically agreed by the parties or incorporated as a result of codes of practice of trade associations, national or international.

The advantages of arbitration are:

(a) *Privacy* – proceedings are private as opposed to litigation proceedings where the final hearing is in *open court*. Thus private and confidential matters are not revealed to members of the public.

(b) *Expertise/experience* – generally the arbitrator will be selected for his skill and experience in the area disputed.

(c) *Timing of hearing* – the date of the hearing is fixed to suit the parties as opposed to court hearing dates which are fitted into the court 'lists' and may not be convenient to the parties.

(d) *Cost* – (in theory) less expensive than litigation although not necessarily so.

(e) *Informality* – procedural rules are generally less cumbersome than in litigation.

(f) *Speed* – (in theory) disputes can be settled more quickly although this is not always so.

The disadvantages are:

(a) *No certainty of outcome* – each case is decided on its own merits and previous decisions are not followed in the same way as judges' decisions.

(b) *Limited right of appeal* – although this may also be considered an advantage as the arbitrator's decision is by and large final and thus the possibility of deferring payment pending the outcome of an appeal is reduced.

(c) *The arbitration procedure may be abused* – the dominant party may invoke an arbitration clause to force the weaker party to give up his court action, for which he may get legal aid, and to enter arbitration, for which no legal aid is available.

(d) *No legal aid for arbitration* – thus the dominant party who can afford specialist legal advise has an advantage over the other.

(e) *Arbitration can still be formal* – thus making it difficult for the parties to represent themselves.

124. *TRIBUNALS*

124.1 *Administrative tribunals*

Until the advent of Legal Aid the courts of law were said, like the Savoy Hotel, to be open to all! (i.e. to those who could afford the enormous costs involved). There are, however, considerations other than cost (which, despite the existence of Legal Aid, is still a problem) which affect the suitability of the courts as institutions for the settlement of all disputes.

The procedure followed in the courts of law is still rather cumbersome, and the rules of evidence are incomprehensible to litigants who wish to appear in proceedings on their own behalf. Equally, the judges who preside over the courts are drawn almost exclusively from the ranks of the Bar, and are thought by many to be either unable or unwilling to determine certain types of dispute in a satisfactory manner, e.g. in the areas of labour and welfare law, in which they have little or no experience.

Tribunals, on the other hand, are staffed by persons with some experience of the cases involved, together usually with a legally qualified chairman. Cases on average are dealt with in a matter of weeks rather than months, or even years taken to settle cases in the ordinary courts. Although the tribunals will take into account evidence which would be admissible in a court of law, they are not bound by either strict rules of evidence or procedure.

The major advantage of tribunals is, therefore, that they are cheap, quick and informal. It was hoped that this would encourage litigants to appear in person, but in practice many of them (despite the absence of Legal Aid) continue to use the services of professional lawyers.

There were fears that the informality and flexibility of the tribunals would lead to inconsistent and perhaps unreasoned decisions but, since most of the recommendations of the Franks Committee in 1957 have been implemented in legislation (at present the *Tribunals and Inquiries Act 1971)*, most of these fears have proved to be unfounded.

The main proposals of the Franks Committee were that a Council on Tribunals should be set up to review the operation of tribunals and make recommendations where necessary to improve their performance. It also recommended that a legal chairman should head each tribunal (to ensure a fair hearing and impartial reasoning) and that reasons should always be given for decisions. The existence of a reasoned decision is essential to enable either an appeal to a higher body, or court, or judicial review by means of the prerogative orders.

Amongst the most important tribunals are:

(a) *Industrial tribunals* – deal with a variety of complaints in the field of employment law, e.g. unfair dismissal, redundancy, race and sex discrimination, equal pay and maternity rights.

(b) *Rent tribunals* – dealing with disputes between landlord and tenant, e.g. on rent review, on security of tenure.

(c) *Supplementary benefits tribunals and National Insurance Commissioners* – deal with appeals from the decisions of DHSS insurance officers concerning state welfare benefits, e.g. unemployment benefit, supplementary benefit, invalidity allowances, sickness benefits, and pensions.

(d) *The Lands Tribunal* – deals with is sues such as the compulsory purchase of land, e.g. by local authorities.

(e) *The Criminal Injuries Compensation Board* – awards compensation to the victims of crime.

(f) *Mental health review tribunals* – deal with requests for release by patients held in hospital on grounds of mental illness.

124.2 *Domestic tribunals*

These are bodies set up by groups of individuals to regulate their own affairs. They cover a wide variety of bodies ranging from the committee of the local social club, or trade union, to the professional disciplinary bodies such as the General Medical Council or the Law Society.

The jurisdiction of these tribunals may be established either by statute or by contract. In the latter case the individual members agree to disputes being settled by some tribunal or committee in an informal manner. If they have agreed to be bound by the decisions of such a body (which will often be a condition of membership) they will be bound to comply with any decision made, and in most cases will have no right to appeal from the decision to a court.

There may be a stipulated procedure, making some provision for a right to appeal either to another body within the organisation or even to an outside body, e.g. an independent arbitrator. Recourse to the courts cannot be completely excluded because it is unlawful, as being against public policy, to attempt to oust the jurisdiction of the courts.

As the courts have an inherent right to interpret contracts, they can always review the decisions of bodies where jurisdiction is based on contract, to ensure that they have interpreted the contract of membership correctly in reaching their decisions (e.g. an expulsion from membership). The courts will also require these bodies to observe the principles of natural justice which require a fair hearing to be given before an impartial body.

LLB

ENGLISH LEGAL SYSTEM

LESSON 13 (STUDY)

131. *CRIMINAL APPEALS*

131.1 DIAGRAM OF CRIMINAL COURTS
131.2 INTRODUCTION

132. *APPEALS FROM SUMMARY TRIAL*

132.1 APPEAL FROM THE MAGISTRATES' COURT TO THE
CROWN COURT
132.2 APPEAL FROM THE MAGISTRATES' COURT TO THE
QUEEN'S BENCH DIVISION
132.3 APPEAL FROM THE CROWN COURT TO THE QUEEN'S
BENCH DIVISION
132.4 APPEAL FROM THE QUEEN'S BENCH DIVISION TO
THE HOUSE OF LORDS

133. *APPEALS FROM TRIAL ON INDICTMENT*

133.1 APPEALS FROM CROWN COURT TO COURT OF APPEAL
(CRIMINAL DIVISION)
133.2 ATTORNEY-GENERAL'S REFERENCE
133.3 APPEALS FROM COURT OF APPEAL TO HOUSE OF
LORDS

134. *CRITICISMS AND REFORMS*

134.1 THE DOUBLE APPEAL SYSTEM
134.2 LENIENT SENTENCES

135. *CIVIL APPEALS*

135.1 DIAGRAM OF CIVIL COURTS
135.2 APPEALS FROM MAGISTRATES' COURT TO NIGH COURT
135.3 APPEALS FROM COUNTY COURT TO HIGH COURT
135.4 APPEALS FROM COUNTY COURT TO COURT OF APPEAL
(CIVIL DIVISION)
135.5 APPEALS FROM HIGH COURT TO COURT OF APPEAL
135.6 APPEALS FROM HIGH COURT TO HOUSE OF LORDS
135.7 APPEALS FROM COURT OF APPEAL TO HOUSE OF LORDS
135.8 APPEALS TO PRIVY COUNCIL
135.9 APPEALS TO EUROPEAN COURT

131. *CRIMINAL APPEALS*

131.1 *Diagram of criminal courts*

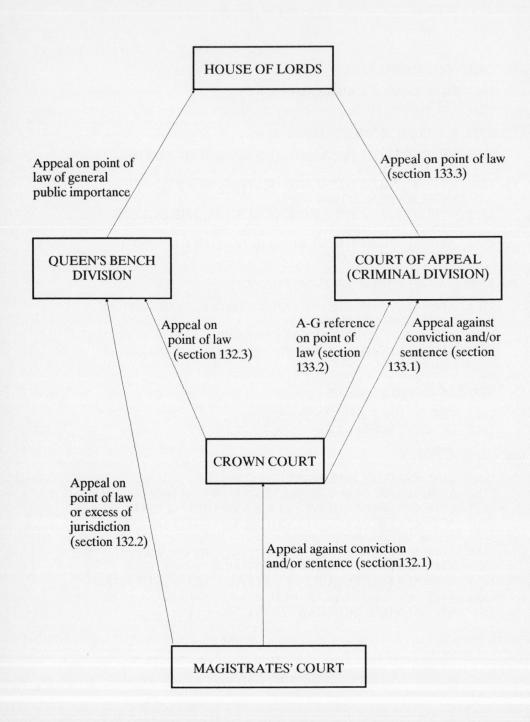

HOUSE OF LORDS

Appeal on point of
law of general
public importance

Appeal on point of law
(section 133.3)

QUEEN'S BENCH
DIVISION

COURT OF APPEAL
(CRIMINAL DIVISION)

Appeal on
point of law
(section 132.3)

A-G reference
on point of
law (section
133.2)

Appeal against
conviction and/or
sentence (section
133.1)

CROWN COURT

Appeal on
point of law
or excess of
jurisdiction
(section 132.2)

Appeal against conviction
and/or sentence (section132.1)

MAGISTRATES' COURT

131.2 *Introduction*

The course of an appeal depends upon whether there was summary trial in the Magistrates' Court, or trial on indictment in the Crown Court. In the diagram the continuous line represents appeals from summary trial, the broken lines represents appeals from trial on indictment.

132. APPEALS FROM SUMMARY TRIAL

132.1 Appeal from the Magistrates' Court to the Crown Court

Only the accused may appeal, and leave to appeal is not required if lodged within 21 days of sentence. Outside this time leave to appeal must be made to a judge of the Crown Court. If the accused pleaded 'not guilty' and is found guilty of the offence, he may appeal to the Crown Court against conviction and sentence. This will take the form of a complete rehearing where fresh evidence may be introduced.

If the accused pleaded guilty, he may also appeal to the Crown Court but only against the sentence.

The judge will sit with at least two lay magistrates, but not the same as those who heard the original case. The decision is by a majority.

The court has the power to increase the sentence as well as reduce it.

132.2 Appeal from the Magistrates' Court to the Queen's Bench Division

Either the convicted person or the prosecution may appeal on a point of law or question of jurisdiction 'by case stated' to a Divisional Court of the Queen's Bench Division.

By case stated written application must be made to the clerk of the Magistrates' Court within 21 days requesting the magistrates to state a case for the opinion of the Divisional Court, i.e. a concise statement of the facts as found by the magistrates. Magistrates must then state a case unless the application is frivolous. The case must be stated within three months although, if magistrates state a case after three months, the Divisional Court may extend time to enable them to hear it. The Divisional Court is bound by the magistrates' findings of fact and no new evidence is admissible.

132.3 Appeal from the Crown Court to the Queen's Bench Division

This only lies when the Crown Court is considering an appeal from the Magistrates' Court (see section 132.1).

Both the prosecution and defence may exercise the right which is by way of case stated on a point of law.

The normal time limit for the application is 14 days, but this may be extended.

132.4 Appeal from the Queen's Bench Division to the House of Lords

An appeal lies from the decisions of the Divisional Court to the House of Lord s either by the defence or by the prosecution. The party who wishes to appeal must:

(a) establish that the case involves a point of law of general public importance by obtaining a certificate to that effect from the Divisional Court; and

(b) obtains leave to appeal either from the court itself or House of Lords.

In practice appeals to the House of Lords in criminal cases are very rare.

If the Divisional Court does not certify that a point of law of general public importance is involved, then it is not possible to obtain the certificate from the House of Lords.

Once an appeal is brought to the House of Lords it seems that the House is not restricted to considering the particular point certified by the court below.

Application to the court below for leave to appeal must be made within 14 days from date of decision of that court. If the court below certifies that a point of law of general public importance is involved but refuses leave to appeal to the House of Lords, an application to the House of Lords for leave must be made within a period of 14 days after refusal by the court below.

The House of Lords and the court below may, upon application made at any time by defendant (but not by prosecution), extend time within which an application may be made for leave, but this right to extend the time does not apply to any case involving the death sentence.

The appeals take place in a committee room with their Lordships sitting unrobed, but counsel is, however, robed.

After hearing the appeal the Lords who presided discuss the case amongst themselves in committee and vote on their decisions. They then write their speeches which might take a few weeks. They then assemble in the Chamber of the House of Lords each stating his decision, which results in whether they would allow or dismiss the appeal. These decisions are not strictly 'judgments' but speeches in support of the members' vote on the motion made by the Lord Chancellor (who is the Speaker of the House of Lords). The House of Lords has no power to pass judgment. It may only remit the case to the trial judge with its recommendations, which must then be turned by the judge into a judgment, e.g. five Law Lords sat on appeal, three voted to allow accused's appeal and two voted other way. This majority will be announced by trial judge and accused has, therefore, won his appeal.

133. *APPEALS FROM TRIAL ON INDICTMENT*

133.1 *Appeals from Crown Court to Court of Appeal (Criminal Division)*

Appeals must be heard by not less than three judges and are always heard by odd numbers in order that, when the judgment is given, there will never be any deadlock in the decision. There must be not less than eight nor more than 18 Lord Justices appointed to the court at any one time.

The appeal

(a)   Only the accused can appeal (see 133.2 below).

(b)   He may appeal against (i) conviction, and/or (ii) sentence:

    (i)   *Conviction* – no leave is required to appeal on a point of law alone, but leave to the Crown Court (trial court) or of the Criminal Division is necessary to appeal against conviction on a question of fact or mixed law and fact.

    (ii)   *Sentence* – an appeal against sentence requires leave of the Criminal Division.

(c)   Time for appealing is 28 days from date of conviction or sentence.

Under the terms of the *Criminal Appeal Act 1968* the court may:

(a)   *Dismiss the appeal* – and confirm the conviction either because the appeal lacks any merit or because, even if some technical irregularity took place during the trial (e.g. the admission of improper evidence) the court considers that no miscarriage of justice resulted.

(b)   *Allow the appeal* – if the court considers the conviction unsafe or unsatisfactory, or some irregularity in the conduct of the trial resulted in some substantial miscarriage of justice. (Bear in mind that the court is reluctant to disagree with the findings of a jury.)

(c)   *Orders a retrial* – the court may allow the appeal but order a re-trial of the case, usually where evidence has come to light which was not available at the time of the trial, but which is of such a nature that it could affect the outcome of the case. (If the evidence was available at the time of the trial but was not called, a retrial will not usually be ordered – unless the court considers it essential in the interests of justice.)

(d)   *Vary the sentence* – the court may confirm the conviction but vary the sentence imposed by the Crown Court. The Court of Appeal will not vary a sentence unless they believe it to be totally wrong in principle. (The court can no longer increase the sentence imposed but, where it believes the appeal to have been totally frivolous, it may order that time spent in prison pending the appeal should be disregarded in computing the sentence.)

133.2 *Attorney-General's reference*

By *s.36(1) Criminal Justice Act 1972* the Attorney-General, on behalf of the prosecution, may refer (technically not appeal) a case from the Crown Court solely on a point of law following an acquittal on indictment. Whichever way the Court of Appeal decides on the point of law in question (in favour of the accused or against him), this will not affect the accused's acquittal, but will provide authoritative guidance on that aspect of the law for the future.

The Home Secretary is putting forward proposals which would allow the prosecution to appeal against sentence to the Court of Appeal. However, the decision of the Court of Appeal would not affect that particular sentence; it would merely act as a guideline to judges in the future.

These proposals feature in the *Criminal Justice Bill 1987* although there are moves to allow the Court of Appeal to increase a lenient sentence.

133.3 *Appeals from Court of Appeal to House of Lords*

Either side may appeal on a point of law of general public importance.

A certificate that such a point is involved is required from the Court of Appeal, and leave is needed from either the Court of Appeal or the House of Lords.

The appeal is conducted in the same way as that from the Queen's Bench Division (see section 132.4).

134. *CRITICISMS AND REFORMS*

134.1 *The double appeal system*

At present there is the possibility that a party that loses an appeal in the Court of Appeal or Queen's Bench Division can have a further appeal to the House of Lords. It is argued that this leads to delay and uncertainty, in that often the majority decision in the House of Lords will overrule a unanimous decision in the Court of Appeal, e.g. trial judge, three Court of Appeal and two House of Lords judges in favour of one outcome would be overruled by three House of Lords judges in favour of another outcome.

Therefore, some critics have proposed abolition of the House of Lords in its appellate jurisdiction, but there are at present no such plans.

134.2 *Lenient sentences*

There has been a great deal of public outcry over the passing of what is regarded as lenient sentences. In response to such outcry, the Government published its *Criminal Justice White Paper* which proposed to allow the prosecution a right of appeal. This proposal was controversial and had formed part of the *Prosecution of Offences Bill* but had been vetoed by the House of Lords. However, the General Election of 1987 meant that the *Criminal Justice Bill* could not be passed in its entirety, and so the debate has continued.

The new *Criminal Justice Bill* will contain some form of prosecution appeal. What remains to be seen is whether it will be an appeal for future guidance only or whether the appeal will actually increase the sentence.

135. CIVIL APPEALS

135.1 Diagram of civil courts

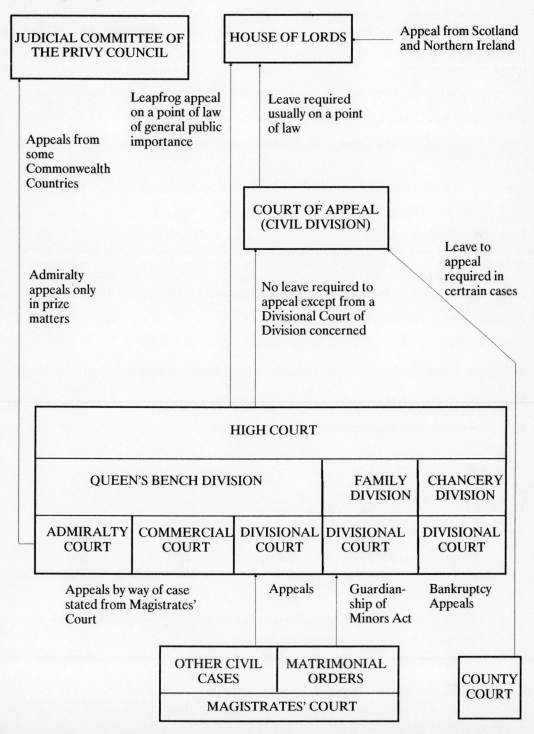

135.2 Appeals from Magistrates' Court to High Court

(a) *Family matters*

Appeals from the Magistrates' Court in matrimonial and family matters lie to the Family Division of the High Court. Further appeal lies to the Court of Appeal and House of Lords, with leave.

(b) *Other civil matters*

Appeal is by way of case stated to the Divisional Court of the Queen's Bench Division.

135.3 *Appeals from County Court to High Court*

Appeal lies to the Divisional Court of the Chancery Division in matters concerning bankruptcy and land registration.

Appeal lies to the Family Division under the *Guardianship of Minors Act 1971*.

135.4 *Appeals from County Court to Court of Appeal (Civil Division)*

Governed by the *County Courts Act 1984*.

Appeal is of right on a point of law. If the appeal is on a question of fact, then leave is required if the sum involved does not exceed one half of the appropriate County Court limit. For example, in contract the limit is £5,000 and leave is needed if less than £2,500 is involved.

135.5 *Appeals from High Court to Court of Appeal*

Appeal lies from the judge' s decision to the Court of Appeal as of right.

If an appeal is from the decision of the Divisional Court, then leave from that court is required.

Appeal is usually by way of rehearing.

135.6 *Appeals from High Court to House of Lords*

In certain cases an appeal will lie directly from the decision of a High Court judge (known as the leap-frog procedure) but only if:

(a) the case involves a point of law of general public importance, and the High Court judge issues a certificate to that effect;

(b) the parties agree to leap-frog the Court of Appeal;

(c) the Court of Appeal is already bound on the issue raised either by one of its own previous decisions, or by a decision of the House of Lords, or the matter involves construction of an enactment;

(d) the House of Lords gives leave to appeal in this way: *Administration of Justice Act 1969*.

135.7 *Appeals from Court of Appeal to House of Lords*

Appeal is not necessarily on a point of law, but nearly always is.

Leave is required from either the Court of Appeal or the House of Lords.

135.8 *Appeals to Privy Council*

Appeal lies from certain Commonwealth countries and from the Admiralty Court in prize matters.

135.9 *Appeals to European Court*

Until 1973 the House of Lords was the highest court of appeal for both civil and criminal matters in England and Wales. Since then the United Kingdom has become a member of the European Economic Community and a new court has acquired jurisdiction over certain types of cases. The vast majority of civil claims will continue to be dealt with solely by English courts applying English law but, where an issue involving European law is raised (which is most likely in the fields of company, competition and discrimination law), the courts will be called upon to apply the decisions of the ECJ and may in some cases have to refer an issue to that court for determination.

A case may be brought before the ECJ:

(a) directly by either a member state or the European Commission under *Art. 169* alleging breach of EEC law by some member state (e.g. on free movement);

(b) on appeal by an individual, company or member state, challenging the decision of some Community institution, or national court, alleging a failure to comply with EEC law (e.g. against a fine imposed by the ECJ for breach of the competition rules in *Arts. 85-86*).

(c) on a reference made under *Art. 177* which provides that, where an is sue of European law is raised which is unclear, any national court *may* refer the issue (not the case) for a preliminary ruling, but a final court of appeal *must* refer the issue.

(If the European law is clear the English courts have an obligation under *s. 2 (1) European Communities Act 1972* to apply it.)

The ECJ is made up of one judge from each of the member states. Its procedure is very different from that of a national court; most of the arguments are set down in writing (and translated into the official languages of the EEC) with only a brief oral hearing before the court preceded by an opinion on the case by the Advocate General, setting out the issues and law impartially to assist the court.

LLB

ENGLISH LEGAL SYSTEM

LESSON 14 (STUDY)

141. *THE LEGAL PROFESSION*

141.1 INTRODUCTION
141.2 SOLICITORS
141.3 BARRISTERS
141.4 QUEEN'S COUNSEL
141.5 LEGAL EXECUTIVES
141.6 THE FUTURE OF THE PROFESSION
141.7 ARGUMENTS FOR FUSION
141.8 ARGUMENTS AGAINST FUSION
141.9 RIGHTS OF AUDIENCE
141.10 DIRECT ACCESS
141.11 CONVEYANCING
141.12 ADVERTISING
141.13 INCORPORATION AND MIXED PARTNERSHIP

142. *LEGAL SERVICES*

142.1 UNMET LEGAL NEED
142.2 LAW CENTRES
142.3 CITIZENS ADVICE BUREAUX
142.4 LEGAL AID AND ADVICE: CRIMINAL CASES
142.5 LEGAL AID AND ADVICE: CIVIL CASES
142.6 THE GREEN FORM SCHEME
142.7 ALTERNATIVES TO LEGAL AID

141. *THE LEGAL PROFESSION*

141.1 *Introduction*

The legal profession is divided into the main branches of *solicitors* and *barristers*. Solicitors are assisted by *legal executives*.

141.2 *Solicitors*

A person who has served a period of articles to a solicitor and who has passed the examinations prescribed by the Law Society may be admitted as a solicitor by having his name entered on the rolls of solicitors. He thereby becomes an officer of the Supreme Court. In practice he takes his instructions directly from lay clients, gives advice, drafts documents and consults barristers *(counsel)* in difficult cases. The scope of his activities is wider than that of a barrister, though he is not allowed to appear as advocate in the courts, except in the Magistrates' and County Courts. In excepted circumstances he may be granted a right of audience in the Crown Court where an accused is appealing from the Magistrates' Court.

The Acts regulating the organisation and remuneration of the solicitors' profession were consolidated by the *Solicitors Act 1974*. The Law Society has power, with the concurrence of the Lord Chancellor, the Lord Chief Justice and the Master of the Rolls, to make regulations about education and training for persons seeking to be admitted or to practise as solicitors. The Council of the Society is required to make rules, with the concurrence of the Master of the Rolls, for regulating the professional practice, conduct and discipline of solicitors. The Solicitors' Disciplinary Tribunal is appointed by the Master of the Rolls. It now includes both solicitors and lay members. Appeal by a solicitor struck off the rolls lies to the High Court, and thence to the Court of Appeal.

A committee including the Lord Chancellor, the Lord Chief Justice and the Master of the Rolls may make rules regulating the remuneration of solicitors in non-contentious business.

In addition, the Law Society administers the Legal Aid and Advice Scheme and maintains a Compensation Fund out of which it may make a hardship grant to any person who suffers hardship through failure of a solicitor to account for money due. There are proposals to remove responsibility for Legal Aid from the Law Society: *Legal Aid White Paper 1987*.

The Law Society is constituted under a Royal Charter of 1845, as amended, with the objects of *promoting professional improvement and facilitating the acquisition of legal knowledge*. Membership is voluntary. It is governed by a Council of 70 elected members.

141.3 *Barristers*

A person who has joined one of the four *Inns of Court* and has passed the examinations required by the *Council of Legal Education* may be *called to the Bar* by the *Benchers* of his Inn and thereby become a barrister.

Recently the entry requirements have been raised, requiring persons desiring to be called to the Bar to possess at least a second class honours degree, unless they can show exceptional circumstances.

The Inns of Court now require a person intending to practise to serve 12 months' pupillage in the chambers of an established barrister, and not to accept a brief until he has been a pupil for six months. A barrister may appear as advocate before any court in England and Wales. His practice will also consist to a varying extent of drawing up legal documents and giving expert advice in his chambers. According to professional etiquette which is judicially noticed, a barrister may take instructions only from solicitors and not directly from lay clients; and he is not entitled to sue for his fees, though he may refuse to take work unless he is paid in advance. Barristers practise individually and not in firms or partnerships. The Attorney-General and the Solicitor-General are, for the time being, considered to be the heads of the Bar.

Barristers, and to a lesser extent solicitors, tend to specialise in one branch of the law or another. Thus, of barristers practising in London, the Equity or Chancery barristers will generally be found in Lincoln's Inn and the Common lawyers in the other Inns.

The four Inns of Court, namely *Inner Temple, Middle Temple, Lincoln's Inn* and *Gray's Inn* are unincorporated bodies of medieval origin, owned and controlled by *Masters of the Bench (Benchers)* for the time being.

A Senate of the Inns of Court was established by agreement in 1966, and in 1974 this became the *Senate of the Inns of Court and the Bar.* The Senate regulates admission to the Inns, and the policy of legal education for Bar students. The Council of Legal Education organises syllabuses, tuition and examinations qualifying for call to the Bar. The Senate also regulates standards of professional conduct through its disciplinary committee on behalf of the Benchers, who act in this capacity on behalf of the judges the Senate exercises disciplinary powers over practising barristers.

The Senate of the Inns of Court and the Bar, constituted in 1974, exercises by its disciplinary committee the customary disciplinary jurisdiction of the Benchers of each of the four Inns of Court over barristers in respect of professional misconduct, other than the actual carrying into effect of any sentence. Appeal by a barrister against an order disbarring him or suspending him from practice continues to be heard by the judges as *Visitors of the Inns: Re S (A Barrister) (1970).*

141.4 *Queen's Counsel*

Nowadays when a barrister has had considerable practical experience and thinks that he has attained some distinction at the Bar, he may, provided he has been continually practising for at least ten years, apply to the Lord Chancellor for permission to *take silk.* If permission is granted letters patent are issued, he is sworn as a QC *(Queen's Counsel)* and is called within the Bar of the Supreme Court wearing a silk instead of a stuff gown. In future he will undertake less routine work and will generally have the assistance of junior counsel in court.

It is no longer compulsory for a QC to appear with a junior, and there have been calls to abolish the distinction.

141.5 *Legal executives*

The Institute of Legal Executives was established in 1963, and its members carry out highly skilled work in solicitors' offices. Legal executives cannot join solicitors' partnerships, but enjoy professional status within solicitors' firms and good positions in the legal departments of corporations, local authorities, national industries, etc.

Members are students, or associates, or fellows. Progression is by examination.

141.6 *The future of the profession*

Unlike many countries, England has a divided legal profession. Barristers and solicitors have different functions, and in most litigious matters, a client will need the services of both branches of the legal profession. Many people have put forward the view that this division is not in the best interests of the client, and that the profession should be fused, i.e. a lawyer would be competent to handle all types of legal work.

As the number of suitably qualified persons continues to increase at a rapid rate, both solicitors and barristers face increasing competition. Not unnaturally both branches have sought to make inroads into areas previously regarded as the exclusive domain of the other. Until recently both branches had been steadfastly against the idea of fusion, but recent developments in other areas have reopened the issue.

141.7 *Arguments for fusion*

(a)   The barrister is too remote from the client, and there is often a breakdown in communication.

(b)   If one lawyer were involved, he could deal with the case from start to finish, and would thus be better prepared.

(c)   There is delay between the initial consultation with the solicitor and the barrister handling the case.

(d)   Confidence in the system would increase since the client would build up a relationship with his lawyer, which would not be interrupted by the case being passed to counsel.

(e)   Last minute instructions would be rarer.

(f)   Costs would be lower for one lawyer than for two.

(g)   The experience of other jurisdictions, especially other common law jurisdiction, e.g. the U.S.A., suggest that fusion will not automatically plunge this country into judicial chaos and ultimate tyranny. Indeed arguably the U.S. system is in some respects superior to the English system and something must be owed to the fused profession there.

(h)   Fusion will finally open the door to solicitors to join the bench: a hitherto jealously guarded privilege of the bar. This can only be a good thing and add not only numbers but also increase the quality of the bench.

141.8 *Arguments against fusion*

(a)   Advocacy is a skill, which needs constant practice. The solicitor deals with many other areas and would lack the necessary expertise in advocacy. Consequently standards would fall.

(b)   If solicitors appeared in court more often, clients would experience difficulty in contacting them in their office.

(c)   Small firms of solicitors would not have the experience necessary to deal with the range of cases presented to them. At present all solicitors have access to the specialist Bar.

(d)   If there was fusion, large firms of solicitors would be able to pay lucrative salaries to attract members of the Bar, leaving smaller firms to struggle.

(e)   Solicitors' firms would become larger. Local firms would find it difficult to compete, and may go out of business.

(f)   It would become more difficult to appoint to the judicial Bench, and the special relationship between the Bench and Bar would be lost.

(g)   The experience of other jurisdictions show that the natural tendency for the efficient working of the legal profession is separation. In the U.S.A. there is increasingly developing a class of lawyers referred to as 'trial lawyers', who by and large fulfil the functions of the barrister. Further in Australia – especially Victoria – although the profession is legally fused, there is an informal but strict separation between solicitors and barristers in practice. The argument can be put therefore that even if lawyers are fused they tend to separate themselves for the greater efficiency of the system.

(h)   Increasingly in international trade contracts where the parties have little or no connection with the English jurisdiction, choice of law and jurisdiction clauses choose England as the jurisdiction for the settlement of disputes. This certainly reflects the superiority of the English judicial system and, it is argued that, the separated legal profession must have contributed to this.

(i)   From the above it is also arguable that the English system is not expensive, as it does not deter foreigners from choosing the English courts. Indeed it is a fact that the primarily fused U.S. system is more expensive.

The Royal Commission was unanimously against fusion, and the committee on the Future of the legal profession (July 1988) was against fusion.

141.9 *Rights of audience*

As mentioned earlier, the Bar had exclusive rights of audience in the superior courts. As solicitors faced increasing competition from each other and outside forces such as accountants, banks and conveyancers, they looked for new areas into which to expand. The obvious area concerned representation in court.

Many solicitors have specialised in litigation, representing clients in the County and Magistrates' Courts. They saw no reason why they should not handle cases in the higher courts if competent to do so: after all, a solicitor with 20 years' experience of litigation would probably be more competent than a junior barrister with little experience.

The Royal Commission considered the extension of solicitors' rights of audience, and rejected the idea by a 10:5 majority. The main reason was a fear of the standard of advocacy declining, although the effect of competition on the junior Bar was also an influential factor.

However, solicitors have continued to campaign for greater rights of audience and the matter became national headlines because of a case called *Abse v Smith (1986) 1 All ER 350.*

Briefly, the facts were as follows. In June 1982, at the time of the Falklands crisis, Mr Cyril Smith MP gave a radio interview in which he made remarks about Mr Leo Abse MP and other MPs which they considered defamatory. Accordingly they issued a writ for libel. More than two years later they agreed to settle the action by reading in the High Court an apology by the defendant. Ironically, it was at this point that the trouble began. The statement was prepared and agreed and all that remained to be done was to have it read. Mr Smith wanted his solicitor to read it, but only barristers have a right of audience in that court. Considering that the fees being quoted for the performance of this task were exorbitant, he applied to the court for leave to have his solicitor read the statement. This was refused, and Mr Smith appealed to the Court of Appeal.

The Court of Appeal refused to extend the rights of audience of solicitors. However, on 9 May 1986 a *Practice Direction* was is sued which allowed solicitors to appear informal or unopposed matters in the High Court.

The Law Society is presently conducting a campaign for further extensions, which, not surprisingly, are opposed by the Bar. The Committee on the Future of the Legal Profession, chaired by Lady Marre, reported in July 1988. It has recommended by a majority to extend solicitor's rights of audience to the Crown Court. The Bar are opposed to this aspect of the report, fearing that it would lead to fusion.

141.10 *Direct access*

At present it is not possible to approach a barrister directly for his advice or representation; the client must use a solicitor. This rule was introduced as a *quid pro quo* for barristers taking exclusive rights of audience.

It has been suggested that the Bar would gain from direct access, and the Bar's opinion is in favour. However, the Law Society would only be in favour if this led to a removal of exclusive rights of audience.

The Bar would stand to lose far more if solicitors gained rights of audience than they would gain by direct access. They lack the organisation, finance and experience to compete with solicitors to provide legal services to the general public. The Committee on the Future of the Legal Profession has recommended that members of specialist professions other than solicitors should have access to the Bar.

141.11 *Conveyancing*

It was illegal for anyone who was not a qualified solicitor to offer to undertake conveyancing work for reward: *Solicitors Act 1974*. This meant that the final transfer of rights in land had to be effected by a solicitor, although most of the preliminary work would be done by unqualified personnel.

Critics argued that conveyancing was a straight-forward transaction for which solicitors, because of their monopoly, were charging exorbitant prices. Solicitors argued that the monopoly was necessary to protect clients from fraud, maintain standards, and to facilitate transactions as banks, etc. would rely on solicitors' undertakings.

The Royal Commission on Legal Services recommended by a narrow majority (8:7) to maintain the monopoly, and the Law Society was quick to prosecute unqualified persons who tried to compete.

A Labour MP, Austin Mitchell, introduced a Private Member's Bill to abolish what he saw as an anti-competitive, restrictive practice. The Bill received unexpected support and the Government were forced to introduce their own measures. They established a committee under Professor Farrand, and that recommended the establishing of a Council for Licensed Conveyancers. This body would set standards to be attained, and rules of ethics and conduct to be followed by its members.

The Farrand proposals were substantially implemented in the *Administration of Justice Act 1985*.

Therefore, solicitors must now compete for conveyancing work with Licensed Conveyancers, although the Law Society have managed to limit the effect of this by persuading the Government that banks and building societies should not be able to offer conveyancing to persons borrowing money from them in order to avoid a conflict of interest.

141.12 *Advertising*

In order to allow more effective competition, the rules against solicitors advertising have been relaxed. However, the advertising must be 'tasteful'.

141.13 *Incorporation and Mixed Partnerships*

The Law Society is considering allowing solicitors to incorporate and to have mixed partnerships with other professionals. It has decided to allow incorporation with safeguards for clients to include insurance, and to allow renumeration agreements with other professionals, provided no partnerships are formed.

142. LEGAL SERVICES

142.1 *Unmet legal need*

Whilst many people realise the need to consult a lawyer in order to seek redress of grievance, many sections of society have difficulty in that they either do not recognise that the law could assist them or, alternatively, they are deterred from consulting a lawyer.

The Law Society has issue pamphlets describing the services provided by solicitors, and these have been published in many languages. However, they do not overcome the suspicion with which many members of the public regard a lawyer. The image of the profession, the fear of the cost involved and the fact that traditional firms do not usually offer the services most in demand, i.e. immigration, welfare, housing law, has led to a large unmet legal need.

142.2 *Law Centres*

The Neighbourhood Law Centres of the 1970s were an attempt to meet the demand for legal services. They were independent of central government control and were staff ed by qualified solicitors. Finance was by local authority grant and donations from charities. They were situated in inner city shopping centres where they would be readily visible to the public, and they specialised in welfare law, an umbrella term for the specific areas listed above.

Their position was precarious in that, at least initially, the Law Society disapproved strongly of them and also because they were operating in a harsh financial climate in which donations from charities became fewer and public spending cuts greater. But there was no doubt that they proved the existence of a need for legal services.

The Royal Commission on Legal Services recommended reorganisation of the scheme on a national basis and the 'Citizen's Law Centres' should be funded by central government, although be independent of it.

The Government response was that it would examine the proposals, but nothing was done, and Law Centres have suffered badly with the abolition of the GLC and other Metropolitan councils who provided a lot of funds.

142.3 *Citizens Advice Bureaux*

These are centres staffed by competent lay advisers backed up by professional lawyers which aim to provide general advice to persons experiencing problems. They exist in most towns and, although they help people with potentially 'legal' problems, the solutions provided do not usually end up with litigation. They assist people with form-filling and letter-writing and making the system of bureaucracy easier to handle.

The Royal Commission recommended the continuance of the scheme and, although recently hit by cut-backs in expenditure, it looks as if both Citizens Advice Bureaux and Law Centres will receive a boost with the Government's Proposals of Legal Aid and Advice. If implemented it could see an end to solicitors in private practice dispensing advice on welfare matters under the Green Form Scheme. All such advice would have to be sought initially from Law Centres and Citizens Advice Bureaux who would then refer complex cases to a solicitor.

142.4 *Legal Aid and advice: Criminal cases*

Now governed by the consolidating *Legal Aid Acts 1974 & 1979* and the *Legal Aid Act 1982.* Costs are funded by the Home Office. Application is made to the appropriate court together with a statement of the applicant's means. A Legal Aid order must be made if these means appear to be inadequate and, if the interests of justice so require, Legal Aid is seldom refused (except on financial grounds) where the charge is a serious one, and it must be granted on a charge of murder.

Legal Aid includes advice by a solicitor on a preparation of the defence, and usually consists of representation by solicitor and counsel, or by solicitor only in Magistrates' Courts. An assisted person may be required to make a reasonable contribution after his case has been dealt with, regard being had to his commitments and resources.

The *Legal Aid Act 1982* contains provisions relating to duty solicitors. In 1980/81 there were duty solicitor schemes operating in over 130 Magistrates' Courts. Most of the schemes were run by the sub-committees of local law societies. Such schemes were operated within a framework set up by such local sub-committees. Further, such duty solicitors gave their services either free of charge or under the Green Form Scheme.

Under the 1982 Act duty solicitor schemes are now provided with a statutory framework. The Act now enables the Law Society, in a scheme under *s. 15 Legal Aid Act 1974*, made with the approval of the Lord Chancellor, to provide duty solicitors for Magistrates' Courts. It may do this by the setting up of committees to ensure that the duty solicitors are available in those Magistrates' Courts which appear to require them. Provision is also made for duty solicitors to be paid for their services.

An important provision is contained in *s. 1 (5)* of the Act which empowers the Lord Chancellor to give directions to Magistrates' Courts to set up duty solicitor schemes where he thinks this is necessary. Before the Act there was no compulsion to set up a scheme and a considerable number of Magistrates' Courts did not operate one even though there was an obvious need for one.

The Act has introduced an important reform to cover cases where an application for Legal Aid is refused by a Magistrates' Court. Before the Act, if an application was refused, all the applicant could do was to make a fresh application. Now, on refusal, the Act states that the applicant may apply to 'such other court or body as may be specified in the regulations'. It is not yet clear what court or body is intended. It could be the Crown Court or a Legal Aid Committee. This will be for the regulations to specify.

This reform should do much to introduce uniformity in the ultimate granting of Legal Aid. The discrepancy in the attitude of Magistrates' Courts towards applications for Legal Aid has, in the past, attracted much adverse criticism.

The *Legal Aid Act 1974* provided for contribution towards the cost of Legal Aid in criminal cases but orders to that effect were not often made. Despite considerable opposition from some quarters, which argued that defendants should not be required to make a contribution to their own defence, the 1982 Act provides that the court must order a defendant to make a contribution out of capital and in the form of instalments out of capital. The order for contribution is to be made where the defendant's capital or income exceeds certain prescribed limits. Previously it was within the court's discretion whether to make such an order. Now it is mandatory.

142.5 *Legal Aid and advice: Civil cases*

Governed by the *Legal Aid and Advice Acts 1949 & 1960*, which made provision for a service of Legal Aid and advice in civil cases, administered by the Law Society under the direction of the Lord Chancellor. Legal Aid in civil cases is also governed by the *Legal Aid Act 1974*, as amended by the *Administration of Justice Act 1977*, and the *Legal Aid Act 1979*.

Legal Aid covers representation by a solicitor and, where necessary, by counsel, in the preparation of claims and the conduct of litigation (excluding defamation, and undefended divorces), in courts generally, including domestic cases in Magistrates' Courts.

Note: It is not available in tribunals other than the Lands Tribunal, though the 1979 Act provides that the Lord Chancellor may by order extend it to such bodies.

The Law Society, in consultation with the Bar Council and under the general guidance of the Lord Chancellor, acts through Area Committees and Local Committees composed of solicitors and barristers. The cost is met out of the Legal Aid Fund. Solicitors and barristers are paid for their services out of the fund, receiving a percentage of their usual fees. This 10% reduction has created dissatisfaction in the profession, which regards Legal Aid work as underpaid.

A means test determines whether an applicant needs financial assistance. The Social Security Advisory Committee assesses the applicant's disposable income and disposable capital for this purpose. A person who is granted Legal Aid may be required to make a contribution towards his own costs. If he is unsuccessful in the action, his liability for his opponent's costs will be limited to the amount (if any) which it is reasonable in all the circumstances for him to pay.

An applicant whose financial position entitles him to Legal Aid must satisfy the Local Committee that he has reasonable grounds for taking, defending or being a party to proceedings. Against a refusal to grant a certificate he may appeal to the Area Committee.

Legal advice is governed by the *Legal Aid and Advice Act 1949* which among other things provided for the setting up of legal advice centres where oral legal advice could be given by solicitors in non-litigious matters.

The Government has issued a *Legal Aid White Paper 1987* and has proposed that administration of the scheme be removed from the Law Society and that more advice should be given by Law Centres and Citizens Advice Bureau instead of by solicitors in private practice.

142.6 *The Green Form Scheme*

A new scheme was set up by the *Legal Advice and Assistance Act 1972.* People of low income and limited capital, as defined in the Act and statutory regulations, are able to obtain the services of a solicitor to the value of £50 with a minimum of formalities (the *Green Form Scheme*). Further help can be obtained with the consent of a committee set up by the Law Society. Assistance does not extend to taking any steps in legal proceedings, since these are covered by the Legal Aid Scheme, except that a County Court or Magistrates' Court may request a solicitor who is present to give, or consent to his giving, such assistance.

No contribution is payable by a person whose disposable income does not exceed a certain amount, or who is in receipt of supplementary benefit or family income supplement, and whose disposable capital does not exceed a certain amount. Otherwise he may be required to make a contribution, within a certain maximum. The Lord Chancellor has power to make regulations by statutory instrument varying these amounts above the statutory minimum.

142.7 *Alternatives to Legal Aid*

The Government has called the Legal Aid Scheme one of the biggest growth areas in public spending. Because it is 'demand-led' expenditure it is out of the control of government attempts to limit public expenditure in the interests of economy.

Two alternatives to civil Legal Aid have been considered but rejected, for the time being:

(a) *Legal insurance*

This involves encouraging individuals to take out 'legal expenses insurance' to cover the cost of litigation. Only a few insurance companies offer such a policy, because of the difficulty in assessing the risk and fixing a realistic premium. The Committee on the Future of the Legal Profession proposed that these schemes should be more widely publicised, and people encouraged to join.

(b) *Contingency fees*

This is the system permitted in the USA, whereby lawyers charge a litigant no fees if they lose a case, but take a sizeable proportion of any damages recovered if they are successful. (The question of fees is said, therefore, to be 'contingent' on the outcome of the case). Such agreements were once illegal in the UK, and are still forbidden in the *Codes of Conduct of Barristers and Solicitors.* Contingency fees tend to encourage exaggerated claims for damages and to discourage settlements of disputes out of court. They also result in some litigants (especially defendants) finding it difficult to retain legal services at a reasonable cost.

The Committee on the Future of the Legal Profession, whilst not in favour of immediate introduction of contingency fees, recommended a close examination of the advantages and drawbacks of such a scheme.

LLB

ENGLISH LEGAL SYSTEM

LESSON 15 (REVISION)

151. *REVIEW OF LESSONS 11-14*

    151.1 SUMMARY OF PROBLEMS DEALT WITH

152. *REVISION QUESTIONS*

151. *REVIEW OF LESSONS 11-14*

151.1 *Summary of problems dealt with*

Read through each section of Lessons 11-14, pausing at the end of each paragraph to recall what you have read. If you cannot recall it adequately and in detail, read and check your knowledge until you are satisfied.

When you have completed this task, test your knowledge further by answering (in your head) the questions on the next page.

152. *REVISION QUESTIONS*

1. When is jury trial available?

2. Is the jury system a good one? What are its defects, if any?

3. How does an accused come to be sentenced?

4. What is the purpose of sentencing?

5. What sentences are available to the court?

6. Do you consider sentences should be harsh?

7. What methods are there of resolving civil disputes?

8. Explain the pre-trial procedure in the Queen's Bench Division.

9. What is the procedure in the County Court?

10. How are judgments enforced?

11. Are tribunals a good idea? Do they achieve justice?

12. What are the ways of appealing from the Magistrates' Court?

13. What is the difference between a barrister and a solicitor?

14. Is fusion of the legal profession a good idea?

15. How easy is it for the man on the street to get the legal advice he needs?